Thomas D. Clark

To Stanley Ferger –
To while away the
tedious hours of con-
valescence. Congratulation
on your good fight.

H. B. Wiley

May 4th '39

# THE RAMPAGING FRONTIER

THE RAMPAGING FRONTIER

# THE RAMPAGING FRONTIER

## Manners and Humors of Pioneer Days in the South and the Middle West

THOMAS D. CLARK

Dionysius 11

THE BOBBS-MERRILL COMPANY
PUBLISHERS

INDIANAPOLIS          NEW YORK

10/15/48

TO

BENNETT

VERY BIG GROUPS CAN'T FIGHT QUIETLY

VBG CFQ

# CONTENTS

# ACKNOWLEDGMENTS

I wish to acknowledge the generosity of Mrs. Louis Lee Haggin and Mr. and Mrs. James Molloy of Mt. Brillant Farm who permitted me free access to the excellent file of the *Spirit of the Times* which was collected by the late Colonel Louis Lee Haggin. Mr. J. A. Estes of the *Blood Horse* permitted me to use his file of the *Spirit of the Times* and *Porter's Spirit of the Times*. Mr. and Mrs. Virgil Steed have given me much of their time and have encouraged me in making this study. A. B. Guthrie, Huntley Dupre, William H. Townsend, Samuel M. Wilson, J. Winston Coleman, Sarah Blanding, Robert G. Lunde, A. M. Bower and Ellery Hall have either read parts of the manuscript or assisted me in other ways. Franklin J. Meine of Chicago, who is preparing a definitive work on western humor, has made many useful suggestions regarding materials. Miss Norma Cass of the University of Kentucky Library patiently borrowed many rare books for my use. Mr. D. L. Chambers and Mrs. Jessica Brown Mannon of the Bobbs-Merrill Company, and Professor Kenneth C. Kaufman of the University of Oklahoma were of real assistance in preparing the manuscript for publication. My wife, Elizabeth Turner Clark, has spent many hours reading and checking my manuscript.

# PREFACE

Too long the historian has neglected the earthy elements of humanity which went into the making of the West. He has written hundreds of learned essays and pamphlets about them, but seldom has he danced with their gals, or rolled on their camp-meeting floors. He has never drunk with the colonels, drilled with the privates, nor dodged their horses in main street and highway races. All of this to the learned fraternity of historians is frivolous, and above all historians must never be frivolous. Of recent years a few bold ones have dared break away from traditional formality to tell some of the rich yarns which amused another generation. This departure has broken the ice, and the dignified brethren have listened with increasing interest to what apologetic chairmen of program committees have labeled "light stuff."

My story is human, and it is buckskin, but if there was ever anything in America that was more buckskin than the frontier and its society it has not yet shown its head. There may be those who will ask: Was there not broadcloth? Yes there was. It is hard to tell at times where it began and where it ended, but I know it really existed. I have come to grips with it. Once I turned patiently through hundreds of records, most of which had to do with teaching Latin, Greek and dogma, of a pioneer institution of learning in the West. I also assisted in collecting material for a history of pioneer medicine from which I found out about the abominable cowpox which was transmitted on woolen strings to innoculate hapless victims against the small-pox. Even a state legislature learned of this cultural advance and undertook to check it with an omnipotent act. Many times I have stood before beautiful fan-sashed Georgian colonial door-ways, built in an early day, and admired the beautiful lines, and

I have sat lightly on rare antique cherry chairs, decorated with ancient needle point, which were made from patterns of Duncan Phyfe and Chippendale. I know there was broadcloth, but there was more—much more—buckskin.

There is no richer source for the study of human activities on the frontier than its thousands of humorous stories. Fortunately William T. Porter began publication of the *Spirit of the Times* as a general sporting magazine in 1836. He opened its columns to everybody who had something original to contribute. Hundreds of backwoodsmen were attracted by the idea, and they contributed either their reminiscences or accounts of what was happening around them at the moment of their writing. I have spent many long and pleasant hours digging in this rich mine. My file case bulges with hundreds of stories which I can never use, but they are there to fortify those which I present in this volume.

Few incidents recorded in my narrative cannot be duplicated by at least a half-dozen more of a kindred nature. I have examined all of the major travel accounts which literate natives and foreigners have left. Some of these are splendid, some are good but caustic, and some are downright vicious. Acts of state legislatures are filled with human stories, diaries and journals yield pay dirt in abundance, and innocent preachers have told more than they ever supposed in their memoirs. Newspaper editors, even the devilish George D. Prentice of the Louisville *Journal,* are disappointing. They were too busily engaged in fighting the cause of partisan politics. Too, these public servants had to live in the community where their papers were published, and they could not afford to take chances by publishing too much about the intimate social life of the times. When an editor needed either an anecdote or a filler he could always crack a joke on an Englishman or fill in with the latest antics of the sea serpent. Advertisements occasionally threw light on what was happening, and, sometimes, a story of an escapade in a distant community found its way into print.

Generally I have kept my story west of the Allegheny Mountains, and within the boundaries of Tennessee and south of the Yankee line in Ohio, Indiana and Illinois. I have gone as far west as the ends of Missouri and Arkansas. On two or three occasions I have gone kidnaping beyond my boundaries and fetched home such choice morsels as "A Wisconsin Debating Society," and the "Iowa Brides." Of course no story of the frontier would be complete without frequent forays into Natchez and New Orleans. This account of the frontier is highly flavored by the Kentucky influence, but so was frontier society. My period covers generally from 1775-1850. There might be an argument that frontier conditions did not exist in some of this region during the latter decades, but after all, the terms frontier and pioneer are relative ones.

The predominant features of social development in the old West have governed the organization of my study. I have fitted my parts into a whole, presenting what I hope is a well-rounded picture of the life of the common man. The frontier is the central theme, and hence the thread which holds it together. I have selected my stories, first because they are good stories; second, because they amplify the body of my narrative. These stories are the literary beginnings of the Mississippi and Ohio Valleys.

At no place have I been guilty of laughing at the people who broke through the mountain barrier to plant a new society along a new frontier. It has ever been my hope to march humbly in lockstep with them and to help tell their human story with as little prejudice as possible and no levity. I cannot refrain from being envious of them of their land and their fun. My enjoyment of their antics has been vicarious, but complete.

No more is there free land or backwoods to which a man can escape if the pressure gets too great in civilization. Backwoodsmen still exist, but they are rapidly moving out to state and federal highways to run filling stations and roadhouses, or they are finding lucrative positions on radio programs. Panthers, b'ars and bobcats have long ago fled before courthouses and lawyers. Only a virgin source of fine anecdotes, and splendid commentaries on a vigorous system of society of another day remain behind. I have worked this source and have tried to present the picture as I have seen it of this other way of life.

T. D. C.

Lexington, Kentucky. January 8, 1939.

## CHAPTER I

# THE BACKWOODS

A HOMESICK Virginian who had lately moved to Kentucky entertained the English traveler William Faux. He declared to this visitor that the land west of the mountains was inhabited by rogues and cheats. No man's word was of any value, and everyone was trying to live without laboring. Physically and morally the West was a land of human ruination. Back in Virginia, said the unhappy immigrant, it was long ago said that when a man was missing from his community, "He has gone to hell or Kentucky."

West of the Appalachian highlands lay a wide strip of territory which rolled away to the cane-lined channels of the mosquito-infested Missouri, Arkansas and Red Rivers. This land for more than seventy-five years was the great American frontier. Here was developed a new American society and a distinctive native personality which showed to what extent human life underwent changes of manners and humors. Contrary to the discouraging predictions of William Faux's host, this land beyond the mountains was not one of eternal perdition: it was a fertile land of promise to thousands of rugged and eager immigrants who founded there a way of life different from that which they had left behind on the seaboard.

At an early date a westward movement got under way, and a new social world came into existence. Here west of the mountains land was plentiful, water was fresh, timber was heavy, and varmints audacious. In this trans-Appalachian country Indians were bold, but less bothersome, even so, than tidewater taxgatherers, and harassed people of the East sought homes in the new country.

Hunters returned to their cabins on the outer fringe of civilization along the great Appalachian trough to proclaim the glories of the land on the western waters. Pioneer liar of the West was John Findley who took fiendish delight in exciting Daniel Boone's imagination to the breaking point by telling him of the large schools of fish which blocked the great falls of the Ohio, and of thousands of quacking waterfowl which floated over the falls and were dashed to pieces on the rocks. According to Findley's carefully spun yarn, the sickening smell of carrion spread over a large area. These were exciting and gross misrepresentations, but so are most real-estate advertisements. When redbirds happily proclaimed corn-planting time in the Carolinas in 1769, Daniel Boone shouldered his flintlock rifle and left Rebecca and the kids to shift as best they could with the corn patch, for he was off to visit Findley's land of eternal promise. Soon other families were left in a like plight by their head "b'ar-catchers" to root-pig-or-die until these restless sons could determine whether there was another side to the "big hill." Each party eventually returned to describe a land which made pikers of the Israelite land scouts. Tales of these first adventurers tempted even the most timid souls to pull up stakes and move westward. By late 1778 the great trail stretching from Cumberland Gap to the Ohio was becoming well-worn by the treading of ambitious families on their way to build new homes, and to found a new society.[1]

Unfortunately for the inquisitors of today who would record the social activities of the early Westerners, gunpowder and salt were of vastly more importance than paper on which to write accounts of human affairs. Campfires, like roadside taverns of later years, were scenes of much tall yarn-spinning, this we know, but the substance of the yarns we do not absolutely know. We can dismiss the search for early stories of human interest, because those who had paper and could write on it were too busy conjuring up materials describing "injun" fights to waste time in recording for future generations the outlandish yarns of the campfire. One look at the crude journal of the serious-minded William Calk would convince even the most skeptical of this truth.[2]

Of more importance to those who would run to earth the humor of the backwoods are types of human beings who found their way over the trails and down the rivers to Ol' Kaintuck and later to the South and the Northwest. There were wild Irishmen who were ready to fight the Devil and give him both underholds, there were stolid pork-loving Germans who kept both eyes peeled in search of fertile land, there were Scotchmen who searched for opportunity in any form, and there were disgruntled Englishmen who did as Englishmen have always done—they looked for good farmsites and dodged taxes. Up the river from New Orleans and Natchez came jabbering Frenchmen in search of furs and adventure.

Once settled in the western country, German heads of households dreamed and worked to secure enough real property to plant a numerous progeny within sight of their front doors. Englishmen located farms and townsites. Scotchmen, bearing an instinct which came from living on frugal hills, practiced frugality in a land of plenty, and conducted mercantile businesses on their own terms. Irishmen, with traditional Irish recklessness and abandon, gave sufficient reason to justify the building of jails.[3] Surely it was the Irish influence that Mann Butler had in mind when he said that in 1806 he found the western young men equipped with fiddles, packs of cards and pistols.[4]

Distances were great, neighborhoods were scattered, but once the mountains were crossed denizens of the backwoods learned to get along without company. A generation of people came into existence to whom the faint tinkling of a stranger's cowbell or the barking of his dog caused life to become oppressive, and it was time "to be gittin' on." These restless citizens had calluses between their shoulders, worn there from leaning perpetually against dying ring-scarred trees while belled cows grazed for their masters' living in the woods near by. These cattlemen of the frontier who detested crowding were the advance guard of civilization. As these drowsy tree-leaning individualists moved across the face of the western country they developed a language of their own, which, coupled with that of their shiftless friends, the hunters, produced a new American vernacular.

Travelers and foreign land-hunters found the roads filled with poor souls moving westward. Stephen Austin passed barefooted immigrants who struggled on bleeding feet to reach the new country. These were spirited travelers, however, and the burden of trials and hardships sat lightly upon them; they possessed at all times a sense of humor.[5] C. A. Murray, an English traveler, found the West settled by what he believed to be "western Virginians, a wild, high-spirited, and somewhat rough tribe of hunters."[6] He found the Westerners to have greater faults; and their moral features were most broadly and distinctly marked. "They are," said Murray, "generous, proud, frank and hospitable, but apt at the same time to be rough and overbearing and quarrelsome. They are vain of their state, and inclined to play braggart—Birmingham [England] and Pittsburg are obliged to complete by the dirk knife the equipment of the 'chivalric Kentuckian.' I am aware that gouging is exaggerated, and mostly invented—the rough and tumble fight is still permitted by the spectators."[7] The pious Timothy Flint was less understanding of the backwoods for he declared the West was populated by an influx of the immoral and ignorant elements of eastern seaboard civilization.

François Michaux, in 1802, estimated that 20,000 souls annually traveled the Wilderness Road or floated down the Ohio River to perdition in the West.[8] Land speculators and swindlers were actively engaged in attracting settlers westward. Their representatives traveled through the East, England and Europe with beautifully drawn maps which showed rivers and thriving villages which existed only on paper.[9] Many disappointed purchasers arrived in the West to find screaming panthers, canebrakes and spring branches instead of humming and bustling cities and open rivers. Along the east coast, families, companies, and even church congregations moved to the promised land of the West.[10] Speculators bought large tracts for pittances and awaited the rush of settlers, but often squatters moved into the country and took up "tomahawk rights" to land. Fights ensued in which one or the other party got a "laced jacket" or a good whipping.[11]

Hardships did not discourage the ambitious. Charles Fenno Hoffman saw, in Indiana, a family frozen stiff, the father at a wheel of the creaky ox wagon, the mother and her children in the wagon. They faced west, a land, they had hoped, would fulfill its promise to them.[12] These mobile settlers had little property and no sentiment to tie them to the soil. They had log cabins, rude furniture, a drove of hogs, a herd of cows, a scrawny pony and a passle of chickens.[13] To move was a simple matter for backwoodsmen for all they had to do was to call up the hogs and cows, pack the pony, line up the "old lady" and the kids, box up the chickens, call the dog, spit on the fire and strike out.

There was no trick to building a new home, even a lean-to would suffice for a long time. Furniture was homemade, and roughly made at that. No one who could not get a good night's rest on a bough bed or piled up on a flea-infested dirt floor had any business on the frontier. Benches were made from rough half-log puncheons, tables were of the same general construction, and a skillet and a fireplace were sufficient kitchen equipment. Womenfolks were easy to please, they did not need a lot of useless truck such as wardrobes, closets, chests, pots, pans and looking glasses. If a squatter lass was so vain that she had to look at herself there was always the spring or the creek.

The diet seldom varied: there was corn bread, greasy pork, black sugar or honey, mush, rancid butter and, sometimes, indifferent coffee. One traveler who demanded milk was told, "We ain't got none, for the kayws is somehaw got a haunt of not comin' hum." Engaging this drawling and sloven female of the Arkansas bottoms in conversation, our traveler discovered that her husband was a hunter who had moved one jump ahead of neighbors and government all the way through Kentucky, Tennessee, Indiana and Missouri to Arkansas. They had a shabby cabin, a few scrawny cows, a shaggy pony, and a hill covered with wild "kids." The "old man" was off in the woods hunting a "painter"; he had left a little corn and two raccoons "to sarve" until he could return. "Why you have got a surprising quantity of children," said the stranger. "How do you mean to bring them up?" "Bring 'em up?" whined the mother. "Why my husband brings 'em up every Saturday night, I reckon, and then I washes 'em all."[14] When the "painter" hunter returned he explained that he had bought a fifty-dollar horse for which he had agreed to pay fifteen gallons of b'ar oil, twelve deerskins, and to go with a negro to the big bottoms to help catch some wild horses.

Traveling through the West, Timothy Flint saw people in Missouri who had come from every state east of the Mississippi River. There were pork-eating Carolinians, lackadaisical Tennesseans, "titled" Virginians, "red-horse" Kentuckians, Buckeyes, Hoosiers and Suckers. That same year the *Kentucky Gazette* announced that three keel boats loaded with immigrants had arrived in Arkansas from Kentucky and Tennessee. Prospects were that there would be a heavy immigration to the mosquito-ridden bottoms of the Arkansas and Red rivers.[15] Immigrants to the trans-Mississippi West had learned the ways of the frontier. There was no quailing of timid souls for most of them were born while "painters" screamed and b'ars snorted within rifle shot of the cabin. They had learned to cook, to eat, to sleep and to perform other social activities with a minimum expenditure of energy.[16] Strangers who came among them had a difficult time finding accommodations. Sensitive Englishmen and critical Yankees found these denizens of the frontier excellent subjects for criticism. The biggest actual difference between them, however, was the fact that one had learned to take nature at face value while the other had not.

These homely squatters often fooled outsiders. As the frontier was settled and such towns as Cincinnati, Louisville, and

St. Louis became important trading centers, skin-clad trappers were forever appearing on the scene to surprise and embarrass haughty clerks in general trading houses and frontier banks. Early one morning a long-haired, unshaven, and stale-smelling trapper blundered into St. Louis to sell his *cache* of b'ar, painter, deer, beaver, otter, 'coon and buffalo hides. For his truck he received three large checks. "He went into the bank to draw his money. His dress and appearance were those of a backwoods trapper, and the bank room was filled with gentry. They looked upon his greasy buckskin hunting shirt and leggings as though they feared he would touch them and spoil or soil their delicate clothing. After looking around the room and its inmates he threw down his first check; this was cashed. He threw down his second, then his third. The gentlemen began by this time to look at one another, and the cashier said, "Where are you from sir?" The trapper replied, "Just down from the moon, Sir. Why I just greased my hunting shirt, Sir, and slid down a rainbow."[17] There was an obvious absence of fine linen, and perhaps the smell of greasy hides and sweaty bodies was enough to turn such civilized individuals as foppish bank clerks against the whole of unwashed mankind on the frontier. There was an obvious absence of social graces, but there was not lacking a ready wit and a keen sense of humor.

From this basic human structure, a western society was built. Leather-shirted hunters turned in time from trailing varmints, or leaning drowsily against girdled trees and listening to the melodious tinkling of cowbells, to "industry." Civilization caught up with them as wave upon wave of new settlers poured into the country. States were formed, counties were laid out, and courthouses were built. One hunter said that with the coming of courthouses and lawyers, all four-footed "varmints took for" the land beyond the boundaries of the state, and the country wasn't "fitten" for a decent man.[18] Pioneer fathers, like the Levitical fathers at Shiloh, soon founded cities to dwell in and suburbs for their cattle. The land of the Mississippi Valley was fertile, and even indifferent efforts produced a surplus of goods.

The Ohio, Scioto, Kentucky, Tennessee, Cumberland, Missouri, Arkansas and the Red Rivers flowed ultimately into the Mississippi and then to the Gulf of Mexico. Before Americans passed through Cumberland Gap, and down the Ohio to claim the lands in the western valley, Frenchmen had obligingly founded the city of New Orleans. By 1800, representatives from nearly every section of the western frontier floated products, ranging from beeswax to Bourbon liquor, to market in arks, broadhorns, and keel boats. The journey was long and tedious. Whirlpools, snags and sandbars threatened destruction. Boat-wreckers used screaming wenches to lure unwary farmer-boatmen into death traps. Lurking along cane and willow-grown riverbanks were copper-tanned Indian devils who lingered to take final "pot shots" at white civilization. When river currents swept clumsy arks too close to the banks, arrows or rifle balls thinned the ranks of their crews.

Combined with the dangers of the rivers and their tricky channels and currents was the competition of the states for a market. There was a rush of frontier farmers and boatmen for the New Orleans trade. If greenhorns successfully floated to market, and sold their goods over their competitors, they were likely to fall into the clutches of sharpers. Many gawky bumpkins from the up-river country lost a fine corn crop by listening to the seductive love-making of dark-haired, voluptuous and quick-fingered daughters of the new-world Sodom at the foot of the river.[19] Suave gamblers "played green" in order to inveigle cash-laden up-river boys into a friendly drink and game. Northward along the river-road leading home lurked heartless brigands who used methods less subtle than those of buxom New Orleans prostitutes and card-stacking shavers. After living through these experiences, boatmen became boasters. Those who were so fortunate as to steer clear of all the dangers of the river, the big city, and the trail back were entitled to boast of their prowess.[20]

Once permanent settlements were made, pride of state, county and community became a passion. It mattered little where they were found: all backswoodsmen boasted of their land. Kentuckians stood at the head of the braggarts list. One of them said to a visitor: "No, stranger, there's no place on the universal arth like Ol' Kaintuck; she whips all *out west* in prettiness; you might bile down creation and not get such another state out of it."[21] Buckeyes boasted that their state produced "the smartest men—the prettiest women—the fattest hogs—the juiciest grapes—the tallest corn—the most golden oat fields—the slickest rats (hence their fine sausages)—the most musical cats—the best painters—the most celebrated artists. No state or nation in the world can compare with her. We have no doubt when she gets the big telescope in operation at Cincinnati, some distinguished 'porker' will be sent up to the moon to explore that unexplored region. All this and more will be done. Doubtless a lasso will be dispatched to the infernal region to describe what is going on down there."[22]

Meanwhile Hoosiers and Suckers soon came to measure the unassailable virtues of their states in terms of hogs, corn and cattle.[23] Flint heard a preacher struggle for a descriptive word with which to convey to an illiterate audience some conception of the heavenly world, and after considerable sputtering he hit upon the satisfactory explanation that it was a "Kaintuck of a place."[24] Bragging of homeland gained momentum as population movements rolled over the land. Virginians were never modest in their proclamations of being the "best," but they lacked the ability of expansive description which came as a second nature with the frontiersman.

Language west of the mountains was simple and direct. At times words were put to peculiar uses, and often they had different meanings between the person speaking and the person spoken to. When written down on paper much of the language of the frontier becomes a peculiar arrangement of letters and phonetic sounds.[25] Many of the western conversations were impossible to record because of a lack of imagination on the part of literate hearers. At Maysville, Kentucky, in 1813, a fight was threatened between a Yankee and a natural son of

Ol' Kaintuck because the latter applied the term plunder to the Yankee's baggage. This traveler, the actor Ludlow, said that "as soon as I had reached level ground at the top of the slope leading to the river, I beheld a four-horse team attached to a covered wagon standing in front of a store. As I approached the wagon, I observed a stout, rough-looking man coming toward me, I said to him: 'Do you belong to this wagon?' 'No,' said he, 'this wagon belongs to me.' 'Oho!' thinks I, 'a specimen of Kentucky wit, one must speak "by the card" here.' 'Well, Sir,' said I, 'I wish to employ some one to haul a load to Frankfort.' After asking how much load I had and what it consisted of he hesitated a few minutes and then said, 'Well, stranger, I think I can haul your "plunder" for you.' 'Now,' thought I, ''tis my turn to be critical.' So I said, 'Damnation, Sir! what do you mean? Do you take me for a housebreaker? Plunder! What do you mean by that?' 'Mean,' said he, 'I mean I can take your truck for you.' 'Look you, my friend,' said I, 'just be so good as to explain what you mean by plunder and truck. I do not understand your outlandish jargon.' 'Jargon,' said he, squaring himself up and looking me full in the face, 'look here, my young hoss, thar's no use to begin raring and pitching here, because you can't make nuthin' off o' me in that way.' "[26]

The descendants of the Kentuckians "reckoned," "allowed," and "didn't care if they did," while Yankee descendants "guessed as how," and "supposed." Idioms and frontier slang marked western American speech. The West was a world of reality and practicality and direct speech utilized simple terms of comparison and figure. The purist Webster slights such words as sass, coming-it, roarers, ringtails, ripsnorters, passle, ruckus and rassle, yet on the frontier they, with dozens of others, were highly useful and exact in description.

Backwoodsmen were as ingenious as the haughty travelers who came among them. They were quick to "size-up" their visitors and to prime them with misinformation. Estwick Evans portrayed gullibility, and humorous Westerners told him that thornbushes (locust) growing near Vevay, Indiana, produced spikes which could be used in the place of nails. Evans with all the seriousness of a London prelate records this astounding fact in his account of a pedestrian's tour.[27] James Flint, a fault-finding traveler, allowed himself to be completely hoodwinked by a woman on Paint Creek, in Illinois, who told him that the river he had to cross was very deep, and that he would need a horse. She had a horse for hire, and when Flint had paid a good rental fee and crossed over the river it was found to be shallow all the way.[28] On other occasions misinformation was given out for the specific purpose of confusing the person receiving it. On the Indiana frontier a pestiferous sheriff attempted to attach a widow's pigs and she locked him in her stable until he promised to leave her premises. As a parting "favor" she gave him specific directions as to the safest place to cross a flush stream which flowed before her cabin. She was careful to direct him to the deepest crossing where the current was most treacherous with the result that the sheriff reached the other side after an exciting life-and-death struggle in midstream.[29]

Young bloods in Louisville who appreciated the gullibility of strangers obliged the ruffian-seeking Captain Marryat by staging a perfect knock-down-and-drag-out in his behalf. They came to the party armed with the "standard" equipment of young men in western America which included dirks, pistols, knucks, and swords concealed in walking canes. An irregularity at cards was enough to touch off a community holocaust, and Marryat was supplied with enough material for a complete treatise on the delicate art of removing eyes, ears and noses in true gouger style.[30]

The West was a free land: free with morals, free with conversation, free with swearing, free with strangers, and free with the Lord. Westerners had their own ideas of morals and freedom, exercising the latter to the fullest. They butted into private conversations with perfect composure, and if they were snubbed they exclaimed, "This is a free country, and a land of liberty."[31] They were generous, good-natured, and well-armed.

Travelers were welcomed to their bed and board, accommodations for which they often refused to accept cash. Strangers were welcomed by frontiersmen who were always hungry for news and information. Many drowsy travelers were kept up beyond a late bedtime answering questions of "Where did you come from? Where are you going? Are you married? What have you got in those boxes? Are you a merchant? I guess you are a mechanic."[32] François Michaux was both annoyed and amused at this eternal questioning. Westerners greeted Michaux by attempting to set a value upon the horse he was riding, by offering him a glass of whisky, and then by plying him with one question after another.[33]

Strangers traveling through the country were stopped on the road and queried as to their points of departure and destinations, or news of their journey. To picayunish snobs this inquisitiveness on the part of natives grew exceedingly boring, and sarcastic answers often got them into trouble. Anxious immigrants were always curious to find out what was happening in their future homeland. Travelers in Virginia were accosted by the inquisitors who wished to know if they had come from Kaintuck. Isaac Weld, an impatient snob, said that these "people traveled in companies of 50, were armed with rifles, pistols and swords. Had large blankets under their saddles—of all the uncouth human beings I met with in America, these people from the western country were the most so; their curiosity was boundless. Frequently have I been stopped abruptly by one of them in a solitary part of the road, and in such a manner, that had it been in another country, I should have imagined it was a highwayman that was going to demand my purse, and without any further preface, asked where I came from? If I was acquainted with the news? Where bound to? and finally my name." One party greeted Weld with "Stop, mister! Why I guess now you be coming from the new state?" "No, sir." "Why then I guess as how you be coming from Kentuc." "No, sir." "Oh! Why then, pray where now might you be coming from?" "From the low country." "Why you must have heard the news then! Pray now, mister, what might the price of bacon be in those parts?" "Upon my word, friend, I can't inform you." "Aye, aye! I see, mister, what might your name be?"[34]

If Westerners were inquisitive, they were equally generous with news and information. They were glad to tell strangers all they knew, and, sometimes, they were too generous with gossip to the traveling banditti who passed through the back country.[35] Prospects for traveling companions were never overlooked. A perfect stranger might be greeted as was Charles Fenno Hoffman when he passed the place of a Kentuckian who was in his lot saddling his horse, and who yelled "Halloo! Stranger; I reckon you and I are cuttin' out for the same place so hold a bit, and you shall have some company."[36] There was a free off-handedness about the backwoodsmen who moved across the frontier from the Alleghenies to Arkansas that made them likable individuals. They were fearless, ardent and self-possessed.

The rank of a stranger meant nothing to them because they believed neither in gradation of society nor the ranking of mere individuals. Not even the personal secretary of the popular Marquis de La Fayette was exempted from this off-handedness as is evidenced by conversation between Auguste Levasseur and an old Kentuckian living near Cincinnati. This son of the West engaged Levasseur in a conversation concerning Napoleon in which he said it was ridiculous for the unfeeling English Government to approve such shameful treatment of him. The Kentuckian insisted that Napoleon should have come to America where he would have found a hospitable exile. "Here he could have had liberty without disturbance," said the American, "and he could have enjoyed the memory of his distinguished achievements." Levasseur replied, "that you would have found in the character of Napoleon appreciation for both sorrow and pleasure; he would have worked without ceasing to satisfy his prodigious energy, and do you not think that he would have undertaken to subject the resources of this young nation to his will, and would this not have been fatal to your wise institutions?" This would have been an act of folly declared the native patriot, and if the hero of Austerlitz had persisted in destroying American liberty his effort would have proved fatal to him. "See that rifle," (turning, the Kentuckian pointed his finger toward a gun leaning against the corner of the room) "with that I have never missed a pheasant in our woods at one hundred yards;—a tyrant is larger than a pheasant, and there is not a Kentuckian who is less patriotic than I."[37]

Puritan customs were slow in reaching the frontier. The Sabbath was only the seventh day to frontiersmen perhaps. The Lord rested on the seventh day, but the inhabitants of the Ohio and Mississippi River Valleys reserved the right to define "resting." At Louisville in the formative period, a Virginian was reproached for not opening his store on Sundays. The storekeeper said that "one Sunday morning, when we all came in to breakfast, they observed my store was not opened and asked the reason *why*. I answered, because it was the Sabbath day. Oh! they replied, Sunday had not yet come over the mountains. Yes, I answered, it had, that I brought it with me. Well said they, you are the first person who had kept his store shut in this village on the Sabbath day."[38] In Albion, Illinois, Suckers engaged in the sport of the frontier, and did some fancy fighting on the side for good measure. In the English Prairie sections, refined Britishers played the civilized game of cricket, while Americans engaged in a more vigorous pastime. Observers in other sections found the Sabbath "not much observed" for there were no places of public worship, and there was too much drinking and fighting.[39] This was the frontier, and not puritanical New England; people had sporting to do, and there was no better day on which to do it than Sunday.

Sporting was the lifeblood of the frontier. Every man who wore britches, and who amounted to anything, had to shoot straight and hit the mark.[40] Squirrel hunting was a grand sport—not that frontiersmen wanted the squirrels to eat. Frequent notices appeared in the early newspapers announcing squirrel hunts, and later these same papers announced the results. The *Kentucky Gazette* gave notice on May 17, 1796, that "On Saturday last, the Hunters rendezvoused at Irvine's Lick and produced *Seven Thousand Nine Hundred and Forty-one* Squirrels killed by them in one day." The hunting party which produced the most "tails and scalps" was richly rewarded with a choice quarter of beef. Hunters in Illinois were either not such good shots or squirrels had become scarcer for out there a party worked hard all day and could produce only 293 furry tokens.[41] Kentuckians and Tennesseans humorously swore that they could not eat squirrels unless they were shot through the left eyes, for otherwise they were sure to give them indigestion. Really good shots did not puncture the hides of squirrels; they "barked" them by shooting into the tree just under the squirrels' bellies, stunning them by the impact.[42] Shooting matches were lively social events.

These hunts were occasions at which bragging egotists gathered from one side of the frontier to the other. Riflemen assembled around tavern stoves, or at courthouse steps, and proclaimed themselves remarkable shots; if liquor flowed freely they testified to hitting microscopic targets at prodigious distances. Even that "trusted old rifleman," Henry Clay, shot himself into the Kentucky legislature by leveling a citizen's rifle, Ol' Bessie, on a fly speck and fetching a dead center drive. Clay was standing for the legislature in Fayette County, but he found the poker games at the Olympian Springs in Bath County more attractive. News reached him that his political stand was likely to become little more than a wobbly squat unless he passed in his cards and rushed home to meet, face to face, a recalcitrant constituency. When Clay strode jauntily upon the political grounds in Fayette he was accosted by a patriarchal backwoodsman who said to him: "Young man you want to go to the legislature, I see. Are you a good shot?" "The best in the country," replied Clay. "Then you shall go to the legislature. But first you must give us a specimen of your skill. We must see you shoot." Clay replied "I never shoot any rifle but my own." "No matter, here is Old Bess; she never fails in the hands of a marksman. She has sent death through a squirrel's head at one hundred yards and daylight through many a redskin twice that distance. If you can shoot any gun you can shoot Old Bess." "Well, put up your mark!" said the trembling Clay. He took aim and centered the mark! On a chance shot! said a bystander, but the good criminal lawyer Clay stopped all muttering by using the dodge that when they set a better mark he would outshoot them.[43]

Enterprising and patriotic William Marshall advertised in the papers:

### "CITIZENS—SOLDIERS

"In the late war the superiority of our marksmen in the art of shooting was strikingly manifested and not less obvious were the advantages derived therefrom. To this qualification we were chiefly indebted to our victories. When our troops saw that their bullets mowed down the enemy whilst themselves sustained but little injury it taught them to look down upon the boasting veterans from Europe with contempt. Peace has now returned; but again we may be required to take arms. Already has the short-sighted monarch of Spain made to our administration insolent demands which may lead to hostilities, and that too, immediately on our southern borders. Then let us be prepared for the event by cultivation of those arts which have heretofore sustained us—Let us practice sharp-shooting and encourage excellence by offering competent rewards to those who are eminent, until we not only astonish the natives on the other side of the waters, but show them that it may be dangerous to stand in battle array before western militia, who, in the heat of action cannot only hit a man aimed at, but place the ball on the very spot chosen, even the eye. With these views the subscribers proposed to have a:

## "SHOOTING MATCH!

"At Manchester adjoining Lexington, for a valuable two-story brick house and lot, together with a stone Smith Shop, the whole valued at $3000, or thirty shots at $100 each at sixty yards off hand.

"Any person paying the subscribers, either in money or such property as they may agree on, $100, shall be entitled to make one shot, either by himself or friend, with his own gun, and the nearest shot take the house and apurtenances, and a deed shall be made on request.

"Captains of companies are requested to subscribe one shot for each of the companies, and to send forward their best marksmen by which means a spirit of emulation will be excited amongst the gentlemen composing their command.

"The shooting to take place on the second Saturday in March, at which time judges will be chosen, by whom all questions are to be decided.

"Applications to be made to William Marshall or Charles Wilks, to subscribe for shots."[44]

Self-respecting marksmen were quick to claim credit where credit was glory, but if shots were poor they preferred to be credited with clean misses. Three frontier colonels became involved in a dispute as to which one had killed a particular Englishman at the Battle of New Orleans. The most pompous of the trio declared he killed the scoundrel if he were hit in the left eye, but he disclaimed responsibility if he were hit elsewhere. Upon examination it was found that "old left-eye" had nobly defended the honor of the Tennessee Volunteers.[45] There was meaning in the boast of the western volunteer when he swore they would win at New Orleans, in spite of the high and mighty sounding titles which were ranged against them on the side of the British. A messenger through the lines shortly before the battle had informed the American soldiers hanging around headquarters that the English would make quick work of the backwoodsmen because they had commanding them Lord Pakenham, Lord Picton, Lord Keene and Lord Cockrane. The backwoodsmen replied, "We have the Lord God Almighty, the Lord Jesus Christ and the Hero Andrew Jackson, and we can hit a crossbelt at three hundred yards."

When rampaging frontiersmen were not practicing the art of hitting spots they indulged in other sports somewhat less accurate in aim but equally defacing. Gouging was a playful form of sport which bore the highly descriptive and qualitative adjective "Virginia." When Arthur St. Clair's army was stationed in Indiana, across the river from Louisville, one of his officers came in hand-to-hand contact with this exciting art of biting off noses, ears, and gouging out eyes. Major Erkuries Beatty recorded in his diary that in Louisville we "saw the barbarous custom of gouging practiced between two of the lower class of people here; their unvaried way of fighting. When two men quarrel they never have an idea of striking, but immediately seize each other, and fall and twist each other's thumbs or fingers into the eye and push it from the socket till it falls on the cheeks, as one of those men experienced today, and was obliged to acknowledge himself beat, although he was on top of the other—but he, in his turn had bit his adversary almost abominably. . . . It chilled my blood with horror to see this unmanly, cruel condition these two men were left in today from this manner of fighting, and no person, although a number stood by, ever attempted to prevent them from thus butchering each other, but all was acknowledged fair play. Soon after our troops came here, one of the officers being in a public house in Louisville was grossly insulted by one of these Virginia Gougers, a perfect bully; all the country round stood in awe of him, for he was so dexterous in these matters that he had, in his time, taken out five eyes, bit off two or three noses and ears and spit them in their faces—this fellow our officer was obliged to encounter without side arms or any weapon but his hands and the insult could not be got over."[46]

Gougers and gouged were sometimes considerate of each other. On one occasion a gouger was in the act of biting off an ear when he asked his victim if he would give up, to which he replied, "No go ahead and bite it off, I can hear without it." From the frequency with which gouging is mentioned by both native and foreign observers it seems to have been fairly common on the frontier. Isaac Weld saw frontiersmen fight "like bears, biting, kicking, punching and gouging."[47] So vicious did this method of frontier combat become that state legislatures took notice and passed laws forbidding mayhem. The basic law against mayhem, which was followed by the western states, was passed by Virginia. A penalty of twenty days to six months was to be levied upon offenders where combats had mutual causes, and where one had "unlawfully and willfully disabled the tongue, eye, slit or bit the nose, ear or lip of another." While if one purposely, and with malice aforethought shall "unlawfully disable the tongue, put out an eye, slit the nose, ear or lip, or 'member' of any such person with intent to disfigure or disable he shall be imprisoned from one to fourteen years. He shall be fined not more than $1000."[48]

Refined Westerners resorted to the more dignified and detached form of offense and defense. They used dirks, guns, and swords-in-canes in place of lusty thumbs. Captain Thomas Hamilton said that on approaching Cincinnati, an English friend "inquired whether I observed that an ivory hilt protruded from beneath the waistcoat of a gentleman opposite. I answered in the affirmative, and he then informed me that the whole population of the Southern and Western States are uniformly armed with daggers. On my expressing some doubts of this singular fact, he pointed to a number of sticks collected in one corner of the cabin, and offered a wager that every one of these contained either a dagger or a sword. I took the bet, and lost it; and my subsequent observations confirmed the truth of his assertion in every particular."[49] Another visitor saw young men buying dirks and guns, and he saw merchants' store windows lined with both of these instruments of self-protection.

The dirk was the most convenient of the early weapons for it could be worn in a sling placed just under the left arm-pit and under the vest.[50] Again state laws interfered with free indulgence of these instruments of torture. Unimaginative assemblymen passed laws which made it a misdemeanor for "sportsmen" to carry dirks, pistols, swords-in-canes, and other unlawful arms.[51]

At Fredericktown, Missouri, a German tavern-keeper had put a pistol bullet through a Frenchman for insulting him. The magistrate who sat in judgment of the case was an unlettered Kentuckian who fled his home state because of an embarrassing bankruptcy proceeding. He had a natural disdain for lawyers, and immediately a feud broke out between him and the prosecuting attorney. When the lawyer asked the judge to sign a woman witness to the affidavit, the sage jurist misunderstood and replied, "I calculate you must take me for a most almighty fool to suppose that I'm a mind to swar to what's in that ar paper before I've read a word of it, and I ain't a-going to do no sich thing for no lawyer on this univarsal arth." The lawyer denied that the court had the power to bail the prisoner, to which the court replied, "The court knows well enough what it is abaught, it ain't a-going to do no sich thing as read all them law books by no manner of means, and it's no use to carry on so for the court decides all pynts agin you." Following this tirade the judge tightened his lips and sucked air through his teeth. The lawyer sneered that "some folks gets their law from law books, and some folks, I calculate, must suck it in." By this time the judge had up a full head of steam and replied, "Suck or no suck, I swar I ain't a-going to be bully-ragged by no sich talking junisuses as you, a human abhorrence, and that's perfickly intosticated with his own importance—that's the court's candid opinion—if it ain't I wish the court may be etarnally damned."[52]

There were sports on the frontier which left less indelible marks on the participants than gougings and dirkings. There were innumerable games that entertained the energetic sons of the western country. They played leapfrog (high over the head style), ran foot races, threw shoulder stones, tomahawks, hatchets, knives, kicked the hat, flung the rail, wrestled and threw long bullets. Of these sports, throwing shoulder stones and long bullets seemed to be most popular. Shoulder stones was a frontier counterpart to the modern shot-put, while long bullets has no modern descendant. Perhaps long bullets was an adaptation of Scotch bowls. In towns, and along highways where there was a smooth surface, the players rolled a large wooden sphere at which they threw sharp barbs. State laws were passed forbidding the playing of this game either down, or across, public thoroughfares and streets.[53]

More exciting were the sports of bearbaiting, dogfighting and gander-pulling. Crowds which poured into western towns for militia musters, political barbecues and county court days "struck up" gander-pullings to test the stamina of both horses and riders. Long-necked residents of the town ponds and creeks were brought forth, the feathers were plucked from their heads, and they were then smeared with lard. A trellis or a limb was selected to which the gander was hung head down so he would be just barely within hand-reach of a man standing in his stirrups. Riders were then lined up to ride in a continuous circle around the trellis until someone was able to jerk the head off the suspended gander. This game lasted for hours, and it was made sporting by the two "whippers" who stood at the base of the tree or scaffolding and gave the horses a good whacking as their riders reached for the prize.[54]

This was the American frontier, which was anything but dull. Frontiersmen were free to come and go. No other Americans have been so absolutely free of conventions and social restrictions as were those people who pushed the Indians, the b'ar, the painter, and the tall timber back off the land in the great "trans-Appalachian" country. In this process they dreamed fondly of the day when they might answer the critical jabs of blundering travelers with proof that they had made good. It was with more vision than is usual with dreamers when in

1821 a frontiersman said: "Other nations boast of what they are or have been, but the true citizen of the United States exalts his head to the skies in the contemplation of what the grandeur of his country is going to be. Others claim respect and honor because of the things done by a long line of ancestors; an American appeals to prophecy, and with Malthus in one hand and a map of the back country in the other he boldly defies us to a comparison with America as she is to be, and chuckles in delight over the splendors the geometrical ratios is to shed over her story. This appeal to the future is his never-failing resource. If an English traveler complains of their inns and hints his dislike to sleeping four in a bed he is first denounced as a calumniator and then told to wait a hundred years and see the superiority of American inns to British. If Shakespeare, Milton, Newton are named, he is again told to wait until we have cleared our land, till we have idle time to attend to other things; wait till 1900, and then see how much nobler our poets and profounder our astronomers and longer our telescopes than any that decrepit old hemisphere of yours will produce."[55]

## CHAPTER II

# VARMINTS

In 1797 a Kentucky "screecher" went out to cut his wife a broom handle and on the way he encountered a large bear. He undertook to kill the varmint with his ax, but before he could get in a blow the animal snatched the implement of death out of his hand, and the Kentuckian was left bare-fisted before the enraged beast. There was only one thing to do in this emergency and that was to gouge the "critter." The backwoodsman set his teeth in the bear's nose after the fashion of committing a first-class piece of mayhem on an opponent at an election and began "thumbing" his belly and eyes. In a few moments bruin was rendering such pitiful screams that neighbors came running to see who was being murdered. Later a traveler inquired of this native son, "How do you and the bears make it?" "They can't stand Kentucky play," said the vigorous red horse. "Biting and gouging are too hard for them."[1]

Wherever settlers were found there were dozens of yarns of pioneer encounters with "varmints." Daniel Boone and his contemporaries spun hundreds of tall tales about their exploits among the beasts of the fields and the woods. At Lexington, Kentucky, the pedantic Professor John McKinney lived to tell of a hair-raising meeting with a catamount. While McKinney was concerned with his desk, a female wildcat crept silently into the room and sprang upon him, fastening its fangs securely around a rib. The courageous professor smashed the cat's head against a table crushing it under the impact. Neighbors heard the commotion and ran to the rescue. From that day on he was known throughout the West as "Wildcat" John.[2]

"Varmints" in the language of the period were audacious. Like Charley of the Arkansas bottoms most backwoodsmen had a mixed love and fear of the animals. Charley was outspoken in the expression of his attitude. He told the traveler Featherstonhaugh, "I hates them 'ar cursed varmints and cattermounts, as folks calls 'em, a plaguey sight worser than painters, and there's pretty smart scatter of 'em in this cane I'll tell *you*. The cursed critters do beat all for sneaking along seven or eight of 'em together when a sow's going to pig, and they'll git right close to her when she is gitting the pigs and when she grunts at 'em, the blasts set up their backs jist like a *naytural* cat and one of 'em will take one pig, and another of 'em will lay hold of another pig, and I swar, when she is done, she turns around and she ain't got ne'er a pig on the face of the arth. That's the way these onaccountable varmints sarved my sows every so many times, for I reckon they like the woods to pig in better'n the stye."[3] Wildcats, or catamounts, were extremely annoying animals. In many respects they stand out as symbolical of the extremely wild western country. They were less timid about entering a hog pen or a cabin than other varmints. They were even bold enough to attack a grown man when driven to it by hunger.

These animals sometimes sneaked right up into a cabin and laid hold of a child. Many times parents had to rescue children from the clutches of catamounts, and sometimes they were unsuccessful in their attempts to prevent serious injury. Bishop H. B. Bascom on one occasion was seated at a puncheon dinner table when blood-curdling screams from the yard sent the family rushing out to see what was happening. When they reached the yard they found a wildcat bearing off the youngest child. Bascom seized a rifle from the pegs over the door and fired at the animal, but he was too late for already the cat had thrust its teeth through the child and it was dead.[4] On many other occasions these sneaking animals caused grief for western settlers. They were the most predatory of all animals in the western woods, and their attacks often came suddenly and without warning. When cornered they were ruthless and tenacious fighters.

Among the varmints which were to be found on the frontier, there were several which were outstanding. These were bears, wolves, raccoons, foxes, catamounts, polecats, panthers (painters), and snakes. The bear figured prominently in many backwoods escapades. Bears, along the frontier, were like cata-mounts—plentiful and dangerous. Shooting one of these animals was certainly not work for a greenhorn, and it was woe unto one who took a shot and missed a vital spot, because a wounded bear fought viciously until it bled to death. Many a hunter failed to return from the woods because he shot shy of the mark in a bear hunt, and was forced to come to bare-handed grips with an angered bruin. These animals figured in many hundreds of human tragedies in the western woods. William Faux visited a family in Indiana who owned two pet bears. He offered one an ear of corn which it took gently from his hand. A few days before Faux's visit one of these pets broke its chain and entered the house, gathered up an infant and set out for the woods. An aged and bedridden grandfather was the only protection the child had, but when the bear started off with it he followed in hot pursuit and rescued it from the "crit-tur" "unhugged and unhurt."[5]

On the Missouri frontier, a gallant female pioneer made a courageous stand against a determined bear. This woman, a Mrs. Atkinson, lived near the present city of St. Louis. During the night she heard an unusual noise among her livestock and rushed out to discover the trouble. At first she found nothing, but before she could summon her negro to come and take a look she was gathered into a fraternal hug by a huge bear from the Mississippi bottoms. The negro hurried to the rescue and began pummeling the varmint's fat sides with his bare fists, and in a moment it let go of the woman and undertook to catch the negro. It failed, however, to accomplish its purpose and returned to Mrs. Atkinson's house where it was on the verge of renewing its affectionate embrace when the woman's daughter shot it between the eyes with a rifle. This account was written by a native son of that region who looked upon the feat as one of the really great accomplishments of womankind in the western country.[6]

Bears and their habits figured prominently in the life of the frontier. Figures of speech and hundreds of stories were built around them. B'ar's oil was the slickest stuff a frontier dandy ever rubbed on his hair, and a bear hug was the tightest embrace the mind of man could imagine. Occasionally the exciting rumor passed around through western villages and country-sides that *b'ars* were in the neighborhood! This rumor always created a furor, and fetched armed huntsmen to the pursuit. Most of these false-alarm bear hunts, however, wound up with an act of rich comedy. Such a case occurred in a western village on the Ohio when one of the citizens informed the people that he had seen *six full-grown bears* crossing the ridge into the town. Business ceased, and lusty huntsmen oiled up their b'ar guns and prepared their dogs for a bloody affray with the bold long-fanged invaders. Soon an army of hunters equipped with every sort of weapon from a flintlock rifle to a pitchfork was in hurried pursuit of the hungry varmints. Hounds, curs, short-legged, snub-nosed bulldogs, and yelping "fice" were carrying on as though they were in the habit of catching bears every day. For five miles around every man was on a rampage. Live-stock was frightened to death, women huddled young children about them behind barred doors. All day the sturdy band of hunters searched the countryside, but "nary" a b'ar's tail did they see.

At last a loud *halloo* from a secluded strip of woods informed the mob that the game was "treed." "There they are," shouted an excited frontiersman, "there they are! I have seen a bear before today! There's the old one and her cubs! But they have such devilish long faces!" Not only did these "bears" have long faces, there arose from the huddle a most "unbear"-like aroma—an aroma which had a strangely familiar tang. Too, the bears grunted in an unusual manner. When the snorting game was surrounded, and the bloodthirsty riflemen were ready to close in and make quick work of the kill, they discovered that they were totally disgraced. These varmints which they had hunted all day were not "six full grown bears," but six mud-covered pigs "which had been turned out to run at large after getting so besmeared and discolored by the black mire of the sty as to be readily mistaken in the dim woods for their "less harmless" cousins; and as the poor creatures stood at bay, the funny wishfulness on their upraised countenances seemed to say to the chagrined hunters, "What went ye out to see?"[7]

Panthers and wolves aggravated frontiersmen. There were no more treacherous animals on the American continent than the "painter." They sneaked upon their prey without warning, and were deadly in their attacks. A hunter named "Slowtrap" gave Frederick Gerstaecker an account of a venture with a panther back in Kentucky. He said that he was caught in the woods after a deer hunt and tried to get some sleep, but a rascally painter kept him awake. Several times the creature came near enough his campfire to be seen, but not near enough for him to get a shot at it. Finally he dropped off to sleep, and in a few minutes he was awakened to find that he was being covered with leaves. A painter was covering him preparatory to making a strike. "Slowtrap" ran the animal away, covered a bough with leaves and climbed a neighboring tree to await its return. In a short time it was back and sprang upon the covered branch and sank its fangs deep into the limb, and while it was thus engaged he shot it.[8] Hunters who were injured in the western woods, or who were otherwise incapacitated, had a horror of being torn to pieces by these savage beasts.

Wolves were fierce animals when they caught their prey in an unsuspecting situation. Frontiersmen who traveled through the woods with fresh meat in their baggage expected to be hounded to death by these howling demons. One traveler, driving from one frontier settlement to another in a wagon loaded with fresh meat, was kept awake nights by howling wolves who were massed for an attack upon his cargo. A wolf, however, could be frightened away by the use of fires. He would not venture into a camp where there was a roaring bonfire.[9] Occasionally these varmints invaded homes, especially when they were driven to it by hunger. Captain Rankin, a frontiersman, heard a scratching at his door and opened it to see what was causing the disturbance, and was attacked by a large gray wolf. The attack would have been fatal, except for the fact that a neighbor was near at hand, and with powerful hands took the varmint by its jaws, and by sheer strength held its mouth open until it was killed with an ax.[10]

Not all the beasts of the frontier woods were vicious. There were 'coons, 'possums and, tamest of all, polecats. 'Coons and 'possums constituted a valuable staple meat resource, and backwoodsmen spent many nights hunting them to replenish their meager larders. Occasionally 'coon hunters got themselves into pretty "fixes" because these animals were shifty creatures, and "took to tall timber." Not only was timber tall, but it was likewise large around. If the dogs happened to trail a wise old ringtail he caused considerable confusion among them. These old fellows knew the art of "marking" trees and going on, that is, they climbed trees for a short way up and sprang well beyond its roots, thus throwing the dogs completely off their trails. Wise hunters and experienced dogs knew about this playful little bit of deceit and circled marked trees to make certain that the game had not fled.

Rather than do a week's chopping for a spavined 'coon, many hunters preferred to climb trees and shake their prizes to the ground and the waiting dogs. J. B. Finley has left a good account of what happened a thousand times between Virginia and Arkansas. A 'coon was treed, and one of the more venturesome Nimrods volunteered his climbing services to go up and "shake the bushes" a little. The dogs were overcome with excitement and awaited the dropping of the 'coon with anticipation of a good fight. Instead of the thudding of a fat coon, however, there came a cry of despair, "I'm falling!" The imperiled climber's companions called out to him to "pray." "Pray," yelled the suspended brother, "I haven't time; I can't pray." "But you must pray," pleaded a companion. "If you fall you will be killed," mourned a pessimistic companion. Obeying the command to seek divine blessing as a sort of extreme unction in his plight the suspended hunter began, "Now I lay me down to sleep," but the limb gave away rapidly and he made a more practical appeal "to hold the dogs I'm coming."[11] Hunters who climbed trees often took the chance of getting gnawed to pieces by their pot-licker hounds when they came down, unless they took particular precautions to "call them off"; and it was woe unto poor mortals who fell out of trees into the midst of their hungry packs.

Of all the animals on the frontier that stimulated the human imagination, the skunk or polecat headed the list. This varmint demanded respect wherever he went, and usually he was given a free right-of-way to go about his business unmolested. William Littell wrote in his *Festoons of Fancy:* "There is no animal in God's creation less beloved by man than a polecat is, and yet, none is more civilly treated. I have seen a major general, and a judge of a supreme court, turn out of a public road into the brush and mud, in order to let one pass along unmolested; and I believe that if a polecat should come to the capitol, and offer to walk into the representatives' chamber during the session of that honorable body, Roger Divine would hardly call him to order.

"I believe that after he had taken his seat or stand among the members, he would be treated with as much respect as is bestowed on Mr. Speaker."[12]

Appearing before the learned Royal Society of England, Captain Jonathan Carver read a paper in which he declared that the skunk or polecat "is the most extraordinary animal that the American woods produce." After a long descriptive narrative of the beast and its habits, he enlightened the nature-loving members of the Royal Society upon other qualities of the animal. He said that its "extraordinary powers are only shown when it is pursued. As soon as he finds himself in danger, he ejects, to great distance from behind, a small stream of water, of so subtle a nature, and at the same time so powerful a smell, that the air is tainted with it for half a mile in circumference; and his pursuers, whether men or dogs, being almost suffocated with the stench, are obliged to give up the pursuit." The learned Carver further explained to his hearers that the French in America called the varmints *Enfants du Diable* or *Bêtes Puantes* (the stinking beast) and that they were exactly right because a drop of the musk sprayed on clothing ruined it for future wear.[13]

John James Audubon also gave much attention to the polecat, or *Mephitis americana,* the correct zoological classification. This animal figured prominently in the naturalist's humorous jokes. Traveling between Henderson, Kentucky, and Louisville, Audubon and a visiting foreigner, whom he called "D. T.," came upon a handsome animal. The foreigner called it a "beautiful squirrel." Audubon informed his green companion that these "squirrels" were so tame that a person could lay hand on them if he were well gloved. This was sufficient encouragement for the European to attempt the experiment. Audubon recorded in his notes that "I think I see him approach, and laying the stick gently across the back of the animal, try to secure it; and I can yet laugh almost as heartily as I then did, when I plainly saw the discomfiture of the traveller." The poor unsuspecting foreigner was thoroughly showered at close range with a fresh stock of musk which he was never to forget. These were indeed strange squirrels, and from all evidence in hand the visitor believed they should be left absolutely to themselves.

Audubon's frivolous act was to cost him dearly before the pair reached Louisville. First, he had to travel a considerable distance with his "sprayed" and vile-smelling companion, and to sleep in the same bed with him that night. Snow began to fall in the late afternoon, and at nightfall the pair was forced to seek lodging in a roadside cabin. When they stopped at the cabin they were invited in and they found a cornshucking in the process of organization. People were coming in preparatory to the festive activities in the corncrib. During the cold ride, the odor of the skunk had died down, but when the European visitor crowded to the fire and his trousers became warm he sent up a "fragrance" which ran the cornshuckers off to their task ahead of schedule. In short order the cabin was deserted by everybody except Audubon, his odoriferous European companion, and a negro servant who was left behind to wait upon the pair.[14]

. Captain Carver reported other matters of zoological wonderment to the dignified Royal Society. He gave a detailed description of the audacious American rattlesnake, which at this late date sounds "stretched." The poison, said he, ran through the human body causing the victim to feel chilly, and to be shaken by a tremor. Doubtless Carver gathered his information from superstitious backwoodsmen, because he stated that a person bitten by this reptile turned the same color as the snake. Dog days, he declared was the worst season in which to be bitten by a rattlesnake for the poison was stronger at this time than at any other period. To be bitten just above the heel on the lower tendons of the calf of the leg, was to experience almost sudden death. He believed that the poison traveled through the body faster from this place. Carver said that though persons lived through the tortures of being bitten by these poisonous reptiles, their health was never the same for each year there was a recurrence of the pain. "Yet they annually experienced a slight return," wrote the Captain of His Majesty's Provincial Troops in America, "of the dreadful symptoms about the time they received the instillation."[15] This report obviously shows the influence of imaginative American backwoodsmen who either believed these things, or "stuffed" the Englishman with this nonsense.

Among the other reptiles which attracted the British scientist's attention were the *long black snake,* the *green snake,* the *thorn-tail snake,* the *speckle snake,* the *ring snake,* and the *two-headed snake.* Captain Carver described the *thorn-tail snake* as of middle size, and he explained that it had a thorn or stinger in its tail. This snake was the most deadly of all because its victims died almost instantaneously. He was cautious, however, to explain to the learned gentlemen back home that the thorn-tail snake was seldom seen. A two-headed snake had been presented to Lord Geoffrey Amherst, but frankly, explained Carver, little was known of this specie.[16]

Another Englishman, James Flint, discovered a reptilian curiosity in the *Ophisaurus ventralis* or glass snake, which on being struck a hard blow broke to pieces. This strange fragile reptile possessed the unusual power of being able to reassemble itself. In this land of the wonderful "glass" creature there was also the hoop or horn snake, which could grab its tail in its mouth and go coasting around the countryside in the shape of a hoop. Wherever this mobile monster chose to thrust its horn-like stinger sudden death followed. Frontiersmen reported having seen trees die from the effects of the sting. Flint, however, was justly dubious of the fatal powers of this natural wonder, and he witnessed a demonstration pricking by a Mr. Say in which nothing happened.[17]

Nothing frightened a backwoodsman quicker than the whi-r-r-r of a rattlesnake, unless it were coming face to face with one. Dr. Gerard Troost, a noted geologist in Tennessee, was much interested in the reptiles of that state, and on one occasion he was en route to Washington, D. C., from Nashville with two large rattlesnakes in a basket. A Baptist parson, on his way to a big immersion, got on the coach and took a top seat. In a short time the heat of the sun and the vibration of the coach lulled the minister to sleep, and at the same time jiggled the lid of the basket out of place. After a time the drowsy minister was aroused from his slumbers by a strange sensation. When he opened his eyes he found the two rattlers staring him in the face. He jumped astride the driver and swept that worthy down from his seat, and when the two landed on the ground they jumped around screaming in their excitement. Momentarily the passengers inside the coach piled out to see what strange powers had possessed their fellow traveler and the driver. In short order the coach was deserted by all except Dr. Troost and his venomous possessions. The snake-loving geologist nonchalantly threw his coat over the basket and bade his fellow passengers to return to their seats with the soothing philosophical observation, "Gentlemen, only don't let dese poor dings pite you, and dey won't hoort you."[18]

Varmints were commonplace on the frontier. Individual escapades with members of the animal kingdom were so numerous that few journals and other writings of the period go to the trouble to describe them. However, the boys who had a leaning for "spinning" entertaining yarns found in either the natural or extraordinary experiences material for tall yarns. The varmint element of the frontier was the central point of hundreds of early western yarns. When backwoodsmen became reminiscent, they gave due attention to this type of adventure. Painters couldn't stand courthouses and they moved on. B'ars were killed and biled down into grease to slick back the hair on dandified heads, rattlesnakes were burned up in wood fires, and the wonderful specimen described by imaginative natives and greenhorn foreigners never existed. Only *Mephitis americana* adjusted himself to changing conditions on the frontier, and settled down to be reasonably happy in the white man's civilization. Thus today the only remains of the varmint frontier are the yarns, and the polecats.

The following tale is a classic of the frontier varmint stories. Long Jim was an ingenious gouger who could take care of trying situations in fine style. Jim was bottled up on one occasion with a b'ar sitting on top of him, and it took all of his ingenuity to get free.

### LONG JIM PUT THE B'AR BEHIND

Some two or three years ago I was wandering about the far-famed state of Rackensac, hunting, fishing and enjoying myself with whatever came my way; and having heard of the celebrated hunting ground, a place called "Devil's Summer Retreat," I concluded to visit the classic spot in hopes of finding amusement. After arriving in the neighborhood of His Sable Majesty's summer residence, I became most unaccountably lost, and wandered about the best part of a day in hopes of finding someone able to inform me of my whereabouts. At length toward evening I stumbled on a little ruined round-log cabin, which seemed inhabited, at least I judged so from the appearance of two or three acres under fence and partial cultivation. When I had ridden up, a yell brought the owner to the door, who courteously invited me to enter, which I did right willingly, as I was both fatigued and hungry. After eating a hearty supper of bear meat, and feeling somewhat relieved, I commenced admiring the locality, improvements, etc., and, among other things, inquired how long since he first settled on the place?

"Stranger," says he, "I ain't the first settler; I bought this clearing from a fellow called 'Tussle Jim' cause he was sich a rantankerus fighter. Jim said he settled here when the Ingens and B'ar war thick as simmons, and a mity hard time he had on it, trying to keep things straight. His stock wasn't very large, only an old cow and a sow, but the sow littered every month or so, and the old cow had a calf every year—she never failed but once. One winter it was so cold that she concluded to hold over, and not have a calf in the spring but she made it up afterwards, for the next spring she had a calf and a yearling! She was a great cow, Jim said, and considerate. The old sow didn't do so well, the b'ar got to persuasin' of her, and whenever her back was turned, they visited her family and enticed some of them off. Jim didn't like such carryings on, but he couldn't help himself, the varmints never left a track, so Jim had to grin and bear it. Well, one cold winter (the same one the old cow held over) Jim was hunting three or four miles from here, and going around the root of a big hollow tree that had fallen down, he seed some bones that looked mity like his pigs, so he fired his rifle in the hole three or four times, and when he listened he heered a noise like as if somethin' war smothering in blood. Jim thought he'd killed a wolf, and as he wanted a skin for the baby to sleep on, he concluded to crawl in and get the varmint out. So he crept in feet foremost. Pulling his rifle in arter him, and when he got to the 'tuther end, a matter of fifty feet, he felt back and found he hadn't killed a wolf, but a young cub b'ar. Jim war mity glad, and commenced pullin' it out, but before he got halfway he seed the hole darkened, and he knowed it war the old she. Jim was so skeered, he didn't know what to do till she war rite over him, but he fired down her throat and she fell dead. Jim's feelin's war mity relieved at first; till he tried to push her back (cause she filled the hole chock full and he couldn't get over). And he found she wouldn't budge an inch. He thought to cut her to pieces, and felt for his knife— but it warn't there! Scissors, wasn't that a fit! Jim said he war rite down worried; if he could only get the tarnal thing behind him, he wouldn't care a cuss, he'd crawl rite straight out and go home; but she wasn't behind him—so he fell to studying, and studied a long spell, and as there was no other way he took hold of her nose with his teeth and commenced eating and before dark the old she was behind him!"[19]

A wild son of Ol' Kaintuck was sent by his father to the American Bottom in Illinois to make his own living, and to relieve the old man of further responsibility. This whole yarn of young Beechum's exploits was spun in a western courtroom while the judge, lawyers and jury awaited the return of star witness John Haynie. Ellick Smothers, the constable, was the narrator of this story.

### How Bill Beechum Killed the Yaller Rattler

"You see 'Squar, ole man Beechum (spelled Beauchamp, but universally pronounced Beechum in Kentucky, had a mighty big plantation, and a powerful sight o' niggers, down there in Ol' Kentucky, and he hadn't nary child 'ceptin Bill, and seein's they wan't no schools like they now is, Bill kind o' run 'mong the niggers 'cept when he was 'projectin' 'round,' down to Kale Lord's store, on the corners, 'bout a mile from the cabin. Thar he'd stay, nigh 'pon a week, drinkin' ole ry, and gettin' it charged to the ole man, till he got kind o' sick on't, and was bound he wouldn't stand it no longer. So one time old Beechum come over into the 'merican bottom—that's afore they was any State here, ye know, and nothin' much but rattlesnakes and Injuns—and entered a half section, put a nice little chunk of a cabin up, and then went back to Kentuck and tole Bill he mought go thar an' make a livin' or starve, just as he'd a min' ter. Wall, Bill kind o' got his spunk up, and said he'd go, and ax no odds of the ole man. So he cum over and went to work. He'd got one o' the niggers to run away tho' fust, and he had him to help."

"That ar long green o' yourn is mighty nice, 'Squar, but I rather reckoned on its swellin' in the mouth more'n it does; gin us a little more on't." After taking an enormous quid, and, probably through absence of mind, putting the balance in his pocket, Ellick proceeded.

"Bill worked like a hoss for a year and didn't drink none, 'cept ma*bee* onct or twiste, when he went down to the landin' to sell his crap and get a little fixins for the cabin. Thar wor a mighty peert gal lived 'bout five miles off from Bill's. Her father was a Yankee—that is, he wan't one of them skinnin', peddlin' Yankees, like that un that sold me the clock I 'sulted you 'bout 'tother day, nor a perlite York Yankee, like you 'Squar, but he was from the Ohio country somewhar—anyhow he *wor* a Yankee, and Bill didn't like the ideer of courtin' the gal, mostly, 'cause he knew that Yankees ain't no 'count *never*. But when he come to get more 'quainted, he diskivered she were so peert, that he just up and married her, Yankee or no Yankee. Now things went on mighty swimmin' with Bill—craps good, fust one baby, and then 'nother in the sap trough—"

"*Sap trough!* what had that to do with the babies Ellick?"

"Why you see 'Squar—it's 'sprizin' that you didn't know it—in them days they wan't no carpenters, to make nice pine cradles like yourn—"

"Like *mine!* I've no cradle."

"Wall, you orter have," said Ellick, with a wink of intense slyness to the bystanders.

"But, anyhow, they rocked younguns in sap troughs when the country was new. But, as I wor g'wine to say, Bill had got fixed just as nice as anybody on the bottom. Byme bye, when the 'improvements' begin to come 'bout, a feller started a store 'bout a mile from Bill's, to buy tobacker and other produce and sell little knick-knacks and red-eye. Bill grow'd wuss an' wuss, till he got so he'd either be over to the store, or lay in the cabin drunk, with a jug 'long side all day. His wife thought she'd scare him; so she begin to tell 'bout a feller, down whar she come from, that had the man with the poker arter him."

"The man with the poker—what's that?"

"Now, 'Squar, don't interrupt, or I shan't get through in time for the case; but then, I 'spose you don't know 'cause now I mind that Bill's wife gave it a larnt name—she called it *delirrus screamins,* cause they screeches so when they has it."

"Yes, now I understand—go on."

"Wall, when she told 'bout that feller's seein' snakes, and lizards and all them things, Bill called her a damned fool, and said 'twor all 'magination and want of narve. He said he never'd give way to such feelins. He wan't so powerful weak in the loft as that. Still it set Bill to thinkin' mighty hard. Wall, one day in the Spring, when the craps were ready to be put in the ground, and the ole nigger couldn't do all the work, and Bill wouldn't get sober enough to help, Bill's wife put the youngest child in the trough, and tole the other one to be a good boy and stay with pap, while she went out to help Pete plant corn. Bill tole her not to go, but she didn't mind, only she said, 'Bill, if any *snakes* come 'bout the children while I'm gone, be sure to kill 'em all!' This riled Bill, and he swore awful at her. But she went out to the field, and Bill tuk another drink and sot down and begin to think it all over, till he most thought he *did* see snakes. But then he'd rouse himself, and open his eyes wide, and they'd all go 'way. Purty soon, though, he seed a tree-men—just a big yaller rattler comin' in at the door. He come kind o' slow, like he wor looking 'round to see if anybody wor thar, or arter a mouse or some milk. This time Bill opened his eyes wider'n ever, and said, 'Go 'way thar; I won't give up to you, no how.' But the rattler he kep' crawlin' 'long till he got clar into the cabin. By this time Bill got mighty skeer'd, but he was bound not to give up to the man with the poker, so he walked right up to the snake and touched him with his foot, thinkin' he'd go 'way out of his mind as soon as he done that. But 'stead o' goin 'way out he just curled himself up and struck Bill on the leg; but Bill had on a pair o' stout linsey trowsers, and bein' loose too 'bout the legs, the pizen didn't go into him. His hair now stood straight up, but he grappled with ole yaller and they had it 'bout two minutes, Bill thumpin' and choken' him, and the snake strikin' like the mischief at Bill's bare wrists. At last Bill flung him onto the step, dead as he could be. Wall, he went back to his cheer, fairly tuckered out and soberer than he'd been for a year. Still he couldn't 'zactly tell whether he'd reely killed a snake, or the man with the poker was arter him. So he just thought he'd let the carcase lay thar till his wife come; and if she passed by 'thout seein' any thing, then he'd got it, sure 'nough. Wall, when Bill's wife come, and seed the snake layin' thar, she didn't know 'twor dead and gave a big jump and screech'd out so you could 'a heerd her 'cross a quarter section. Then Bill know'd he'd killed a reel snake, and begin to brag 'bout it; but, what 'tween his bein' a little shaky, and not bein' smart 'nough to tell a 'cute lie, he let the whole thing out. Pete, who'd come in right arter Bill's wife, heerd the whole story, and that night, when he went to the store to get some molasses, he told it to a lot o' fellers loafering 'bout thar. Bill didn't go to the store for more'n a week, and his wife begin to think he wor a changed man. But, at last, he got mighty dry, and tuk his jug and went over. As soon's he got in the door, the boys begin to run him so, and ax him to tell all 'bout his tussle with a rattler, that he clar'd out without gettin' a drap; an', from that day to this, he hain't drunk a single glass, so fur's know's."

"Of course, then, he's a much better man."

"Wall, I don't know 'bout that. It 'pears like he's natterally mean, an' when he couldn't meet with the boys an' have rum with 'em like he used to, he took to makin' money and cheatin' everybody, till he hain't got a friend on the hull bottom. Besides most folks think he don't drink 'cause he's so 'fernal mean, and 'cause, every time he goes into a doggery, the boys allers begins on him. They plagued him so, down on the 'merican bottom, that he had to quit thar; so he moved up onto Claypole's, but the story follered him an' I reckon he never will hear the last on't."

"But Ellick, you said the snake 'struck' him on his bare wrists, while he was killing him. Now, why didn't he die of the poison?"

"Lord, 'Squar, didn't you know that snake bites don't hurt drunken men? He had so much pizen in him that a little bit more didn't make no difference. That's why we all keep whisky in our houses—it's all on 'count o' bein' 'fraid o' snake bites."

"But here comes Jack Haynie with all his witnesses. Lord! ain't some of 'em right! Boys, you better look out, they'll be gougin' 'fore the case is through."

An' that's the way that Bill Beechum "killed the Yaller rattler."[20]

When liquor ran short even a Hoosier would run the risk of getting snake-bit for a drink. The following story was told of one of Dr. Thomas' patients at Monticello, Indiana.

## LOOKING FOR A SNAKE BITE

Mr. J. H. S. aged thirty-eight, who stands six feet in his stockings—who by the way is very fond of brandy—had just been bitten on the inside of his left heel by a large rattlesnake both fangs having been inserted in the muscles. I gave him, in the short time alluded to, one quart of brandy and one and one-half gallons of whisky, all without intoxication. He wanted more, and I refused to supply his wants. The next day, Mr. H., his next neighbor, was passing along and saw him barefooted with his pants rolled up and wading around in the weeds and grass with his bare feet. H. asked him if he had lost anything? "No, sir, ain't any liquor only what Dr. Thomas has, and he won't let me have any unless I am snake-bit."[21]

## CHAPTER III

## GREEN UN'S

Measured by certain standards the whole western country was populated by green and inquisitive rustics. The greenhorn of the early western frontier, however, was unlike the tenderfoot of a later period. He was shut off from free communication with the outside world and as a consequence was uninformed of what was taking place elsewhere. At other times Westerners gave the impression that they were nothing more than a bumptious race of crude, brash backwoodsmen. If the accounts of the early English travelers are of any value the West was a land of verdant forest, verdant mud and verdant natives. Everywhere visitors, both native and foreign, met with an eternal stream of questions of "Where did you get that horse?" "What is your business?" Others claimed that they were greeted with "Stranger, will you drink or fight?"[1] If a stranger coming into town had drunk with everybody who wished to pump him of news, he would have remained thoroughly "overseas" during an extended visit.

The traveler Flagg was considerably wrought up over the eternal questioning which he experienced. He referred to these inquisitions as "blessed moments of trencher devotion" in which all the inmates of a log cabin examined him with the thoroughness of a county court lawyer. Everyone took his turn in asking "name and nativity, occupation, location, and destination." Uncle Bill "a little corpulent old fellow with a proboscis of exceeding rubicundity, and eyes red as a weasel's, to say nothing of a voice melodious in note as an asthmatic clarionet," was searching in his inquiries. He exasperated the traveler to such an extent that he preached a forthright sermon on western inquisitiveness. "The curiosity of the Northern Yankee," said the intimidated Flagg, "is, in all conscience, unconscionable enough when aroused; but, for genuine quintessence of inquisitiveness, commend your enemy, if you have one, to an army of starving gallinippers, or to a backwoods family of the Far West, who sees a traveller twice a year, and don't take the newspaper!" Becoming a bit ashamed of his unheroic attack upon his hospitable but curious hosts, Flagg apologized that "I mention this not as a *fault* of the worthy Suckers: it is rather a misfortune; or, if otherwise, it surely 'leans to virtue's side!' "[2]

The boys over west of the mountains may have been a bit green and tedious in their questioning and in their general demeanor, but they lacked nothing when it came to brashness of manner. There were never franker people than those who lived in the great Ohio Valley. If they formed an opinion of a stranger they proceeded to express themselves with the same freedom they claimed for the American eagle. A son of the western woods approached a stranger whom he did not know and had never seen before with the remarkable statement: "Stranger, I don't want to hurt your feelings, but you are the ugliest man that ever was turned out of the workshop of creation." Naturally such a shocking salutation was disarming, and especially so if the person addressed were a Britisher. "Sir-r-r," sputtered the gentleman in wrath and confusion, "if you mean to insult me. . . ." It was now time for the native son to take the defensive and he apologized by saying, "By no means, but the thing was on my mind, and I couldn't help telling you so." He explained further that "I didn't know you were a foreigner, or I should have bewar'd of the British lion."[3]

Green ones were habitually taking things literally, and often embarrassed both themselves and their friends. Frontier orators dealt in high flights, and sometimes rapidly ascending verbal balloons were punctured by well-aimed barbs. Lawyers, politicians and preachers exhibited promiscuously this fine article of oratorical adornment. Finest of all figures in the West was one in which the American eagle flapped his mighty wings and soared in ever-widening circles even unto the uppermost realms of the "ethereal blue." A rampaging speaker shouted to his audience, "Don't you see him, fellow citizens, a-risin' higher and higher?" An uncurried backwoodsman, who stood by and craned his neck until he had permanently warped his spinal column and had contracted a horribly disfiguring case of "sun grins," turned to the orator and said, "Well damned if I can see him!" This unceremonious prick would have completely unhorsed an ordinary chest-pounding vote-seeker, but not so this homespun speaker who descended with his altitudinous eagle long enough to explain, "Hoss, I was speakin in a figger."[4]

Speakers were brought low at times by other equally effective methods. Often opponents in hot political stumpings took advantage of ranting opponents by mumbling behind their backs. There was an old prod which felled even the most brazened orator. An unfeeling heckler would whisper audibly that "I guess he wouldn't talk quite so high falutin' if he knowed how his britches was torn out behind."[5] If there was anything which universal mankind on the frontier responded to without argument it was a whispered warning that his britches had silently given way in their posterior regions.

Greenness was a part of the reality of the frontier. Isolation bred curious manners, and outlandish attitudes at times. There were green ones who, like Mike Shuck, the beaver hunter, were perfectly satisfied and at home in the woods, but a bit confused in company. Michael was a whiteheaded semi-barbarian who followed the frontier in its rising tide westward. No one was able to locate him definitely in any one place; that is, he was never known to be a Kentuckian, a Hoosier, a Sucker or a Missourian. Wherever the beaver went Mike followed. He followed bareheaded, barefooted, and bent under a heavy load of traps. This hardy son of the woods knew more about game and its habits than a whole tribe of Indian hunters. When night came the beaver hunter made his bed, cooked his meal, and slept without a single earthly fear or worry. When the trapping season ended, and the fur was thin this weary huntsman loaded his fall *cache* in a cottonwood canoe and put out for New

Orleans. He could navigate the Missouri, the Arkansas and the Mississippi without mishap. When he appeared in New Orleans Michael was a wonder to behold. There he proclaimed in glowing terms to persuasive bartenders the salubrity of spring water, and damned civilization to city dwellers who pitied him. To the latter he was a comic greenhorn who had never "caught on."[6]

The backwardness of Mike Shuck attracted attention even in the frontier papers. But frontier verdancy was a highly relative thing. Easterners coming into the land showed a marked ignorance of manners and conditions of life. When Sol Smith came west with his theatrical company in the early part of the nineteenth century he ran into a trying situation along the Allegheny River. Sol and his friend Francisco were on their way to the Ohio Valley frontier to begin an engagement when one evening they were halted by darkness. They saw a light in a dwelling near by. They "hallooed the house" and received an answer. When they landed three "ugly-looking fellows" greeted them. These uncouth appearing hosts welcomed them enthusiastically to their cabin. As Smith and his companions trudged up the bank they overheard one of the bullies say, "The devil! They have a right smart chance of plunder!" "Yes," replied another, "these boxes are confounded heavy; wonder which of 'ems got the specie in it?" The woman of the house was a sloven female with a bitter countenance, who scowled at the approaching company. She protested that they had no provisions for travelers, but the head of the meager household argued that they "could make out." He ordered a large fire built, and there followed a series of events which seemed to indicate that these squatters were brigands of the first water.

Sol and his traveling companions repented that they had stopped when they heard snatches of conversation which they took to mean murder. One of the boys asked the old man, "What success had you this evening?" "None at all," grumbled the hoary elder. "Haven't killed a living crittur tonight, though I've been watching since dark. I came very near knocking over a fine fellow but he was alarmed at the hallooing of these strangers and made his escape before I could get a crack at him." Further discussion for the evening's entertainment was to the effect that the guests could easily be cared for "if the menfolks will consent to be separated from their wives." The old man instructed two of the boys to "take the spade and basket and do as I told you." By this time the visitors were convinced that the shovel gang was off on a mission which had to do with grave-digging. Other bits of conversation picked up by the travelers were "How cursed heavy that black trunk of theirs is; they must be very rich. I am sorry we can't give 'em better fare *than what we are providing for them!*" Then there was some mention that "they won't mind when they are sound asleep" and other murderous-sounding suggestions. Later the old man appeared at the door with bloody hands and bawled, "Here boys, I've cut his throat come help me drag him up!" Finally when the travelers were for taking to the woods they had an answer to all the ominous talk which they had heard. The people with whom they were stopping were honest, ignorant and hospitable backwoodsmen who were trying to get together enough potatoes and meat to feed their guests. Instead of digging graves, the boys had gone to the potato patch, and instead of slitting the throat of an innocent traveler who owned "a black trunk full of specie" the head of the household had killed a pet ram.[7] Their visitors, however, had heard hair-raising yarns about the heartless assaults of river bandits, and they had convinced themselves that their moment of destruction had come.

Frontier actors and theaters were curiosities within themselves, but combined with the literal manner in which western greenhorns reacted to the plays there was much high comedy. At Paris, Kentucky, N. M. Ludlow's company was playing the famous tear-maker, the *Gamester.* This play was a prime favorite with sentimentalists in the West who desired a doleful release from the realities of life about them. The sentiment of the play was so clearly portrayed that no one but the greenest of greenhorns could fail to get the point. Before the curtain was lifted there strolled into the theater a jolly round-faced farmer who seated himself midway in the front row, and when the performers reached a new low in creating a melancholy situation this bumpkin regaled the tear-stained audience with a burst of unrestrained laughter. Each time the tragedian executed a masterly recitation of gloom, the rosy-faced patron burst forth with rib-quivering guffaws. His laughing completely ruined the effects of fine acting, and turned the *Gamester* and its troupe into a farce.

It was the custom on the frontier with strolling companies to lead their audiences through a vale of tears with tragedy and then bring them back to a normal state of mind with farce. At Paris the comedians were certain that the raucous disturbers would help make their act a rip roaring success. When the curtain was drawn, however, and the troupe was hitting a merry stride, the jubilant farmer became exceedingly morose. Each light line recited deepened the furrows of melancholy on his face, and soon he was in tears. This behavior was devastating; the tragedy had become a farce, and the comedy had become a tear-drenched tragedy. The actors believed they had been victimized by a smart Reuben and they were in favor of administering a "tanning" to their abnormal patron. They found, however, that this was his first play, and that he had reacted honestly to the lines.[8]

Some time later in this same town, Sol Smith created a disturbance by exciting the fears of a greenhorn theater-goer. His company was playing the *Honey Moon* in which he was brought on the stage as the Mock Duke, or, as had been whispered about, as a wax figure. When the supernumeraries bore the Mock Duke (Sol) onto the stage he was placed within six feet of a "raw specimen" who leaned forward chin in hands to stare at the waxmaker's wonder. The Mock Duke lay staring straight into the eyes of the "Kentuck," and giving way to a devilish temptation he winked at him. This was too much for the staring "Junius" who jumped up yelling, "I'll be damned if it's wax." This outburst surprised and amused the audience so much that attention was completely withdrawn from the "drama" on the stage.[9]

The gambler Morris was impressed in the early 'thirties with the licentious antics of patrons of the western theaters. At Cincinnati he witnessed a rather frisky adventure of a tobacco-chewing "yahoo" whose legs dangled over the ballustrade of the gallery. This nonchalant rustic amplified the thespian attractions of the stage by squirting ambeer onto the heads of the occupants of the orchestra seats. One of the bespattered victims became so enraged that he secured a stone in the streets and felled his spitting antagonist like a lumbering ox into the pit.[10]

A similar affair occurred in Louisville. One of the young bloods became inebriated and extended his naked legs over the balcony rail. He not only displayed a pair of knotty and hairy appendages, but he snored loudly in his drunken stupor. Rowdies in the pit below began yelling "Legs!" "Put 'em out!" "Saw his legs off!" "Pitch 'em down!" and "Grease his nostrils!" This noise and hubbub awakened the drunkard and he began hurling profane and vulgar invectives at his disturbers, and when they knotted themselves into a seething mob underneath the gallery he jumped upon their heads. Three of the booing pitmen were knocked down cold, but the daring blade was pounded into a bloody mass and thrown out of the door.[11]

Traveling away from their native communities, greenhorns were certain to show their lack of understanding to the complete amusement of all about them. At Madison, Indiana, two cautious Hoosier sisters from Mount Vernon came aboard a river steamer for their first visit to the great "outside." They were determined that nothing should escape them unnoticed, and that they would let no sharpers cheat them of their substance. Dad had paid for their comfort, and they were anxious to secure full value from the old man's sacrifices. One of these lassies from the Mount Vernon bottoms was more talkative than the other, and she kept up a constant babble of conversation that soon attracted the attention of everyone around her. The other was a shy and blushing violet who hardly dared open her mouth. At the dinner table these backwoods belles were placed at the head of the table where they were in the center of a hungry male company. The oldest cut her bread into hunks, and with extended arms she dipped it with lusty strokes into the gravy of the beefsteak dish. Her sister was more hesitant and was slow in availing herself of the delicious gravy in the common dish. To fail to sop the gravy was to be cheated, thought the talkative female, and she turned to her sister and commanded, "Sal, dip into the gravy. Dad pays as much as any on 'em!"[12]

The green maidens from Mount Vernon were not the only gawky persons in the Hoosier state. Enemies of Governor James B. Ray said that he was not versed in the fine art of using a cuspidor. In 1825, when General Lafayette visited in Louisville, the chief executive of Indiana went to Jeffersonville to receive the French dignitary. The Governor kept spitting on the floor, to the annoyance of certain polite visitors, so a negro boy was instructed to keep the receptacle pushed around in front of the chief executive. Each time the Honorable Mr. Ray missed the box, and each time the boy pushed it around into a more favorable position. Finally the Governor became exasperated and said to the negro, "You black rascal, take that box away, or, by the powers I'll spit in it."[13]

Nowhere did the frontiersman show his awkwardness more than at the table. The editor of the St. Louis *Pennant* warned a reading public to "let the Kentuckians alone. In fighting they are equal to Hercules— For fun, the rivals of Monus— For the oddity of their blunders up to an Irishman in his best days." This warning prefaced an account of a party of nine Kentuckians who had partaken of a "light lunch" in a St. Louis restaurant. They were feeling "wolfish," said the editor, and were looking around to see if there was any "fighting going on." One of these blustering boys from the other side of the Ohio had sized up St. Louis and knew where all the good places "to liquor" could be found. He chose a popular tavern as a place to give a treat. He lined up his eight buddies of the pole and paddle and awaited the sounding of the gong to march in roughshod over a company of hungry fellow patrons and to demand the waiters to "shell out." The leader informed the company that he had plenty of money, and to eat everything in sight and to "call your wine!" Oranges, roast beef, raisins, gravy, pies, cheese and nuts were washed down with fine wines. For dessert they ordered oyster pies and beef stew, and yelled for more wines. Isaac, the treasurer of this gorging band of wild 'uns, counted his change and again consulted the wine list. The company had drunk several bottles of fine French vintage, and Isaac pored studiously over a list which included "Berryman, LaFitte, Golden Sherry, Golden Madeira, and Hock," along with dozens of other fine varieties. Prices opposite each offering were high enough to shock a cashier in a state bank, and to salivate a Kentucky boatman completely. The Bluegrass bully was baffled by all the large figures and difficult French names. He quickly called for the "bill" and the waiter thought he meant the "bill of fare." Isaac proceeded to add all the list prices together and got the startling sum of four hundred eight dollars. "Whow-w-w," yelled the snapping turtle, "if this ain't strong odor, I'll be shot." Another said, "Let me see," and he added up the column and got the same answer, "Four hundred and eight dollars for wine by God!" His eight well-stuffed friends roared like tigers. They swore to the proprietor, "We'll fight out that amount!" Isaac suggested that the party "go to the bar, I want to whip that fellow into snake tails." Soon the nine Kentucky mudcats were puffing and snarling around the barkeeper like cornered bobcats. When the bill was added correctly it came to twenty-five dollars instead of four hundred and eight as Isaac had supposed. They paid the bill and left the dining room with the sneering observation that their humble friend Isaac was "an infernal smart feller not to be able to tell a bill of fare from a fair bill."[14]

Not all of the sons of Ol' Kentuck were as badly nonplused as Isaac of the "bill-of-fare" escapade. There was that shaggy son who wandered into a Cincinnati banking house from the neighboring Licking territory to make a "singed cat" of the cashier. This hungry specimen was clad in loose-fitting red jeans generously smeared with hog lard and road grime. He gave the appearance of not being worth, red suit and all, more than fifty cents in state specie on a high hide and tallow market. "I say, stranger," said the natural son, "have you got any Kaintuck?" "Any what?" said the pompous cashier. "Why any Kaintuck money—the Ohio trash don't go in our parts," answered the drover. The Cincinnatian said he had nothing shorter than a few five hundred dollar notes, nothing shorter. "Well, how many have you got of them?" "Oh, twelve or fifteen I think," said the banker. "I call you on the whole," said the shaggy son and he pulled out a roll of small bills as big around as a spar on an Ohio steamer. Fifteen five hundred dollar notes were counted out and the Kentuckian stored them away safely in a jeans pocket. From another woolly receptacle he drew a second roll and inquired, "You couldn't see the same amount and go a leetle better, could you, for this pile is so big it bothers me to carry it." The banker was so thoroughly "singed" that he became obstinate and replied, "No I'll be hanged if I can,"[15] and he refused to exchange another bill with his red-shirted neighbor who had bitterly condemned the legal tender of the Buckeye state.

Occasionally a green "whistler between his teeth" wandered into smart stores in 'Orleans to transact a "leetle bisiness" and took smart-aleck clerks for rough rides with their coarse wits. Such was the case of a Hoosier who took a young French clerk in a Chartres Street hardware store for a considerable gallop about a lock. This son of the Wabash found himself among the long counters of the hardware store, and to the impatient clerk he remarked, "Stranger, you go it rather extensive here, in the saw, hatchet and etcetera business." With a superior air the clerk replied, "Rather." This started the green son from up the river on an aggravating tirade which was to "saw the clerk off close" before he left the store. He allowed the clerk "was a

right nice kind of a man. Why your hair is jist as greasy and
as glossy as if you et nothing but b'ar meat, you raccoon looking
crittur you, why on airth don't you make a clearing on your
chin, out West we never leave a stump standing that we don't
cut down." This infuriated the "proper gentleman of Chartres
Street" who took great pride in his imperial beard. "Sir," said
he, "do you wish to buy anything?" "Hain't you got locks?"
asked the Hoosier in a most matter-of-fact manner. After running over the whole list of locks from common padlocks to
double-lock pistols, the corn-cracker informed his brash friend
that he did his shooting with a rifle, but he wanted a "lockjaw,
for I've tried every means to stop my old woman's tongue, and
I believe nothing else will silence her." The clerk replied they
didn't carry such an article in stock. "And, damn you," said the
snag, "why couldn't you say so at first, you half-feathered, half-
starved looking prairie chicken," and he walked out in a huff.[16]
Strangers found it difficult to "come it" over the green boys from
the backwoods. They were coarse, cautious and cantankerous
at all times. A single hint that they were being looked down
upon or ridiculed by an individual who felt himself a little
better was enough to prompt them to do their best to turn the
tables.

There were of course those green and ignorant individuals
who seldom saw a stranger, and who knew little about the
progress the world about them was making. Traveling near
New Madrid, Missouri, H. M. Brackenridge came upon a garrulous squatter who engaged him in conversation concerning
the country's politicians. This "Tom Jones" of the back country
fed his guest hog meat and coarse hominy and threw down a
bearskin upon a dirt floor for his bed. "You hearrin tell, I 'spose
of Braddick's defeat," said the shaggy settler, "well I was one o'
them what fout there. I was from Maryland, but most o' the
milishy was from Virginny— and there was Washington, he
fout like a man—and you hearrin tell arter that I 'spose, how
he got head ginneral o' the army. Then he got president o' the
'nited States— and arter that I hearrin tell o' John Adams—

but he never fout. Whose president now, I don't know." Brackenridge suggested that this old militiaman had never heard of
Franklin, Jefferson and Madison because they never fout. Most
Westerners measured a man's usefulness by his ability to
"fout."[17] Tippecanoe (William Henry) Harrison became great
in the eyes of his western countrymen who remembered how
he "put it over on" the Prophet at Tippecanoe, and how he
"fit" Tecumseh and General Proctor at the Thames. "Ol'
Hick'ry" was great because he fought the British at New
Orleans. It was a green but "fouting" West which loved its
heroes best when they were fighting, or, later, when they were
speaking on behalf of "the people" at Washington. To most,
senators and congressmen were great men and great heroes.

Henry Clay excited his western followers to fever pitch on
many occasions. They followed his political career with much
anxiety and as he succeeded they rejoiced, and as he failed they
were melancholy. In 1844, after Clay had been a national figure
for many years, the erroneous news reached Louisville that he
had carried New York in the presidential election. A great
clamor went up from the assembled Clay partisans for a speech
from the master Whig, George D. Prentice, but he sneaked
away mumbling that all he had to say would appear in the
*Journal* on the morrow. In the meantime a "tight little knot"
of a Kentuckian named Charley had ridden into the crowd
astride a scrub pony, and he sat by watching as calmly as a
post. When Prentice refused to speak, the crowd called for
Charley. He dismounted, handed his reins to a boy, and
mounted a near-by wagon. "Gentlemen," shouted the highly
imaginative greenhorn, "I came here not to make a speech, but
hearing the joyful news, I came to rejoice with you while you
did rejoice, as I have ever wept with you when you wept; but if
you must have a speech, here is at you. . . . Gentlemen I am in
favor of erecting a monument to Henry Clay, and unlike any
other monument I would commence it during his lifetime.

"Let me select the place I would for its base. I would go to
the highest Allegheny Ridge! No, gentlemen, that is not high

enough! I would go west, west, west, till I reached the Rocky Mountains, but although many of those peaks are covered with eternal snows none of them are high enough. I would follow down, down, down, till I arrived at the Andes, and on Cotopaxi's highest peak, there would I erect his monument.

"I would build it of materials more durable than brass, and I would have it ascend beyond the fleeting clouds! Yes, gentlemen, beyond yon twinkling star, on its summit I would place a flambeau which should give light to the whole world, and the first comet that came that way, should be so astonished that he would tuck his tail and fly from his orbit."[18] There were thousands of "green Charleys" on the frontier who did not become quite so ambitious as the equestrian orator at Louisville. But they bellowed forth a stream of nonsense from political and public stumps all over the West. They dragged in everything from the planetary system and the classics to General Jackson and Henry Dodge, either as points of argument or adornment for their speeches.

Thousands of greenhorns were engaged in floating goods to market and walking back home, or, after 1816, returning by steamboats. They could be spotted a mile off, and sharpers of every description preyed upon them. Women took their money by subtle tricks. Gamblers and their heartless cappers herded them into tricky games of chance. These bumpkins were crude and coarse, they were good natural butts of rude joking. They were objects of ridicule by persons who felt superior because of their better opportunities. Nevertheless the western or frontier greenhorn was an important American institution. He rivaled the Irish, the Dutchman, and the excitable Frenchman in his antics, and, except the Irish, he was far more graceful in accepting jokes at his expense.

Many times it was a feeling of inferiority which spurred wild western sons into tantrums of boastfulness. Such no doubt was the case of often-quoted Nimrod Wildfire who in a moment of spasmodic enthusiasm declared, "Mister, I can whip my weight in wildcats—my name is Nimrod Wildfire—half horse, half alligator, and a touch of the airthquake; that's got the prettiest sister, fastest horse and ugliest dog in the district, and can outrun, out jump, throw down, drag out and whip any man in Kaintuck."[19] Nimrod Wildfires were to be found on steamboats, in New York, in New Orleans, all over the West, and, even in Europe. The green frontiersman went everywhere, and made himself known wherever he went.

Tales of the frontier greenhorns have been preserved by the hundreds. These relate stories of all sorts of predicaments from being strung by gamblers to arguing about the humane contributions of Mr. Christopher Columbus and General Washington. All of them were good-natured unself-conscious sons who were "pulled out of season," but who were not afraid at any time to stand up and give three shrill shrieks for liberty.

Greenhorns of the frontier showed their ignorance most away from home. This was especially true if a native son became involved with the "fixin's" of a city hotel. Jacob Gridiron, a correspondent to the New York *Spirit of the Times,* has reported an interesting case of a brash Kentuckian learning the ways of the world.

### OUR FRIEND BILLY GRIDER

Billy was a denizen of the great and growing West, and although he had driven a thriving business in the flatboat line, and was *some* in navigating a team of well-educated oxen, yet he had never left the neighborhood where he had been "raised" except when making his regular trips down the diminutive river, rejoicing in the euphonious name of "Cow-killer," which flowed into the "Mountain Forks," a distance of forty miles, with which distance his peregrinations always ended.

Having toiled and labored unceasingly he had accumulated quite a modicum of the "casting," and having now plenty of leisure he determined to turn his attention a little to the "fine arts," and to "literary" pursuits. Fired at the thought of thus entering upon a new sphere of action he immediately purchased the last "Crocket's" Almanacks, and forthwith subscribed for the "Trumpet of Freedom," the best, although the only paper published in those "parts," and with a laudable generosity, influenced not a little by the bland smile and honeyed accents irresistible, of the insinuating agent, he "took" the "Louisville *Journal*." After carefully studying for many days each and every number of the aforesaid document, his curiosity was raised to the highest pitch on reading the marvelous accounts therein contained of the "grand doings" in the mighty cities of the North, and determined as he had lots of "time," that he would *"jest git on his old mare Bets"* and go see some of those wonderful things. Having attired himself in his best shirt, a new pair of *"cow hides,"* with his *"tother"* coat, and "them copperas colored pants of his'n, what warn't to be beat," he took a look at himself in the *creek* and was perfectly satisfied with the *tout ensemble* of his outer man, with the single exception that his pants were "jest a leetle too short," in fact so much so that to an individual's totally unbiased opinion, it would have been a matter of doubt whether *Billy* was *too long* for his breeches, or *they too short for his* nether extremities! However his ingenuity overcame this difficulty, for with his knife he cut some *strings* of buckskin, that he had shot himself, which strings once inserted in holes perforated in the unmentionables and tied under his *mud-stampers,* he made about as neat a pair of "straps" as you would like to see, though perhaps not quite so dressy as if made by a Broadway tailor.

Ready cocked and primed, off he started, and "landed" at Louisville, and though that city was far beyond anything that ever *his* fertile imagination could have conjured up, he *was* going to New York, he was "bound" to go. He sold the "Mar" for an overcoat made of *red* blanket, a pair of "gallusses," a tickler of *peach and honey,* and ten dollars to boot, and then pitched on board the "Roaring River" steamboat, for Wheeling. He chuckled all the way, to think how he had "come it over" the fellow at Louisville—for *Bets* though a *"splendifferous"* animal, unfortunately was twenty-two years old, broken winded, grievously afflicted with the botts, and, in fact, wasn't worth "shucks." "Pretty good trade *that,* I reckon, Capting," as he remarked to the officer of the boat, "them fellars thought this boy was green, but I reckin I came the *Giraffe* over 'em, and tuk' 'em in a few. By hokey! only to think that Billy Grider away down from *Cowkiller,* diddled, fooled and *rampaciously conflagrated* the darnation cute chaps of the big town of Louisville! But, Capting, this is a fine critter of yourn, this here bellowin' steam flatboat. I reckon she cost *some* dollars. Now if I *could* make a trade, I'd like to take her off your hands, and run her in Cowkiller; what'll you take? I'll give you a ten-dollar bill, genuine and no mistakes, and any amount of b'ar, deer, and coonskins for her, and seein' it is *you,* I'll throw in old Bets' *fourteen*-year-old colt! I will, by thunder!" The Captain put him off, before the bargain was struck. Bill was at Wheeling, where he had good luck to fall in with a friend of his from his country town who was on his way to the North to lay in a stock of goods.

Under his care Billy arrived at New York without displaying many evidences of his verdancy—and when there, he swore he would go to "the Astor, *if that was* the biggest *house of entertainment* in the burgh for, by jingo, he was as good a man as any in the whole *state* of America!" When he heard the gong sound for dinner, he thought the devil was to pay, so he rushed out into the entry and pounced on the innocent waiter with a "What the he— are you kicking up such a racket for? Who is dead? And what is the matter?" After being pacified, and let into the mystery, by his kind friend the merchant, he turned in to dinner. Here he was much interested and completely astonished at everything he saw—a well-dressed and polite waiter showed him to a chair. But Billy swore that "the gentlemen shouldn't outdo Bill Grider in politeness. What *would* Marm Sukey say? No, *Sir,* you sit down yourself, and I'll hunt a squattin' place somewhere else!" The waiter laughed, as naturally he would, and Billy, taking it as an insult, knocked him down! "The unmannerly, audacious, ungrateful son of a *water moccasin!*" His friend again came forward and helped him out of the scrape. The soups were discussed, and all the dishes, whether of fish, flesh, or fowl, that were before him. Billy ate most heartily, swearing that they were d—d fine, but they couldn't hold a candle to the corn doings and chicken fixin's his marm *could* git up. When the time came for removing the dishes and for the dessert, he turned around in his chair to reconnoitre, and after twisting about impatiently for some moments, he thought he saw in the hurrying to and fro of the waiters, all making now for one corner, and now rushing breathlessly to different parts of the room, something important in the way of a scrimmage going on. He couldn't stand it any longer, so jumping up, and rolling his sleeves up to the elbow, he roared out, "B'ar and Ingins, if there is anything in the fighting line a-going on, jist let me show *my* hand, for I'm *some* in a b'ar fight, a considerable quantity *on eggs!* Take care, let *me come?* Whar's the man that says Billy Grider can't swaller him *whole!* Show him out." With this he rushed to the end of the dining saloon, and was about to wallop the affrighted ganymedes, when his friend came up and took him off. He became quiet, only saying now and then that "it was a *tarnal* shame to fool a man in that way, for he had hoped to have a *leetle fun.*"[20]

Another Kentuckian away from home took advantage of his place of birth, and lack of geographical knowledge on the part of a French boat captain, to secure a good meal. This story was published in the *Western Citizen,* and the editor declared that it was a good yarn.

## A KENTUCKIAN PRECEDES A COUNT

We were shown yesterday a letter from a young gentleman— a native of Kentucky who is now in Rome—the Eternal City— to his friends in this state. He gives a graphic description of his journey from Paris thither, and recites one amusing incident of a traveler, which is worth transcribing. He states that in the boat in which he traveled to Rome, from Lyons to Avignon, he was half famished with cold, and nearly whole starved with hunger. He tried to bribe the cook and entreat with the captain—but neither availed him in obtaining a dinner. After pacing the deck for some time, mentally calling anathema on the heads of all Frenchmen in general, and the surly boat captain in particular, whose passenger he was, he hurried down into the cabin for the purpose of getting a segar and puffing it instead of blowing up the captain. There, to his astonishment, and not without exciting his envy he found a tallow-faced Russian count—Count Orlof—discussing a very fine dinner, the obsequious captain standing behind his chair, apparently honored with being permitted to act as his waiter.

"I thought," said the young Kentuckian, casting a scowl at the captain, who understood and could speak a little broken English, "I thought you had told me that you did not furnish passengers with dinner?"

"Pardonne, Monsieur, dis be not one eber-body passenger; he be one grand Russian count."

"And what the hell if he be!" said the Kentuckian, who was as ardent as western sun could make him; "if he be a *count,* I'm a Kentuckian; I'd like to know which should rank higher?"

"Pardonne, Monsieur," said the captain "you be a Kent—what?—dat be title one noble Anglaise, eh?"

Kentuckian and a count—

"No," said the Kentuckian, bluntly, "that is the title of an American sovereign."

"Ah," said the little French captain, shrugging up his shoulders, and bowing his head, "ah, excusez, Monsieur—pardon, I did not know you be one gran nobleman; but now I get you dinner tout suite," and in due time the dinner was brought, to which, with the addition of a bottle of sparkling hock, the young Kentuckian did ample justice.[21]

Debating was one of the devices which the frontiersmen used to let off steam. Thousands of debates occurred in the West on subjects as ridiculous as "Which Conferred the Greatest Benefit on Mankind, Mr. Christopher Columbus, or General

George Washington?" A traveler through the western country sought entertainment and he was advised by the innkeeper to attend the "Debatin' Club" at the schoolhouse.

## A Wisconsin Debating Society

There, mounted upon his throne in that temple of knowledge, sat the village schoolmaster, ex officio the President of the Society—the counterfeit presentment of Dominie Sampson, of "prodigious" notoriety. In front of the old dominie sat the Secretary, as is usual, while near at hand the debaters for the evening occupied the desks of the scholars; back from their line of desks the room was crowded—all J—had gathered there, her beauty and her chivalry.

The house was called to order, the "minutes of the preceding meeting were read and adopted," and Report of the Committee on "Hazekiah Pilcher, charged with non-payment of dues," was offered and laid on the table, when the Chair arose and said:

"Is the house ready for the question?"

"Aye! aye!" cried a dozen voices.

And the Chair proceeded:

"Gentlemen—the question for this evening is, which conferred the greatest benefit on mankind, Mr. Christopher Columbus, or General George Washington? On the affirmative, Messrs. Van Drezzer, Dusenbury, and Penix; on the negative, Messrs. Foster, Milligan, and Sampson. Mr. Van Drezzer has the floor."

Mr. V., the village lawyer, a smart, dapper-looking man, arose, and, taking a sup of water from the tin cup which was before him, did depose and say:

"Mr. President, and Gentlemen, and Ladies—I arise to advocate the affirmative of this question; that is to say, that I affirm that Mr. Columbus did a greater benefit to mankind than General Washington. In order more fully to digest the interrogatory just propounded, to enter fully into the merits of the case, I will give a brief, succinct, and condensed account of Mr. Columbus's life and exploits.

"Sir, who was Christopher Columbus? 'Sir,' echo answers, 'the greatest man of his times.' Sir, Columbus was the offspring of a man of the same name, who was an indignant [sic] basket-maker in a small town called Rome, situated on the river Tigers, a stream which takes its rise in the *Pyranine* Mountains, and flows in a southeasterly course into the Gulf of Mexico. At an early age Columbus evinced a decided talent for the sea, and occupied the leisure hours of his infancy in perusing books of travel and works on navigation; it was while engaged in these pursuits that he inadvertently met with the works of Robinson Crusoe, and Captain Cook, and the definition he made from them was that far away over the trackless main, thitherto untrodden by the foot of man, was an undiscovered country. As he approached manhood, he was filled with a desire to discover that country which he so often saw in his youthful dreams; actuated by this desire, he petitioned the great Pontifical Pope of Rome to give him three yawls and a jolly boat to carry out his design. That distinguished man at first refused, but his wife Cleopatra, being pleased with the promising looks of Mr. Columbus, actuated with a magnanimity which is a caricature of her sex, prevailed upon him to grant Columbus's request, whereupon, providing his vessels with stores and men out of his own pocket, Columbus got ready, and on a certain day of a certain month, and in a certain year, he sat sail from the Holy *Sea* of Rome, and after a long and tempestuous trip, he set foot, at last, upon the Plymouth Rock, in the Island of Juan Fernandez; it was on that occasion that he exclaimed: 'Breathes there any man with soul so perfectly dead as never to himself has said, this is my own, my native land!'

"Sir, Mr. Columbus did not long survive the hardships of that voyage, and was finally taken prisoner by the King of Cannonball Islands, and, with all his crew, cast into chains and slavery, where he died, at an advanced age, an ignominious natural death, with his whole crew, leaving not one to tell the tale. Peace to his ashes and their'n.

"Sir, the discovery of this continent was the greatest invention of the year 1492. Fernandez's Island was the stepping stone to the settlement of this country, Sir. Look around you and behold the populated world, the United States, North and South America, Oregon and Asia, Hindoostan and Belorchistan, England and Turkey, France and China, and many others, too numerous to mention—behold these countries traversed by steamboats, railroads, and telegraphs, and ask yourself, would these things have been if it hadn't been for Columbus? and your reply would certainly be, 'Certainly not, sir.' If it hadn't been for Mr. Columbus, General Washington wouldn't have been born—but suppose he had, what then? What did Washington ever do that was a great benefit to this country? There is much said about his talents for war. To be sure he performed several masterly retreats, but what's that an evidence of?—Sir, it is that he was a coward."

"General Washington a coward!" screamed Foster, the village doctor, in a voice of thunder. "General Washington a coward! Who is so base as dare say it? Look at him at the battle of the Nile, look at him at Waterloo, the Cowpens, on the Plains of Marathon, at the Pyramids, at Stillman's Defeat, at Bad Axe; and, Sir, look at him at the battle of New Orleans!"

"Gineral Washington at the battle of New Orleans!" exclaimed a huge backwoodsman, gesticulating violently. "Mr. Speaker, is thare such a agnoramus in the house? Sir, any schoolboy knows that the battle of New Orleans was fit before General Washington was born. Let the gentleman read Plutarch's lives, the lives of the Signers of the Declaration of Independence, or let him read Arkwright's *History of the Black Hawk War,* and he'll find that *General Henry Dodge fit the battle of New Orleans!*"[22]

Wherever the frontiersman happened to be he made his presence felt. A fine example of this forwardness is S. P. Avery's account of how the Honorable Jack Cole of Frankfort, Kentucky, attended the Marshal's ball in Paris, France. Jack was Marshal of the Census in Frankfort, and when he read in a

Paris paper that there was to be a ball in honor of the Marshals he made ready to present himself at the appointed hour.

## Jack Cole Among the Marshals of France

Among the Americans who attended the late ball given at the Hôtel de Ville, Paris, was Jack Cole of Kentucky. Jack rushed the dress strong, and consequently was the observed of all observers and got mixed up with a party that his friends could not account for. Wherever the Marshals of France went there went Jack, and when the Marshals sat down Jack did the same, always taking the post of honor. The day after the ball Jack called on his old acquaintance, Mr. Mason, our Minister to France, who started up a little conversation in the following manner:

"I hear you were at the ball last night?"

"I was, Sir, and I had a high old time."

"For which you were indebted, I suppose, to the high old company you got mixed up with? By the way, how came you associated with the Marshals?"

"How? By virtue of my office; they were Marshals of France, while I am nothing else than Marshal of the Republic. I showed my commission and took my post accordingly."

"By right of your office! What do you mean?"

"Read that and see."

Here Jack presented Mr. Mason with a whity-brown paper with a seal big enough for a four-pound weight.

"What in the name of heaven is this?"

"My commission of Marshal. I received it in 1860 when I assisted in taking the census of Frankfort."

"You don't mean to say that you travel on this?"

"I don't mean anything else. That makes me a Marshal of the Republic, and I intend to have the office duly honored."

Mr. Mason allowed that Jack was doing a large business on a very small capital.[23]

## CHAPTER IV

## BOOM POLES AND PADDLE WHEELS

FOR more than three-quarters of a century there was nothing in the western country which compared with its rivers. Acme of every "airthly" thing to the average man in the West was the "Ol' Massasip!" A certain eloquent native son pointed with pride, but with a perverted sense of geography, to "The Mississippi! The great big rollin', tumblin', bilin', endless and almost shoreless Mississippi! There's a river for you! I don't care what John Bull may say, or any other ruffle-shirted fellow, about their old castles with their bloody murder legends. I tell you the United States is a great country! There ain't nobody else but Uncle Sam as could afford such a river as that! Where in airth so much water comes from I can't think! Why, it might set in and just rain from January to July and it couldn't make a mud puddle half as big at one end. I'll tell you what I guess about it; you see the geography books tell you about the almighty great stream as runs up along the coast, and is lost near where they catch mackerel; wal it strikes me it just sinks down there in a hole and butts up agin on this side of the mountains, where it's pushed through sich a tight place as squeezes out all the salt."[1] Perhaps all of the salt was squeezed out of the water, but in its turbulent "rollin', tumblin', and bilin'" the "Ol' Massasip" floated some queer characters upon its ample bosom.

Typical of river humanity of the West and its general outlook upon life was that western flatboatman who was caught "tearing up" Donaldsonville, Louisiana. This Kentucky screamer worked vigorously for one night in his effort to destroy peace and happiness in this down-river town. For his trouble he was reported by a humorless Frenchman, and the local court tacked

79

on a heavy fine. Paying the fine caused this rampant son of Ol'
Kentuck little embarrassment, except that it relieved him of his
immediate cash resources. He asked the judge, upon the recess
of court, how much the cost would be if he whipped the Frenchman who "squealed" on him. The court replied that the fine
would be fifty dollars, and the up-river bully asked him if he
would take it in corn.[2]

Center of western commercial activity were the rivers. River
life from the beginning was vigorous, and it was among the
boatmen that such terms as "Kentucks," "red horses,"
"screamers," "buckeyes," "half-alligators," "half-horses," "children of calamity" and "howlers" originated. These were strong
terms, but they were expressive of the unrelenting hardships
combated by boatmen.

From 1775 to 1860 the Mississippi River and its tributary
streams were channels in which thousands of boats of every
description floated southward to markets. First in order there
were the pirogues, bateaux, canoes and skiffs. As pioneers moved
westward to settle Kentucky, Tennessee, Ohio, Indiana and
Illinois they used flatboats, arks, broadhorns, rafts and keelboats.
On these crude and clumsy craft an empire floated to a new
home west of the mountains. Families floated down the river
from Pittsburgh to begin life all over in the Mississippi and
Ohio Valleys. It was not unusual to see several boats floating
by a given point daily, loaded with women, children, cows,
horses, hogs, sheep and chickens; and with "plunder" and farm
implements.[3] Far more settlers floated westward than trudged
over the Wilderness Road.

While peaceable citizens were floating slowly to landings in
the new settlements, there came with them a procession of
banditti. James Flint in his letters says that the Ohio River
was an open thoroughfare on which a constant throng of bandits floated, under cover of night, to the western communities.
There were horse thieves, jailbirds, counterfeiters, black legs,
boat-wreckers and scalawags of no specific classification. These
cowardly rascals came into the West without their true charac-

ters being known, and without anyone's taking too much trouble in advance to investigate them. Some of these knaves proceeded to throw off all moral restraints in the new country where law-enforcing agencies were either poorly organized, or within their control. If one of this fraternity of cheats landed in jail, he remained there as long as he was satisfied with the accommodations, and then broke out and put off down the river to a new field of nefarious endeavor.[4]

There were, also, those hardy individuals, many of whom could scarcely name the place of their birth, who followed river-boating as a trade. They learned by constant association with the river about the snags, shoals, eddies and sandbars. They mastered the art of steering their craft clear of Indian attacks along the west banks, a danger which was ever present until Wayne's victory in 1794. These professional rivermen became distinct characters in a land which had already become famous for its rugged personalities. They were boastful of their prowess with pole and paddle, and they believed steadfastly that they were "some" when it came to dealing with boat-wreckers, cheating gamblers, and bandying prostitutes from Pittsburgh to 'Orleans.

It was generally conceded that Kentuckians, Buckeyes and Hoosiers were past-masters in the use of poles and at handling clumsy ill-shapen rivercraft which floated southward with the current and were loaded to the gunwales with heavy plunder. The French, however, were more temperamental and they mastered the more exact science of the paddle. A Frenchman could take a pirogue and journey from the headwaters to the mouth of a river without serious mishap, while a Kentuckian, Hoosier or Buckeye could not even "mount" this type of boat without a ducking.[5]

Often in traveling down the Ohio and Mississippi Rivers, boatmen were caught in blinding fogs. These were frightening because there was danger of butting into another craft, or of being snagged or beached. To keep from colliding, boatmen blew their long tin horns continuously until the cloud lifted.

When other boats were known to be in the vicinity, these horn-blowing boatmen kept up a din that would have put the idiots of bedlam to shame. Alexander Wilson wrote a friend in 1810 that he had stood on the bluff overlooking the Kentucky River on a foggy morning, and was highly entertained by the terrific furor created by the boatmen blowing their horns.[6]

Sometimes boatmen became confused in fogs, and if they had the misfortune to pass through the mouth of a lateral stream their craft sometimes got caught in an eddy which headed them in the wrong direction. When this happened they were unable to establish their location, and stubbornly refused to admit their confusion. If by chance there were settlers or squatters along the bank the boatmen were subjected to ridicule. Timothy Flint heard one such conversation between his boatmen and inquisitive settlers along the bank. Flint's crew had fallen victim to a strong eddy and were floating in the wrong direction when a squatter, perceiving their predicament, yelled, "Where from? How ladened? Who's captain? Where bound?" To this last question the crew answered, "To New Orleans," and it was with extreme difficulty that the boatmen were convinced that they were in the wrong river. There was a common "smart-aleck" answer given by boatmen all along the river to the eternal questioning of the settlers. When they were asked "Where from?" by the settlers they replied "Redstone," "What's your laden?" "Millstones," "What's your captain's name?" "Whetstone," "Where are you bound?" "Limestone."[7]

Conversation between boatmen and landsmen was not always so refined as it might reasonably have been, and they would shout vulgarities of the coarsest sort back and forth. The common practice was to call each other base and vulgar names, a practice which sometimes resulted in an exchange of rifle shots. Flint saw a boatman level his rifle on an aggravating, bank-tramping squatter who had a little better imaginative power in a heated exchange of mellifluous names. The boatman leveled his rifle on his antagonist, and when his intended victim stepped discreetly behind a tree he was abused in the coarsest terms for being a coward.[8]

The Reverend Mr. Flint found before he had floated far southward from Pittsburgh, that he had employed a hard-fisted set of oarsmen whose continuous swearing was repulsive to his sensitive ear. These oarsmen, however, were not devoid of a keen sense of humor, and on one occasion they did a masterly job of verbally strafing a lackadaisical, but thirsty, settler who lolled upon his front piazza when the boat first came in sight. He saluted: "Hallo, the boat!" To which the boatmen responded: "Hallo, the house!" And to add interest to their exchanges they asked, "Have you got any potatoes for our boat?" "None," said the settler. "Have you got any whisky aboard that boat?" "Plenty." "Well I will trade you some potatoes for whisky." "What do you ask for your potatoes?" "A dollar a bushel." "That's too high." "Well, I will let you have a bushel of potatoes for a gallon of whisky!" The boatmen carried on this badinage with the potato-grower as long as they could make themselves heard. They dickered with him on the price of his potatoes until he was willing to give them almost any quantity for a small portion of whisky.[9]

Since 1787, a vast produce trade went to New Orleans from the upriver country. In that year, James Wilkinson, a new-comer to Kentucky, went to New Orleans and through a series of agreements with the Spanish Governor, the port of New Orleans was opened to the admission of some western produce. By this date western fields were producing bountiful crops of corn, wheat, hemp, flax and tobacco. Likewise there was a bristling trade in livestock, cured meats, skins, leather and whisky. Shipping products to market by way of the river was a matter of vital concern to every settler in the western country. These early farmer-rivermen, in crafts of their own making, floated their produce to market, where it was sold, and the boat was disposed of for timber or fuel, after which they walked back home by the overland trail.[10]

Boatmen living above Louisville and the treacherous Ohio

Falls had the problem of getting their heavily ladened craft into the "lower river." If the water was high the danger was increased, and, if the river was at low stage, they had to unload their boats and haul their goods to Shippingport, reload them and set afloat from that point. The falls were treacherous in several ways, they threatened danger to both boats and cargoes, or there was the expense of a portage involved. One danger, however, was not localized at the falls, and that was the presence of brigands who either stole the shippers' goods or rushed down the river to "hide-outs" to inform boat-wreckers that rich cargoes were on their way.[11]

Colonel Flueger, or Colonel Plug, a native of New Hampshire, was one of the well-known and much-dreaded pirates, who inveigled innocent bargemen into traps for the purpose of murdering and robbing them. Plug knew the art of screaming pitifully for help from a stranded flatboat; also, he was able to "drill" boats in tow by boring holes below the water line so they sank in midstream leaving much of the cargo afloat. This heartless wretch was as bloodthirsty as the murderous Harpes, or his notable competitors, the outlaws of Cave-in-Rock.[12] At Cave-in-Rock, green but sporting rivermen were tempted by one means or another to land their boats for a short "social" visit. Here they were made drunk, or were involved in gambling and were murdered for their trouble. Their boats were floated southward by picked freebooters who sold their produce and returned to the "Rock" to divide the booty. The "Cave" and its bloody gang was for a long time under the watchful care of a conscienceless scoundrel named Wilson. After several years of continuous pillaging of boats and of destroying their owners, an indignant shipping public raided the pirates in their hang-out and dispersed their gang. Sixty skeletons were found in the rear of the cavern. At least sixty boatmen had fallen victims to the outlaws of the lower Ohio, and no one can ever know how many scores of skeletons are imbedded in silt at the bottom of the river.[13]

It took not only courage, but a keen sense of humor to make

the hazardous trip to Natchez and New Orleans. A traveler through the western country was told of two flatboat disasters at the falls of the Ohio. Each of these crafts contained the fruits of a full year of labor on the farm. When the first was swept into the rapids it was churned to pieces, and it was with extreme difficulty that the crew was rescued. The owner, however, accepted the whole matter as an act of Providence, and crawled out of the water to cast a doleful countenance in the direction of the rapids and to exclaim:

"Hail Columbia, happy land!
"If I ain't ruined, I'll be damned."

The second disaster occurred in practically the same way, except that the owner was a bit less poetical in accepting his loss. As the last logs of his boat rushed headlong through the rocky shoals he philosophized: "She's gone to the devil, anyhow, but she made a most almighty rear of it, didn't she?"[14]

François Michaux estimated that it was 2100 miles by river from Pittsburgh to New Orleans, and that merchant boats, broadhorns and arks required from forty-five to fifty days to negotiate the trip downstream.[15] It would have been startling indeed to that boastful Englishman who engaged Robert J. Breckinridge in conversation concerning the length of the Thames River as compared with those in America, had he made a thorough examination of Zadoc Cramer's *Navigator*. Dr. Breckinridge was traveling up the Thames when his garrulous native companion expressed pride in his country's streams. "Sir," said he, "it may seem incredible to you, but it is nevertheless true, that this prodigious stream is, from its mouth to its source, not much, if at all, short of one hundred and fifty miles." Dr. Breckinridge said, "I looked steadfastly in his eyes to see if he jested; but the gravity of deep conviction was upon it indeed. John Bull never jests." He inquired of this expansive British traveler if he had ever heard of the Ohio, the Missouri and the Mississippi. Except for the Mississippi "John Bull" was a bit hazy in his knowledge even of the names. He was quite startled, however, when his "unreasonable" American friend explained to him that he might see a steamboat come down the Ohio "a thousand miles, and there meet another steamboat of the same class which has come in an opposite direction twelve hundred miles down the Missouri, and then, after going fifteen hundred miles more, down the Mississippi, he may see that flood of waters disembogue by fifty channels into the sea." This "tall" description of American rivers was too much—it was utterly uncalled for—in the eyes of the Englishman. He took this account as a personal affront and "let down his visage into a contemptuous pout," said Dr. Breckinridge, "and regularly cut my acquaintance."[16]

To thousands of rugged rivermen who pulled their lives away steering stubborn boats free of shoals, eddies, snags and sandbars, Dr. Breckinridge's estimate of the length of American rivers was modest enough. Boats from Pittsburgh to the mouth of the Ohio were generally fifteen days in passage, if conditions were favorable.[17] From the mouth of the Ohio to New Orleans required more time because of the rapid and treacherous current. There were more eddies, and below Natchez the river became exceedingly hazardous. When conditions were unfavorable, of course a longer time was required all along the river. Extremely low water made it dangerous to travel at night, and high water obliterated the channel. Many of the larger flatboats traveled only in the daylight, but others traveled every night, for the rivermen believed a boat floated faster at night. Mounted as the boats were with long side sweeps, and a powerful tiller, or gouger, they could not be pulled into shore with a reasonable amount of safety and precision. Keelboats made fairly good time on the down trip, but the upriver pull was almost unbelievably difficult. An account of the keelboat travel at the turn of the century was given by James J. Audubon, who estimated that it took from March first to July first, or, sometimes, October first for keelboats to go from New Orleans to Louisville. Some of these boats came ladened with bags of coffee, while others bore not more than one hundred small hogsheads of sugar. Keelboats usually carried crews of ten men and a patroon. In open water the men used poles which they set and at the order of the patroon they forced their way from stem to stern and ran back to their original places over the "runners" to repeat the process.[18]

When the going was exceedingly difficult, the crew on keelboats took out the line and cordelled the boat by walking up the riverbank pulling their craft behind them while one member of the crew kept it far enough out in the stream to miss snags and other debris. Sometimes gaff hooks were used to pull the boats along from one snag to another, or, at times, the crew "bushwhacked" them along by catching hold of low branches and pulling themselves forward.[19]

It is little wonder that the water fronts at Pittsburgh, Wheeling, Cincinnati and Louisville became veritable hells, because rivermen who had wrestled with every conceivable hardship on the river relaxed by taking in stride the fastest entertainment the towns offered. These rivermen celebrated their arrival at the various meccas of entertainment with a sense of taking the pleasures at hand instead of looking forward to either economic or celestial security. Hard pulling on oars and poles, a boiling sun, heartless snags, eternal sandbars, swirling eddies, and a stubborn current were trying. Timid souls never succeeded on the river because they wavered, and in wavering, they were lost.

River ruffians who extracted a livelihood from their poles and paddles were faced daily with peril, and soon became the devil's own cousins. They learned to express themselves in a language which lacked nothing in color, if it often lacked veracity. Timothy Flint, in his *Western Monthly Review,* attributes the "half-horse, half-alligator, snapping turtle" boast to H. M. Brackenridge, but Brackenridge was certainly not responsible for all the tall talk of the rivers.[20] A southern congressmen returning to the national capital on a coastwise vessel met a Kentucky flatboatman who spoke hyperbolically, in tropes and figures. This ring-tailed roarer from the famous Salt River bottoms of the old red-horse state informed his listeners that he was a man who could "jump higher, squat lower, dive deeper, stay under longer, and come up dryer; who could whip his weight in wildcats, and let a zebra kick him every fifteen minutes."[21]

A traveler in the West found the rivermen tougher than "whit leather." These rivermen called themselves the "genuine Mississip" of which Ol' Kentuck was but a part. He found that they claimed to be "the genuine and original breed, compounded of the horse, alligator and snapping turtle. In their new and 'strange curses,' you discover new features of atrocity; a race of men placed on the extreme limits of order and civilization." This observer heard the boatmen talk casually about mutilations and bloody physical combats as a common occurrence. "Indeed," said he, "I saw more than one man, who wanted an eye, and ascertained that I was now in the 'region of gouging.'" The "best" man in the settlement was one, who, in the Kentucky sense of the word, had either whipped or could whip everybody in the community.[22]

Another traveler, the Englishman Woods, formed some definite opinions of the rivermen. They might not have been so extreme in their roughness as his account, but doubtless they were "rough and ready." He said they were a coarse set given to drinking much whisky, "and fighting, and gouging, that is, they fight up and down, trying to put each other's eyes out with their fingers and thumbs, and sometimes biting off each other's noses and ears."[23] These descriptions, while truthful to a great extent, are doubtless overdone. The rivermen were rough, but they were human, and fighting has never been a favorite manner in which to take daily "constitutionals."

Figurehead of all the flatboatmen was Mike Fink. This hardy patroon of the Ohio and Mississippi early became an entertaining figure. So entertaining has he now grown in frontier history that it is difficult to determine whether he was as rugged as he is pictured, or whether he was the most imaginative soul afloat in the West. Under other circumstances Mike might have become a great novelist. He loved whisky (a gallon every twenty-four hours), women, frolicking and fighting. He was a master with the pole, the rifle and a pair of oar-scarred fists. He was a liar convincing enough to make a gullible farmer give up a number of choice sheep because they had a black murrain—in this case nothing more serious than a healthy pinch of snuff. Mike was frolicsome enough to make a fool of the "honorable court" at Louisville which submitted to his outrageous demands that he be hauled into its august presence in a boat. By his own description he possessed the fine talent of being able "to outrun, out-hop, out-jump, throw-down, drag-out and lick any man in the country." "I am a Salt River roarer," said Mike, "I love wimming and I'm chock full of fight."[24]

Drifting around the wide sweep of river which is Giles' Bend, men who had struggled with their boats came in sight of their first down-river stopping place, Natchez. They saw not staid and dignified Natchez which sat atop the foot of the Chickasaw Bluff with its churches and "decent society" like a plume atop a militia colonel's hat, but more alluring and exciting "Natchez-under-the-Hill." Danger, at least from the river, was behind the rivermen, and here they found a market for their produce, and fun which ran the whole category from drinking freely of raw liquor to alluring and painted Delilahs who had "entertained" and fleeced a whole generation of Kentuckians, Hoosiers, Buckeyes and Suckers.[25] "Natchez-under-the-Hill" in its heyday would surely have put to shame those hellholes of antiquity, Sodom and Gomorrah. Modern eighteenth and nineteenth-century vice showed a "marked development." This town on the Mississippi was located at the foot of the great bluff which overshadowed the river. There was one main street which ran from the road ascending the "hill" to the water's edge toward the bight of the great Giles' Bend. Lining either side of this muddy thoroughfare were rows of wooden shanties which were alternately gambling houses, brothels and barrooms. The sunken sidewalks were blocked day and night with fashionably dressed dandies from the plantations back of the hill, rough, crudely dressed river bullies who smelled of a hundred days' perspiration, sailors and foreign merchants, and tawdrily arrayed, highly rouged and scented females who could not recall the day of their virginity.[26] Life in the underworld was cheap, gamblers cheated at cards and shot protesting victims without mercy, boatmen, blear-eyed with bad whisky or green with jealousy over deceptive whores, bit, kicked and gouged one another. The town under the hill knew no God, no law, no morals.

Speaking of the pacific stretch of river which lay before the landing at Natchez, Alexander Wilson said, "This part of the river and shore is the general rendezvous of all the arks of Kentucky boats, several hundred of which are lying moored there, loaded with the produce of the thousand shores of this noble river. The busy multitudes below present a perpetually varying picture of industry; and the noise and uproar, softened by the distance, with the continual crowing of the poultry with which many of these arks are filled, produce cheerful and exhilarating ideas. The majestic Mississippi swelled by his ten thousand tributary streams, of a pale brown colour, half a mile wide, and spotted with trunks of trees that show the different threads of current and its numerous eddies, bears his depth of water past in silent grandeur."[27] At New Orleans this scene was compounded. The levee was as rowdy a place as was ever found in an American town. So notorious were the river traffic and the rivermen, that the most opprobrious slur in New Orleans society was to say a person was as coarse as a "Kentucky boatman."

Just as the ark, the broadhorn and the keelboat supplanted the pirogue, the bateau and the canoe, the steamboat eventually drove the smaller craft from the rivers. Many dull, but convincing, statistics could be cited to prove the economic and social significance of the flatboats and their lusty crews, but these would add little that is human to their departed glory. The year 1811, and the steamer *New Orleans* ushered in a new river regime, and "get up steam," "reverse your wheel," "bust a biler," and "a nigger on both pop valves" became popular figures of western speech. Of equal importance with the maiden trip of the *New Orleans* was the successful upriver trip of the *Enterprise* which ended at Shippingport on May 30, 1815.[28]

Scoffing flatboatmen denied that the first upriver voyage of the *Enterprise* proved that steam was practical for navigation against the current. They claimed that Captain Shreve had taken advantage of high water, and that he had followed slack water through the inundated countryside, and away from the swift main channel. Next the *Aetna* and then the *Dispatch* made round trips between Louisville and New Orleans, but it remained for the sturdy *Washington,* a magnificent two-decker, to silence the scoffers who hopefully predicted failure for upriver navigation. The *Washington* crossed the great Ohio Falls in September, 1816, and in 1817 she performed the marvelous feat of making the round trip from Shippingport to New Orleans in forty-five days![29] The age of the steamboat was now a reality.

The coming of the steamboat to the western waters influenced greatly the movement of commerce on the rivers, and changed the whole society of the western country. Western Pennsylvania, Virginia, Ohio, Kentucky, Indiana, Illinois and Missouri farmers produced vast quantities of agricultural products which they now hurried away to rich southern markets. There were flour, corn meal, pork, bacon, hams, salted beef, apples, cider, dried apples, peaches, salt, iron, cotton bagging and rope, and slaves; from Ol' Kentuck and Pennsylvania there was red liquor![30]

Travelers boarding western steamboats found the decks littered with freight, humans and varmints. There was always a great commotion at leaving time; drunken firemen just returned from shore leave kept up a furor in the holds, mates and deckhands yelled and swore above the crying of rusty wenches and taut hempen fore, stern and breast lines. Bells clanged, and captains bellowed orders from texas decks which could be heard over the entire area of a county.

Among the passengers scattered about the decks from fo'castle to stern, from boiler deck to pilot house, were fine ladies, crimson ladies, gentlemen, blacklegs, bumpkins, slave-traders, actors, circus performers, and riffraff. There were two general classifications of passengers, "cabin passengers" and "deck passengers." This latter group were often flatboatmen who were returning from the southern market; and there were immigrants, and coffles of slaves. Baird said there was the "half-horse, and half-alligator Kentuckian boatman, swaggering and boasting of his prowess, his rifle, his horse, his dog, and his sister. One [passenger] is sawing away on a fiddle all day long; another is grinding a knife or razor; here is a party playing cards, and in yonder corner is a dance to the tune of a jew's harp."[31] Passengers on the cabin deck were separated after a fashion. Women, preachers and such other sedate and timid gentlemen as might be aboard were placed in the "ladies' cabin." Hardened sinners who had come aboard to transact other business than that of traveling, found ample and varied accommodations in the great entertainment halls.[32]

Thousands of gamblers, cheats and blacklegs followed river gambling for a livelihood. Formerly they had remained stationary in the river towns, and there took advantage of landing flatboatmen and travelers. Captains were supposed to watch out for those rascals and to see that none of their passengers were tricked, and if a blackleg got aboard he had instructions from the owners to "bank" him at once. Few precautions, however, were actually taken, and gambling on board the steamboats was as commonplace as stopping for wood.[33] Sometimes the boats' officers were *en league* with the sharpers, and always put them off at the "right time" and at the "right woodyards."[34] Next to gambling, excessive drinking and the "entertainment halls" were notorious vices of river travel. These two evils combined were the means of many innocent "gulls" losing personal fortunes within the scope of a short voyage.

Most of the early steamboat crews were ex-flatboatmen, and they set the precedents for steamboat conduct. Captains had poled Kentucky boats along the river or had served as patroons on keelboats, pilots learned about the river from the decks of flatboats, and machinists learned their trade as they traveled. There was a hierarchy of authority on board, at the head of which stood the captain. Most of these officious gentlemen were rivermen who had come up through the ranks, and their ability to knock a deck hand down surpassed their capacity to carve gracefully as the head of the boats' tables. If a passenger irritated these dignitaries, and that was easy to do, he was put off at the next landing. Arguments between captains and woodchoppers sometimes took a nasty turn. Rifles were kept loaded and conveniently located behind cabin doors in case arguments over wood arose. The poor swamp dwellers were often treated by the boatmen as though they were entirely devoid of human sensibilities.[35]

Perhaps next to the captain, the most explosive individual in the crew was the mate. This lordly creature ordered the march of armies of wood-passing deck passengers at every woodyard where he raved and ranted for them to trot faster. He also was lord and master over the deck hands, and the matter of pulling in lines and clearing the deck convulsed this impulsive creature many times a day. Although he went through the ordinary routine of landing and departing from the bank often in the course of a voyage, the mate's show of temperament gave inexperienced travelers the impression that the success of the whole western steamboat industry depended upon his raising hell at the landings.

Most captains prided themselves upon two accomplishments: keeping ahead of competing boats, and setting fine tables. Racing on the river created as intense excitement as anything that happened during the first half of the nineteenth century. Thousands of dollars' worth of property and hundreds of lives were lost by this sport. Racing captains taxed their boats beyond endurance, and boilers exploded, dispatching many souls to eternity. C. A. Murray, an English traveler, said: "I read an account of the bursting of a boiler a few days previously, lower down the river, by which thirty or forty persons were killed or missing; I heard a rough Kentuckian chap relating that he had been on board the steamer at the time of the explosion—'It was damned lucky,' said the Kentuckian, 'it was only a parcel of these Dutch.' "[36]

No captain could maintain self-respect and engage in that most hated of all river professions called "belly robbing." They set tables well supplied with good food. Captain Hamilton was served "joints, turkeys, hams, chops, and steaks. Brandy bottles were located at handy intervals."[37] Many passengers traveled round trips on the steamboats for the sake of enjoying convivial company and extraordinarily good meals.[38]

A new industry grew up about the steamboat and the river. Furnaces consumed wood by the thousands of cords, and the principal rivers of the West were lined with woodyards. C. C. Arfwedson saw a Kentucky squatter and woodcutter on the river whose "exterior bespoke a man about forty, though he had seen sixty winters: all he knew of himself and his age was that he was born in the eighteenth century. His looks had a wild expression, without exciting awe; his hair fell in long dark ringlets from his back. His costume was singular, consisting of a coarse green coat, waistcoat of variegated colors, wide chocolate-colored inexpressibles, no cravat, high shirt collar, following the impulse of the wind and a low-brimmed hat."[39] This squatter had been driven from place to place by his dislike of neighbors. He could not bear them closer than one hundred miles. "I have no elbow room," said the wood-cutting squatter, "I can't move about without seeing the nose of my neighbour sticking between the trees. Thou doest not understand, stranger, what liberty is; don't meddle with it! I cannot bear a close-confined town air, and laugh at the fool who submits to wear chains."[40]

A fairly impartial American observer said that upon stopping to wood he had seldom seen such wild grotesque creatures as those that issued from the forests. He found these children of the woods as peculiar a race of human beings, as those who shoved the wood they cut into the furnaces of the steamboats. They lived in unhealthy isolated places where they were absolutely out of touch with organized society. "Their forms," said the observer, "are shaken by fevers till the flesh departs from their rickety limbs; while the drooping rotundity of their persons in front contrasts strangely with their sunken cheeks, whose hue seems still more sallow from the lank black hair that hangs in elf-locks over them."[41]

The boatmen of the West contributed much to the development of the region. They were rough in their manners, they disturbed complacent society wherever they went, but underneath their uncouth habits and their eternal drinking and fighting they carried with them the will power of western civilization. They were endowed with a spirit of defiance which made of them noble pioneers. No better case can be made for the defiant character of the western riverman than the tale of the "ducked screamer" who missed the plank and landed in the river at Concordia, Louisiana. The Concordia *Intelligencer* carried the story that "a fellow was walking ashore from that splendid boat *Harry of the West,* all his bundles in one hand and five dollars in specie clinched in the other, on a single plank, and heedless of his way, he tripped and fell souse into the river. In an instant recovering himself he struck manfully for the shore. He waded out in full view of the boat, shook himself like a huge water dog, opened his hand and found but two shiners left. He was angered at the plank, mad with himself, furious at the loss of his money, and more furious at the monstrous Mississippi. He looked at the plank, the boat, the river, his money, and wound up the survey by venting his spleen as follows: 'I've got five dollars in this-here bundle, two dollars in my hand, have jist been ducked—stand five feet ten in my stocking feet—tolerably stout for my age—rayther mad—and dog my cats if I can't flog any man on that boat fa'r fist fight or rough and tumble; who'll say yes? Whoop! Whoop! Hurra for Ol' Kentuck.' "[42]

The editor of the *Western Boatman* obtained a firsthand account of the wild antics of the early flatboatmen. Keeping a wild mob searching for beef off his boat was a puzzle to one flatboat captain until he recalled the fear of the great scourge—smallpox. News that the crew was sick with this disease sent the irate natives scurrying to the woods in fright, and permitted the boatmen to be on their way with a supply of fresh meat.

### Jim Girty's Beef Story

It took Jim Girty to show how to hook beef in flatboat times. On a trip up the Tennessee River, Jim and his crew got out of meat. They could not think it fair play to be without meat in a cane country where there were so many fat cattle.

So, as usual, they selected the best and fattest beef they could find; they obtained one that weighed about seven hundred pounds. They dressed it neatly and took it on board. About three hours afterward, fourteen men came down to the boat with rifles, charging Jim with having stolen beef. Jim did not show fight. The crew paid no attention to what was going on; some were sitting on the running boards, with their feet dangling in the water; several were lying upon the deck on blankets—everyone seemed dull and stupefied. Jim was seated on the bow of the boat, his head resting on his hand, when again assailed.

"I say, your men have been stealing the best beef in all these parts."

"There must be some mistake," said Jim very quietly.

"You lie, your men were seen skinning it."

"There is strangers about there, maybe," said Jim.

"Yes, yes, we know there is strangers here, on this very boat—they have the beef on board, and we will have it off."

"The boat is open, go look for yourselves, gentlemen, but you will find a mistake, certain—but satisfy yourselves, gentlemen, on that head."

"That we will, and in an instant order have the beef."

So at it they went, first having placed three men as a guard, to see that the crew did not play some trick. The others made a search by rolling and rerolling everything in the boat, and still no beef was found. One fellow declared that they had left no place untouched where the fore-quarters of a cat could be hid, let alone a big ox.

The same gravity was preserved by Jim; he wished the gentlemen to be satisfied.

The fact was while the crew was skinning the beef one of them discovered a man watching him from behind a tree. They took no notice of it, but when they came to the boat, they told Jim that they were caught.

He scratched his head a while, and then prepared for just such a visit as he received.

He placed the four quarters of beef on the deck of the boat, and spread the hide over them; on this he spread all the blankets, and four men lay down on these blankets. Jim, as before stated, was on the bow of the boat, continually wishing "the gentlemen to be satisfied, but they would find a mistake, certain."

"Look about and be satisfied, gentlemen—look where you please and be satisfied, gentlemen; but there is one thing I must ask of you, not to disturb them-there sick men—we buried two yesterday, with smallpox, and them four are very sick—very sick indeed, gentlemen, and I must beg of you not to disturb them; it always is the worst thing you can do, to disturb a sick man, especially if he be near his last; it kind of makes the blood fly to the head, to be disturbed." But long before Jim closed his speech he had no listeners.

If ever there were pale faces, fallen jaws, and ghostly looks, among a set of men, it was about that time and place—they marched off without speaking a word. Jim got clear of his visitors, and kept the beef.[43]

The next yarn is an account of the son of a double-breasted catamount who did a little free-for-all gouging. This Arkansas wildcat was a terror in his community and a detriment to society in general. The story is told by an observer who claims to have seen the fight which he describes.

### AN ARKANSAS FIGHT

Once upon a time we were coming down the Mississippi River on our way to this city. Bunyan has written about a certain delectable spot, situated somewhere in Utopia; but had the Pilgrim seen the Arkansas landing we are just now speaking of, he would have thrown down his scallop shell and staff, and cut dirt as if the gentleman in black, on a streak of double-milled electricity, was after him. Two flatboats constituted the wharf and they were continually butting their heads together. Such was the energy and regularity of their movement against each other, that for a moment we fancied the doctrine of Pythagoras was true, and that the departed spirits of two antagonistic rams had entered the timbers of the flatboats, and thence the combative symptoms above spoken of. As soon as the steamboat was moved alongside the floating wharf, the rush to board her was tremendous. One man, dressed in a hunting shirt of coarse homespun, and a coonskin cap, with a knife, something like that which sailors wear, sticking to his girdle, was the first to get on the plank that led from the flatboat to the steamer, and in his hurry to get on board he was pushed into the water, by a gigantic fellow in a bearskin coat, a coarse wool hat, and a pair of green baize leggings. The immersion of the gentleman in the hunting shirt was altogether accidental, but it was sufficient foundation, in the estimation of the cavaliers of Arkansas, for the tournament ground to be marked off, and the trumpets to blow "largesse" to the knights of the coonskin cap and the green baize leggings.

As soon as the ducked man arose from the top of the mulatto-colored river, he clenched one hand above his head, and hallowed, "Hold on there—you thin-milk-livered skunk! Hold on till I get on shore, and may I be cut up for shoe pegs if I don't make your skillet-faced phizcymahogany look like a cabbage made into sour-kraut!"

"See here, stranger," replied the offender, "your duckin' was axesighdental; but if you want a tussel I am har—just like a fin on a cat-fish's back!"

"The plank was mine by seniority, as the doctors say, old cat skinner, and may I be ground up into gunpowder, if I don't light on to you like a bull bat on a gallinipper," remarked the dripping man, as he shook himself like a Newfoundland dog, and stepped on shore.

"Stranger," said the causer of the accident, while his eyes gleamed like that of an enraged panther, and his fists clenched so forcibly that his nails were driven into the palms of his hands, "perhaps you don't know that I'm the man that fought with Washington Coffee, and dirked wild Jule Lynch."

"May I run on a sawyer, and may my brains fall down into my boot heels as I am walking up a stony hill, if I care if you had a rough and tumble with the devil. You pushed me off the plank and you must fight," was the peaceable reply of the wet gentleman.

"See here, man," said the opponent of Washington Coffee, as he bared his breast and pointed to a large scar that ran across three or four of his ribs, "Wild Jule done this, but I laid him up for a time—these big scratches on my face was got through my trying to hug a young b'ar—and this arm has been broken twice. I'm a cripple, but if you will fight, why strip and let's be at it."

In an instant a ring was made, and the two combatants, when doffed of their clothing, looked like middle-aged Titans, preparing for battle. The younger, who had fallen into the water, was about twenty-eight years of age, and his opponent was thirty-four or five. With eyes made fiery by anger, and lips quivering with intense passion, the younger dealt his adversary a tremendous blow in the breast. Until this affront the elder man had maintained a strange coolness and manifested a disposition rather in favor of an apology than anything else; but the instant he felt the blow his nostrils became white, and twitched like a steed's scenting the battle. Closing his teeth hard together, he planted himself for the attack, and as his adversary approached him, he dealt him a fierce lick on the side of the face with his iron-bound knuckles, that laid his cheek bones as bare as though the flesh had been chipped off by an ax. Smarting with rage the other returned the compliment, and as the blood gushed in a torrent from his mouth, he turned around and spit out one or two of his teeth that were hanging by the gums, and with a "rounder" as it is technically termed, he hit the younger man a blow on the temple that laid him on the beach with a dead, heavy sound, like that of a falling tree.

"Thar, I hope he is got enough," said the elder of the two, at almost every word stopping to spit out some fragment of his broken jaw. One of his companions handed him a flask of brandy, and with a long deep-drawn swallow, like that of a camel at a spring on an oasis, he gulped down enough of the fiery liquor to have made a common man mad.

"Enough," cried the other party, who had been in a like manner attended by his friends. "Yes, when I drink your heart's blood I'll cry enough, and not till then, come on, you white-wired—"

"See here, stranger, stop thar. Don't talk of my mother— She's dead—God bless her! I'm a man from A to izzard—and you—you thin-gutted wasp. I'll whip you now if I die for it!"

With a shout from the bystanders, and passions made furious by hate and deep draughts of liquor, with a howl the combatants again went to work. Disengaging his right hand from the boa constrictor grip of his opponent, the younger brute buried his long talon-like nails directly under the eyelid of his victim, and the orb clotted with blood hung by a few tendons to his cheek! As soon as the elder man felt the torture, his face for an instant was as white as snow, and then a deep purple hue overspread his countenance. Lifting his adversary in the air as though he had been a child, he threw him to the earth, and clutching his throat with both hands, he squeezed it until his enemy's face became almost black. Suddenly he uttered a sharp quick cry, and put his hand to his side, and when he drew it away it was covered with blood! The younger villain, while on his back, had drawn his knife and stabbed him. As the elder of the combatants staggered up, he was caught by some of his friends, and holding him in their arms, with clenched fists they muttered curses toward his inhuman opponent, who being shielded by his own particular clique made for the river and plunged in. When about halfway across, he gained a small island, and rising to his full height, he flapped his hands against his sides and crow'd like a cock.

"Ruo-ru—oo-o! I can lick a steamboat! My fingernails is related to a sawmill on my mother's side, and my daddy was a double-breasted catamount! I wear a hoop snake for a neck handkerchief, and the brass buttons on my coat have all been boiled in poison! Who'll Ru—oo—ru—ooo!"[44]

## CHAPTER V

## SOMEBODY IN MY BED

A TRAVELER arriving at a frontier tavern inquired of an indifferent innkeeper:

"Have you something to eat?" "I guess whisky is all the feed we have for sale." "Have you any meat?" "No." "Either cold or hot will make no difference to me." "I guess I don't know." "Have you any fowls?" "No." "Fish?" "No." "Ham?" "No." "Bread?" "No." "Cheese?" "No." "Crackers?" "No." "I will pay you any price you please." "I guess we have only whisky feed."[1] This greeting engendered little cheer in saddle-worn or stage-jolted travelers of the western country, since there was little or no competition, and some tavern-keepers could see no earthly reason why even the most timid souls couldn't exist on whisky alone. America had no more democratic institution than the tavern. When the eastern or foreign traveler set foot westward, either by way of the mountain road to Pittsburgh, or the Wilderness Road through Cumberland Gap, he had the choice of either sleeping "out," or spending his nights in overcrowded taverns.[2] These early hostelries were neither famous for their fine springs and soft mattresses nor the excellency of their culinary departments. A clearing was made in the woods by the roadside, a large log house was constructed on the spot, and a crude wooden tavern sign hung on a leaning skinned pole to wag an indifferent welcome to weary travelers. There was a large room which had many uses, among which were tap, entertainment, and as a sleeping room for late arrivals or stubborn cusses who refused to brave the rigors of the big bedroom upstairs.[3] A wide fireplace at the end of the hall was the center of activity; here early arrivals took seat, and refused to push back or "open up" for others to get even a glimpse

102

of the fire. These entrenched brigands of the fireside had every advantage except one—they were liable to a spattering from distressed tobacco-chewers who had either to spit over the heads of those monopolizing the hearth positions into the fireplace, or strangle.[4] Here at the fireside, liars were active in practicing their fascinating art, pranks were organized, political discussions grew hot enough to cause dirkings, and, most important of all, news from "furrin'" parts was "passed on." It was indeed a wise traveler who went through the western country equipped with the trinity of the road: news, pistols and bed sheets.[5] He found the tavern crowded with rugged restless individuals. To the localities, the taverns were public gathering places. Saturday nights they were scenes of high cavorting and rude frolicking.[6] On such occasions when a scraping and whining fiddle signified that a shindig was in progress the harassed traveler in the upstairs bedroom was assured there would be no sleep for him before daybreak. Heavily-shod dandies kept up a thunderous pounding of puncheon floors to the galloping tunes of *"Fisherman's Horn Pipe, Sweet Barbara Allen, Leather Britches, Old Dan Tucker,* and *Old Joe Clark,* while buxom western vixens lent a romantic gusto to the wheeling and stampeding breakdown. Not all the fun came from promenading puncheon floors with arms full of perspiring damsels for there were those who imbibed "Old MonHghahela" and began "to 'spile" and "run over" for a little fancy Virginia gouging, or rough-and-tumble-with-no-holds-barred. These knock-down-and-drag-outs were exciting; lusty maidens screamed at the top of shrill western voices, while horny-handed and seasoned sons of the woods swore with vigorous abandon. What did it matter to them if a cranky traveler did lie awake upstairs, he would catch up with his sleeping before he died!

No traveler knew when he "pulled-in" at a tavern yard how many bedfellows he would have to nudge over for an advantage of shuck mattress space before the sun came up on the morrow. Of one thing he could be certain: there would be no dearth of bedfellows, of both humans and insects. And there was no false

modesty on the part of the sexes, for women soon learned that
they either had to sleep in the common dormitory rooms or the
woods, and often the woods were cold and damp. Male travelers
were annoyed nightly by chattering women who kept them
awake and disturbed. Fortescue Cuming had to share the room
with a man and his wife, and when this amorous couple believed
him asleep "they continued to talk to each other on the most private and domestic affairs as though there had been no other person in the room."[7]

Unfortunate was the patron of the backwoods tavern who
had to sleep three-deep in a cord bed. The cords sagged, and
the man in the middle became a "rope-sawed" scotch between
oppressive and snoring brethren.[8] The middle man was fortunate indeed to survive the night. William H. Herndon, Abraham Lincoln's law partner, said of the frontier taverns: "Remember to travel on the circuit from 1837 to 1856 was a soul's
sore trial, down here away at least, no human being would now
endure what we used to on the circuit. I have slept with twenty
men in the same room—some on the bed ropes—some on
quilts—some on sheets—a straw or two under them; and oh—
such victuals—Good God! Excuse me from details of our
meals."[9] To add to the miseries of crowded bedrooms was
the eternal chewing of tobacco and spitting, even after patrons
of the inns had gone to bed. Tavern architects never heard of
pegs on which to hang clothes, and these luxuries were obviously
left out of building plans. A fastidious sojourner could do one
of two things—he could sleep in his britches or he could step out
and leave them where they hit the floor. There was always the
certainty that he would be unable to recognize them in the
morning because of the generous covering of ambeer showered
upon them during the night.[10]

Occasionally visitors to the West came upon good accommodations. Faux reported that he found a good brick tavern on
the White River in Missouri. Here he was given excellent fare,
and a comfortable bed. Perhaps he discovered the secret, however, when he reported that the owner had been a widow who

married a Yankee soldier with a knapsack on his back. Yankees looked for opportunities on the frontier, and a widow with a tavern was a good start. Faux's Yankee host was able to supply him with "buck venison, fowls, whisky and coffee." On the night which the English farmer spent at this tavern the Yankee landlord had organized a corn shucking and got his whole corn crop husked without much cost.[11]

Many taverns in the West were kept by rowdies who robbed their patrons. Birbeck reported such places to his friend Wheeler. One traveler going from Illinois to Missouri had been disturbed twice during the night by a robber who came into the room. He came in each time with an ax on his shoulder, but the traveler drove him away with a pistol. Mr. Birbeck said that many of these outlaw tavern-keepers would charge exorbitant rates for their accommodations, and make their patrons pay it or rob them.[12] Featherstonhaugh had pretty much the same experience in Arkansas. Hignite's tavern in that state was little more than a gamblers' and robbers' hangout. Bullying brigands remained about the place to scalp innocent travelers either by beating them with cards, or by relieving them of their property at the point of a pistol.[13]

Bed sheets—when there were such things—constituted a real problem to the more fastidious patrons of the back-country hostelries. Perhaps many innocent persons suffered the indignity of the French nobleman who raised a pertinent question with his prospective landlord concerning a certain suspicious off-colored spot on the sheet, "which he (the landlord) had the impudence to say was only soiled by pigeon dung while drying on the fence." The Frenchman said "his own senses told him it proceeded from a different biped." "Pigeon dung," insisted the obstinate landlord. "No sare," said the snobbist Frenchman, "man dung!" Following this warm debate the high-strung Latin proclaimed, "This is indeed one infamous country, in Russia, where I have lived lately, which has the character of being barbarous compared to civilized Europe, if a gentleman is insulted he can order the knout at his pleasure, but here you

are worse than Hottentots—you have not a spark of civilization—no government, sir—it is no country for a gentleman—I
will take my monkey, I will take my parrots, I will take my wife
and go back to Russia."[14]

There were ever-present and ravenous bedbugs and fleas.
François Michaux found fleas in the western taverns that covered him with the same anxious crawling and jumping as they
would have the fattest dog.[15] Bedbugs were plentiful—even
in newly-built taverns. They seemed to come of spontaneous
origin. Boarders were given the privilege of leaving the beds
when they could withstand the nocturnal attacks no longer, and
when the bugs were too ferocious the beds would all be deserted,
and guests would be strewn upon the floor. The common bedrooms became scenes of clawing and blaspheming victims who
attempted to stay the siege of bloodthirsty habitués of the mattress and crevices. A humane Kentuckian gave to the public
press a recipe which he believed would "be the means of saving
a great deal of innocent blood from being spilled. The Kentucky merchants by sad experience know the danger they have
to encounter without being able to guard against it in traveling
through Pennsylvania, Ohio and part of their own state. This
recipe will protect them against the most formidable enemies—
I mean the bold and abominable *bed bugs*." The recipe: "Dis-
solve corrosive sublimate in whisky as it can be made, and
with a feather or small stick touch the cords and bedstead. The
bugs will disappear instantly. This mixture is used in all eastern
cities."[16]

Thousands of restless patrons of the frontier taverns tossed
night upon night from being mashed to pieces by "scrouging"
bedfellows, and eaten by a voracious army of bedbugs. No native
ever denied this pestilence, but for downright angry expression
the English patrons were not excelled by any writers of the early
period in America. Basil Hall rented a room in a tavern which
had two beds, and paid for both of them in order to be free
of bedfellows. Hardly had he nestled into the blankets of the
"least dirty-looking of the beds" before an onslaught of savage

bugs sent him scurrying. He said there "forth rushed from tester, pillow, and post a horde of those 'blasted wonners' whose name I abhor to write." The brave Hall, however, bestowed hundreds of random blows upon this army, but even then every part of his body showed marks of the combat. He slew five of the ringleaders, but the "rebel rout" returned to gain an easy victory over him.[17]

Next to being consumed alive by voracious bedbugs or being disturbed by inconsiderate bedfellows was the experience of sleeping in a feather bed. Perhaps a new well-filled feather tick was the most luxurious bed that could be offered a traveler through the West, but an old, half-filled mattress was torturous. These beds conformed to every hard object underneath them, and the sides turned in to smother the sleeper. To Englishmen and other foreign travelers a feather bed, like hot corn bread, was something which had to be endured. The actor Ludlow said that he awoke from his slumbers after he had dreamed that he was consigned to the lower region, and that the devil had instructed that he be put in the hottest cauldron of oil. He rushed to the barkeeper's room and got that explosive dignitary out of bed. The irritated host asked, "What the hell do you want?" "That's it," responded Ludlow, "I've just come out of hell and I wish you to show me some other place." "Look here, Mr. Showman, if you want to play any of your jokes you'd better hunt up some other person——" was the barkeeper's answer. When the actor explained he couldn't sleep on a feather bed the host shouted, "Hark ye, if you don't take your damned show carcass out of this house, I'll put you out! I tell you there are no better beds in the county, and you have one of the best in the house."[18]

Few frontiersmen could see any reason why a feather bed was not the finest mattress that the hand of man could manufacture. These luxurious couches were reserved for special guests. In private homes strangers were put to bed in feathers, and no family which had any social standing or ambition ever permitted a minister of the gospel to sleep on a hard mattress.

This perhaps accounts for some of the realistic pictures of destruction by fire and brimstone which they were able to paint in their sermons.

Travelers who moved across the frontier with their womenfolk faced many trying situations. Margaret Van Horn Dwight has left an entertaining account of her journey from New Haven, Connecticut, to Ohio in 1810. Her party stopped for the night at an Ohio Valley tavern, but for a time it looked as though they were going to have to sit up in their wagon. When rooms were secured the party was separated. Miss Dwight and a Mrs. Jackson were put to bed in the landlady's room. The common room was filled with drunken wagoners, and when the women got to bed one of these drunken rascals came and lay down beside the young girl for the purpose as he said of becoming acquainted with her. Before the night was over crawling wagoners invaded every woman's room in the house. The landlord took for the timber because his drunken guests proposed throwing him in the creek if he interfered with their fun. Before long women were running about the place in their nightgowns and stocking feet screaming for help. When morning came the men threatened the marauders of the night with prosecution, but they were in the employ of an influential Pittsburgh merchant who got them out of their scrape without a lawsuit. Only two of these wagoners were offenders, said Miss Dwight, and one of them was "the vilest, worst, most blasphemous wretch that ever lived."

This same fair traveler believed that Dutchmen and Pennsylvania wagoners were profane beyond description. She had the experience of sleeping on barroom floors with these profane wretches and of being taunted by the uncouth patrons of the bar about getting married. Everywhere she went people prevailed upon her to marry. Little did she know at the time she was recording her ordeals in the western taverns, in which she learned to drink hard liquor and eat raw pork, that during her forty-four years of life she would mother thirteen children. Fortunately she never attempted to return to New Haven with her numerous brood, because if she had her difficulties in frontier taverns might have been quite different.[19]

Irish adventurers, French wanderers, and "escaped" Englishmen turned to the business of bar and tavern-keeping. The Irish kept a well-stocked bar, and set a "heavy," if not attractive, table. The Frenchman was sure to furnish plenty of wine and to brag about his mediocre food. The Englishman carved with a lusty stroke, spilled gravy on his customers and lied about his world travels. When he had finished the carving he could throw his managerial dignity into the corner along with his greasy apron and swing the giggling gals in a toe-smashing hoe-down. These dignitaries were not only tavern-keepers, but often colonels of militia, justices of the peace, sometimes jailors, and in the absence of better hands, they could take a text and do a bit of ordinary exhorting.

The tavern was the community center; if it were located on the roadside the "turn-in" was deeply worn, and if it were in town it was generally the central building on the square. As the West developed, the "dog-hole" taverns of the Great Laurel Ridge along the old National Road gave way to the more "refined" inns, before which stood weaving signposts proclaiming to expectant travelers that the hostelries were the "Indian Queen," "General Washington," "Mad Anthony," "Fried Meat," "Sheaf of Wheat," "General Pike," "Henry Clay," "General Jackson," "Liberty Bell," "Mount Vernon," and every other historical and classical name. From experience innkeepers learned how to control their guests. Some of them posted rules:[20]

1st.  All gentlemen shall give their names to the barkeeper.
2nd.  No gentleman shall enter the dining room until the second bell rings.
3rd.  No gambling in the bedrooms.
4th.  The doors close at ten o'clock, except on the nights of public entertainment.
5th.  No gentleman shall take the saddle, bridle or harness of another gentleman without his consent.

These were strange rules, but strange gentlemen were traveling in the West. Wise innkeepers knew their "ways" and their habits. As for good measure some ingenious managers posted signs that "Gentlemen learning to spell are requested to use last week's newsletter." Other tavern bulletins bore a miscellany of information which informed literate customers that "My liquor's good, my measure's just. But honest Sirs, I will not trust," and, natives were told that the colonel would hold a militia drill, or that on a given date "there will be RARE SPORT at which time a HE BEAR will be baited by relays of five dogs every thirty minutes, and that a SHE BEAR will be barbecued for dinner."[21]

The dining rooms were scenes of mad scrambling. The bell was rung once for attention, and twice for meals. The bellman hardly finished his task before the hungry boarders were seated and were gorging themselves with the food nearest at hand. The inn tables were democratic—everybody from the governor to wagoners grabbed a seat and "fought his face." The tables groaned under burdens of wheat and corncakes, beef, pork, venison, wild turkey, poultry, cucumbers, onions, cabbage, beans and preserved fruits. This varied assortment of food was gulped down ahead of generous "eye-openers," "phlegm-dispensers," "gas removers," and "toddies." Rough-handed dirk-wielding citizens knifed choice morsels of meat with a steady arm, and damned delftware for dulling their precious cutlery. Fastidious foreign travelers were horrified to find that they hardly had time to serve their plates before the dining rooms were deserted. Many times meticulous visitors asked politely that a fowl be passed them from the far end of the table, and before it reached its destination gorging gourmets spearing with razor-sharp skinning knives stripped it of the choice meat.[22]

Captain Marryat stopped at the famous "Snake Hollow" tavern on the Mississippi where he got a definite, if not, perhaps, an accurate impression of the Americans and their hostelries. "Americans," wrote the garrulous Marryat, "are the grossest feeders of any civilized nation known. As a nation, their food is heavy, coarse, and indigestible, while it is taken in the least artificial form cookery will allow. The predominance of grease in the American kitchen coupled with the habits of hearty eating, and of constant expectoration, are the causes of diseases of the stomach which are so common in America."[23] Later another Eglishman found great fault with the American at the table. Charles Dickens observed that his fellow travelers (Americans) were generally "dyspeptic ladies and gentlemen who eat unheard of quantities of hot corn bread (almost as good for the digestion as a kneaded pincushion), for breakfast and for supper. Those who do not observe this custom, and who help themselves several times instead, usually suck their knives and forks meditatively, until they have decided what to take next: then pull them out of their mouths: put them in the dish; help themselves; and fall to work again."[24] Dickens and Marryat, of course, were extremely critical, but doubtless the American on the frontier, like many Americans of the twentieth century, were shocking in their table habits.

Regular commercial taverns along the early roads in the Ohio and Mississippi Valleys were bad enough, but seldom were they as crude as the combination taverns and homes. Settlers attempted to augment their incomes from farms or trades by keeping a "travelers' rest." One native observer in the Mississippi Valley said that often a traveler could be seen riding up to a one-story, one-room cabin, twelve by fourteen feet. In this single room slept "the man, his wife and fifteen or twenty children." But fastened to a tree was a board bearing a legend painted with charcoal, "Akomidation fur man and Beast."[25]

Another sojourner in the West had a doleful experience in an "accommodation" tavern. The landlord welcomed this visitor to his house, but informed him he "had nothing for him to eat," but that he was welcome to what there was if he could eat it in the room with half a dozen sick children. Bacon and greens constituted the diet and the host poured out a hot cup of coffee. While the traveler sat munching his meager fare his hostess passed about among the sick family, with a baby in her

arms, administering to each member's wants. The father made
the gloomy observation that "these are the only relations I have,
I feel concern to get them on their feet again; for I want to
raise the whole of them."[26] It took a traveler with an iron constitution to enjoy or even relish food under such circumstances.
Often the strangers had to pile up in bed with two or three children, and sleep in the same room with a dozen more, including
the "old man and old lady." The dignified and haughty Fortescue Cuming spent a night cooped up in one room with a
family which had five children in one bed, and the rest slept
in another.[27]

The taverns with their crowded and "buggy" bedrooms, their
noisy "common" rooms, and their tobacco-chewing, knife-tot-
ing, and ravenous patrons were symbolical of the spread of white
civilization along the frontier from Cumberland, Maryland, to
the Widow Meredith's "dog-hole" in the Arkansas bottoms.
Heavily "tanked" with applejack, rum, wine and liquor, guests
of the selected fireside circle spun yarns of fact and fiction. Within this sacred pale, and under the influence of the spirits of the
time, heavy-fisted, but sharp-eyed, riflemen made the best shots
of their lives. "Saliva-dispensing" tobacconists boasted of spattering spots that were every bit of twenty feet away. Tobacco-
covered britches, confusion of shoes, and anxiety among female
bedfellows were accepted philosophically as a matter of course.
The tavern was an institution which the West couldn't get along
without and didn't want to.

Women patrons of western taverns caused consternation, and
if one of them accidentally got into the wrong bed there was
a riot. An itinerate book peddler has left a splendid account of
such a happening in his description of life about a tavern stove.

### SOMEBODY IN MY BED

I just dropped in at a comfortable looking inn where I concluded to remain a day or two. After a good substantial meal,
I lit a "York County Principle" (the like of which sell in these
regions at the rate of four for a penny), and seated myself in the

ring formed around the barroom stove. There was a brawny butcher, the effeminate tailor, a Yankee fiddler, two horse dealers, a speculator, a blackleg, the village Esculapius, and "the captain," who in consequence of being able to live on his means, was a person of no small importance, and therefore allowed to sit before the firestove with the poker to stir the fire—a mark of respect granted *only* to persons of standing.

Yarn after yarn had been spun and the hour for retiring had arrived—the landlord was dozing behind his bar,—and the spirit of the conversation was beginning to wane when the doctor whispered to me that if I would pay attention, he would "topp off" with a good one.

"I believe, Captain," said the doctor, "I never told you about my adventure with a woman at my boarding house, when I was attending the lecture?"

"No, let's hear it," replied the individual addressed, who was a short, flabby, fat man of about fifty, with a highly nervous temperament, and a very red face.

"At the time I attended the lectures, I boarded at a house in which there were no females, but the landlady and the old colored cook—" (Here the doctor made a slight pause, and the Captain, by way of requesting him to go on, said "Well.")

"I often felt the want of female society to soften the severe labors of deep study, and dispel the ennui to which I was subject—"

"Well," said the Captain.

"But as I feared that forming acquaintances among the ladies might interfere with my studies, I avoided them all—"

"Well."

"One evening after listening to a long lecture of physical anatomy, and after dissecting a large negro, fatigued in body and mind, I went to my lodgings—"

"Well," said the Captain.

"I went into the hall, took a large lamp, and went directly to my room, it being then after one o'clock—"

"Well!"

"I placed the light upon the table, and commenced undressing. I had hardly got my coat off when my attention was attracted to a frock, and a quantity of petticoats lying on a chair near the bed—"

"Well!" said the Captain, who began to show sign that he was getting deeply interested.

"And a pair of beautiful small shoes and stockings on the floor. Of course I thought it strange, and was about to retire— but then I thought it was my room, I had at least a right to know who was in my bed—"

"Exactly," nodded the Captain. "Well!"

"So I took the light, went softly to the bed and, with a trembling hand, drew aside the curtain. Heavens! what a sight! A young girl—I should say an angel, of about eighteen, was in there asleep—"

"Well!" said the Captain, giving his chair a hitch.

"As I gazed upon her, I thought that I had never witnessed anything more beautiful. From underneath a little nightcap, rivaling the snow in whiteness, being a stray ringlet over a neck and shoulders of albaster—"

"Well!" said the excited Captain, giving his chair another hitch.

"Never did I look upon a bust more perfectly formed. I took hold of the coverlid—"

"Well!" said the Captain, throwing his right leg over his left.

"And softly pulled it down—"

"Well!" said the Captain, betraying the utmost excitement.

"To her waist—"

"*Well!*" said the Captain, dropping the paper and renewing the position of his legs.

"She had on a nightdress, buttoned up before, but softly I opened the first two buttons—"

"*Well!*" said the Captain, wrought to the highest pitch of excitement.

"And then, ye Gods! What a sight to gaze upon—a Hevepshaw! words fail me. Just then—"

"Well!!!" said the Captain, hitching his chair right and left, and squirting his tobacco juice against the stove that it fairly fizzed again.

"I thought that I was taking a mean advantage of her, so I covered her up, seized my coat and boots, and went and slept in another room."

*"It's a lie!"* shouted the excited Captain, jumping up and kicking over his chair. "It's a lie! I'll bet up to fifty dollars that you got into the bed."[28]

Taverns were always surrounded by both sportsmen and liars. Contests of all sorts were organized, and much excitement prevailed at the firesides. In this particular tavern a young blood arrived at suppertime and created a general commotion in the process of getting himself free of a heavy brown overcoat and a fur cap. His boasting provoked one of the local citizens to challenge him to a spitting contest in which the supercilious young man was completely singed.

## WILD WESTERN SPORTS

"Lodgings for the night," said he to the landlord, "and have my horse well fed."

Then approaching the fire, he spread himself, and tapping his boot with his whip, gave a supercilious look at the little knot of men around, who had made way for him.

"Devilish cold night," said he, unbuttoning his coat. "Why don't you have more wood on here?"

"That was a great shot of Billy Robinson's," said an old man in the corner, peering over his spectacles at the stranger, "but I'll bet ten dollars that I can outshoot, outride, outwrestle, outrun, or outwhip anybody about your diggin's."

No one replied to this banter, and at last the old man, who stood about six feet high, said:

"We don't fight much about here, stranger, except with Indians; but, as you appear keen for a bet, I'll bet you ten dollars that I can beat you spitting at a mark, at the distance of six feet."

"Done," said the stranger, "I'll take the bet."

And the money was forthwith put up, the distance measured off, and a cross made on the floor with a piece of chalk for a target.

"Well, go on," said the old man; "you spit first."

The stranger took his position, and calculating the distance with his eye to the mark, spat within an inch of the chalk cross.

"Well, beat that," said he with a look of triumph.

"That's just what I'm going to do," said the old man and taking his place, fixed his eyes firmly on his nose, knelt upon his knees, and stretching out his hands as far as he could leaned over and spat plump on the cross.

"I rather think I drove the center that time," said the old man, resuming his seat; while the party around, who had been watching the sport, roared with laughter.

The old man quietly pocketed the stakes, while the stranger, with a grave-yard countenance, simply remarked, "Is that the way you do things here?" and retired to his lodgings.[29]

The West was a land of "smart" people. Occasionally a frontiersman was caught in some awkward situation, but most often he did the catching, especially if he were on home ground. Nothing delighted a Kentuckian more than teasing a Frenchman or an Irishman. Kappa declares that this account of a Frenchman looking for a tavern actually happened in Henderson, Kentucky.

## You Can Go to Helle

It seems a person from the "land of krout" kept a public house or tavern in the place, and the said host rejoiced under the cognomen of Jacob Helle. One evening a Frenchman rode into town fatigued and dusty, and was anxious to put up for the night. Stopping a passer-by, whom we will call Simpkins for the sake of euphony, and who was a bit of a wag, he asked to be shown to the nearest tavern. Simpkins proceeded to direct him —with, "There's Jo Muggiono's house round the corner, and

Dick Pearson's at the end of this street, Abe Mosley's house about half a square further on and, if you don't like any of these, then you can go to Helle," pointing with his bony index to the establishment of that best-named individual just across the way. The latter part of this speech "riled" the Frenchman, who did not understand, and jumping from his horse he drew a formidable-looking cowskin, with—"By gar! You means to geeve me ze insult; I will geeve you ze horsewheep"—and he would have wolloped poor Simpkins handsomely had the latter not hastily explained that it was to the hospitalities of the host and not to the "warm locale" he would consign his mortal coil.

"Oh, oui! je suis satisfait, by gar! vat a peeples."[30]

The panic of 1837 created chaos on every hand. None were more disappointed, however, than those who speculated in western lands. One of these Easterners has left an interesting account of how he was cheated of his lands, and humiliated by a Sucker who had no table manners.

### TABLE ETIQUETTE IN ILLINOIS

While in Illinois, I happened to buy a couple of Sections of Land of a genuine "sucker," who had been for the last twenty years in the western wilderness, and was, consequently, a trifle behind the age in politeness and fashionable movements. After the purchase it became necessary for him to go with me to Quincy to arrange the papers with the lawyers; and, as he was under my charge, or rather, as I liquidated the transitory expenses we "put up" together at the Quincy House, kept by Munro, in a manner not inferior to any house west of the Alleghanies. As I heard much of this house, my headquarters during my peregrinations in search of desirable lands (and be damned to them) I was acquainted with nearly all that fed thar, who were mostly from the East, and preserved a certain degree of politeness and etiquette! Being disposed to make my "sucker" friend as comfortable as possible, I introduced him to a number of my acquaintances, all of whom conversed with him freely, but any attempt on his part to start a conversation with any one to whom he had *not been introduced,* happened to prove a failure, and he soon made the discovery that it was a useless expenditure of breath to talk to people in that place without first being introduced.

At dinner he appeared much astonished to see knives so clean, and the fork was a perfect enigma to him, he could see no possible use for it. He was singularly impatient during the discussion of the soup, which he disdained to touch as being altogether too vapid for use, but amused himself in devouring his bread.

After the soup was removed and he was bountifully supplied with meats and vegetables, and was stowing them away with a great "gusto," he stopped suddenly, and I thought he was choked; but, after looking about the table, and at the waiter for some time, he says to me with the greatest possible gravity, *"I wish you would introduce me to this gentleman* [pointing over his shoulder to the waiter] *for I want some more bread and I am not acquainted with him."*[31]

Getting rid of an undesirable bedfellow was a fine art on the frontier. Nothing was more annoying than having to sleep piled up in bed with several strangers. Many travelers developed a fine technique in securing the sole use of tavern beds. Lice and itch were two sure-fire gags which travelers used.

## GETTING SHUT OF A BEDFELLOW

A gentleman was traveling in the West some years ago and it so happened that about nightfall one evening he unexpectedly arrived at a little French village on the inquiry for a public house, and was soon directed to one close by. The wayfaring man soon found, from appearance of "the crowd" after supper (the barroom being filled with a number of dark-complexioned gentlemen, some of whom declared to be "half-hoss, half-alligator, steamboats, etc."), and the house being a very small affair, that the best thing he could do was to get over "double trouble" by turning in, and therefore asked the major-domo of the establishment to be kind enough to show him his sleeping quarters. The landlord made himself very useful, and soon had his guest furnished, as he remarked with a private room, in size about eight by ten, with a single bed, which the polite old Frenchman informed him was the only empty bed about the house. The tired traveler needed nothing more, and without further ceremony pop'd into bed. He had been there but a few minutes, when he heard someone blundering through the dark toward his room; and, to his great surprise, one of the "steamboats" from the barroom "rounded to" in his private bedchamber, puffing and blowing off steam, high-pressure fashion. The intruder was what is known in this country as a "Gumbo Frenchman," and, as we would say in "Old Kaintuck," of the "low-flung" order at that.

"Hallo, my friend," said our traveler, who began to think it was time to inquire of Mr. Gumbo what his business was in his private apartment, "what are you going to do?"

"Do!" says Gumbo. "Sacre, Got d--n! 'Spose I am goin' to lay in de bed."

"What!—with me?" said the traveler.

"Yas, sa," said Mr. Frenchman.

"Yes, but, my friend, see here; you certainly don't want to sleep with a sick man; I am diseased—I am diseased—I have got the itch!"

"Oh! dat's nothing!" said Gumbo. "I has got worse and more as dat, for I had got de dem louse like de dev!"

The cunning traveler was beat at his own game.

"I give it up," said he; "you can take the bed, sir, and I'll hang up on a nail."

"Ah!" says Gumbo, "you no like de sleep two in de bed, eh?"

"As to that number," said the ousted man, "I could probably get along with it; but, from your own account, you and 'de louse' number more like two thousand. Good night."

"Adieu, Monsieur," said Frenchy, as he hid himself beneath the bedclothes, and whether the poor cheated traveler found another bed that night, this deponent saith not.[32]

## CHAPTER VI

# SERVANTS OF THE PEOPLE

"ROTATION in office, and frequent election, salutary principles which disjoint the schemes of usurpation, and frustrate the systematic continuations of power," was the toast of a rampant frontiersman at a Washington's birthday celebration.[1] This utterance was greeted with thunderous applause, lengthy swigging at the jug, and a sustained fire by the militia. "Rotation in office" and "frequent elections" were indeed "salutary principles" of the frontier. Western polls were storm centers of political activity. Fight after fight occurred during elections. Kentucky alone followed the time-honored precedent of Virginia and prolonged the delectable process of selecting public officials by keeping its polls open three days. By the time the Bluegrass State had endured a three-day bender its eyes were reddened for months to come.[2]

Strangers visiting in Kentucky during elections were frightened out of their wits. Fortesque Cuming had to pass through Carlisle where he said: "I counted above a hundred horses fastened under trees—I was induced to hasten past this place as the voters in that sterile part of the country did not appear quite peaceable and orderly as those in Paris. Some of them might have been moved by the spirit of liquor to challenge me to run a race with them or to amuse the company with a game of rough and tumble, at both of which the backwoods Virginians are very dexterous."[3] One would be led to doubt Cuming's statement of affairs in Kentucky during elections if it were not for the fact that other travelers, and, likewise, native observers, have left similar accounts.

Nothing could have provoked more excitement than a three-day election at which the voters made their choice known to the clerks viva voce. Cuming found the election in Lexington quiet. "It was the day of election for representatives in the legislature of the state. The voting was very simple. The county clerk sat within the bar of the courthouse, and the freeholders as they arrived gave their names, and the names of those voted for."[4] This was at Lexington, a town of more refinement, but down the river James Flint contrasted conditions in Indiana and Kentucky. He said: "A few days ago I witnessed an election of a member of congress from the state of Indiana—members for the state assembly and county officers, and the voters for the township of Jeffersonville were taken by ballot in one day. No quarrels or disorder occurred. At Louisville in Kentucky the poll was kept open three days. The votes were given viva voce. I saw three fights in the course of an hour."[5]

Usually the candidates sat inside the enclosure with the clerks of the elections, and when the voters appeared they announced their choice by turning to their favorite candidates, and with a patronizing smile said, "I vote for you, Sir," to which the candidates replied, "Thank you, Sir, and may God bless you, Sir."[6]

Candidates were able to keep tab on their standing at the polls by the viva-voce method of voting, and they stimulated their constituents' choice by administering frequent and generous potations of the best bourbon which all the land of famous bourbon liquor could supply. Liquor barrels stood within easy reach of the polls, and ham-fisted bullies gulped down deep draughts and cast fighting epithets at less intemperate voters. Along with liquor which flowed as freely as mountain branch water there were other coveted commodities. Gingerbread, pawpaw, and trinket salesmen surrounded the polls. There were loafers, huckster women, "niggers," and horse jockeys all milling around the grounds. By nightfall they were all drunk and craving excitement. The candidates bought all the gingerbread available and sent the crowd home loaded to return the next day in even higher spirits. By the second day the election contests grew warm, and a two-day drunk began to tell on the nervous temperaments of the minions of democracy. Fights broke the tedium for election clerks, and even for the candidates who waited for each new crop of citizens to make up their minds. If by chance the candidates were running nose and nose down the homestretch on the third day, liquor flowed more freely, and each side lambasted the other with fiery vocal fusilades. Treats were passed out to all within reach, and voters were bullied, badgered and openly intimidated. Fighting ruffians tumbled to and fro before the clerk's stand and at many polls ears were bitten off, noses impaired and eyes gouged. Benjamin Drake in describing a third-day election fracas in Mason County, Kentucky, said the highly excited partisans of each of the candidates were shouting "Huzza, the Little Red," "Well done, Bald Eagle," "Go it, Captain," "Nail him, Coffin." The native son of Old Kentucky in this particular contest saw that his chances for success were becoming more uncertain with the passage of each hour. He bought two barrels of "stout" liquor, rolled them into the courtyard where he mounted one and proclaimed to the crowd that his father was a "pyore canebrake" pioneer, that he himself was a native son who had been rocked in a sugar trough and raised on "possum fat and hominy." He was a captain of the "melishy" and waded in muck and mire up to his belly for his country. He declared his opponent to be a "New Englander by birth, a college-learnt dandy schoolmaster, who carried his sheepskin in a tea cannister." To his gaping audience this "sugar-trough" scion flung the opprobrious denouncement that his opponent was a hawk-billed "blue belly." To top this thunderclap, he invited "all true sons of Ol'Kentuck to come to the trough and liquor!" This fiery brand of the Limestone bottoms leaped from his barrel-head platform, and knocked the ends out of his mellow prizes and ladled out the "spirit of democracy" by the gourdful to gasping "citizens." Shouts of "Huzza for old Kentuck" and "Down with the Yankees," filled the air. The opposition, undaunted by this eleventh-hour show of strength, answered the militia captain's free-handed generosity with, "stones, clubs and brickbats [which] were hurled by the assailing party, and returned with equal violence; half-horse half-alligator encountered all Pottawattamie—a Mississippi snag was loosened from its moorings by a full-grown snapping turtle—the 'yaller flower of the desert' bruised the nose of 'Old Tecumseh,' 'Bill Corncracker' walked right into 'Yankee Doodle' and made the 'claret' run in torrents; in short, so hot waxed the patriotism of the belligerents, that many of them were trampled under foot, some were gouged, others horribly snake-poled and not a few knocked clear into a cocked hat."[7]

George D. Prentice started an editorial fight in Kentucky which lasted until 1842. Prentice had witnessed an election in Frankfort which he described in detail in his "Letter of a Strolling Editor" to the *New England Weekly Review*. The editor of the Cincinnati *Advertiser* was the first to publish this letter in the West and it was later republished in the Louisville *Advertiser* under the exciting title of "Prick Me a Bull Calf Until He Roar."[8] This letter paints a lusty picture of democracy at work in the West:

"I have just witnessed a strange thing—a Kentucky election— and I am disposed to give you an account of it [said Prentice]. An election in Kentucky lasts three days, and during that period whiskey and apple toddy flow through our cities and villages like the Euphrates through ancient Babylon. I must do Lexington the justice to say that matters were conducted here with tolerable propriety; but in Frankfort, a place which I had the curiosity to visit on the last day of the election, Jacksonianism and drunkenness stalked triumphant—'an unclean pair of lubberly giants.' A number of runners, each with a whiskey bottle poking its long neck from his pocket, were busily employed bribing voters, and each party kept half a dozen bullies under pay, genuine specimen of Kentucky alligatorism, to flog every poor fellow who should attempt to vote illegally. A half a hundred mortar would scarcely fill up the chinks of the skulls that were broken on that occasion. I barely escaped myself. One of the runners came up to me, and slapping me on the shoulder with his right hand, and a whiskey bottle with his left, asked me if I was a voter. 'No,' said I. 'Ah, never mind,' quoth the fellow, pulling a corncob out of the neck of the bottle, and shaking it up to the best advantage. 'Jest take a swig at the cretur and toss in a vote for Old Hickory's boys—I'll fight for you, damne!' Here was a temptation to be sure; but after looking alternately at the bottle and the bullies who were standing ready with their sledge-hammer fists to knock down all interlopers, my fears prevailed and I lost my whiskey. Shortly after this I witnessed a fight that would have done honor to Mendoza and Big Ben. A great ruffian-looking scoundrel, with arms like a pair of cables knotted at the ends, and a round black head that looked like a forty pound cannon shot, swaggered up to the polls and threw in his bit of paper, and was walking off in triumph. 'Stop, friend,' exclaimed one of the Salt River Roarers, stepping deliberately up to him, 'Are you a voter?' 'Yes, by G-d,' replied he of the bullet head. 'That's a lie,' rejoined the Roarer, 'and you must prepare yourself to go home an old man, for I'll be damned if I don't knock you into the middle of your ninety-ninth year.' 'Ay, ay,' replied the other, 'come on, then; I'll ride you to hell, whipped up with the sea sarpint!' They had now reached an open space, and the Salt River bully, shaking his fist a moment by way of feint, dropped his chin suddenly upon his bosom and pitched headforemost toward the stomach of his antagonist with the whole force of his gigantic frame. Bullet Head, however, was on his guard, and, dodging aside with the quickness of lightning to avoid the shock, gave the assailant a blow that sent him staggering against a whiskey table, where he fell to the ground amid the crash of bottles, mugs, and tumblers. Nothing daunted by this temporary discomfiture, the bully gathered himself up and with a single muttered curse renewed his place in front of his foe. Several blows were now given on both sides with tremendous effect, and in a few moments the Salt River boy, watching his opportunity, repeated his maneuver in which he had first been foiled. This time he was successful. His head was planted directly in his antagonist's stomach, who fell backward with such force that I had no expectation of his ever rising again.

'Is the scoundrel done for?' inquired the temporary victor, walking up and looking down on his prostrate foe. Bullet Head spoke not, but with the bound of a wildcat leaped to his feet and grappled with his enemy. It was a trial of strength, and the combatants tugged and strained and foamed at the mouth, and twined like serpents around each other's bodies, till at length the strength of Bullet Head prevailed and his opponent lay struggling beneath him. 'Gouge him!' exclaimed a dozen voices, and the topmost combatant seized his victim by the hair and was preparing to follow the advice that was thus shouted in his ear, when the prostrate man, roused by desperation and exerting a strength that seemed superhuman, caught his assailant by the throat with a grasp like that of fate. For a few moments the struggle seemed to cease, and then the face of the throttled man turned black, his tongue fell out of his mouth, and he rolled to the ground as senseless as a dead man. I turned away a confirmed believer in the doctrine of total depravity."

This is an extreme account perhaps. However, a sane critic of another era has said that this description by Prentice is valid.[9]

Stump speaking was a necessary part of the process of electing officers. There were no occassions like log rollings, muster days, barbecues, burgoo dinners, and court days for collecting crowds. Candidates went to log rollings with hand sticks over their shoulders and took an active part in the labors of the day. Later they took "the stump" and bellowed forth speeches, many of which had neither rhyme nor reason. Politicians, however, had to be witty. Governor Thomas Ford, of Illinois, said that these stumping "thunderers" faced men who were "drunken, cursing, swearing, hallooing, yelling, huzzaing favorite candidates." "Whole-hog" men, said he, were lined up against "bare-back" politicians. Many times candidates received votes because their constituents were voting *against* someone rather than *for* a man of their choice.[10] Politicians who could use odd phrases, catchwords, bywords, figures of speech and vulgar innuendoes were most likely to succeed. Such artisans were known, in the vernacular, to "carry gourds of possum grease" with which they greased and swallowed the credulous.

There are extant many samples of the rantings of the "flat-top" stump speakers who sought public favor by their peculiar brand of persuasiveness. Some of these which remain may be fictitious, others perhaps are authentic recordings. Governor Ford has preserved the speech of Adolphus Frederick Hubbard who sought the governorship of Illinois over the opposition of Ninian Edwards. "Fellow Citizens," shouted the eloquent Adolphus, "I offer myself as a candidate before you, for the office of governor. I do not pretend to be a man of extraordinary talents; nor do I claim to be equal to Julius Caesar or Napoleon Boneparte, nor yet to be as great a man as my opponent Governor Edwards. Nevertheless I think I can govern you pretty well. I do not think it will take an extraordinarily smart man to govern you; for to tell the truth, Fellow Citizens, I do not think you will be very hard to govern nohow."[11] This speech had the virtue of being a very frank argument to the effect that the Suckers should elect just an "ordinary" man to the governorship.

In Arkansas voracious sons entranced their hearers with discourses, which neither the speakers nor the listeners could possibly understand; nevertheless they got right down to business. "Feller Citizens," began a slouchy, shock-haired mud turtle, "this are the day for the people of Wolf's Mouth, and I mought say, if I warn't modest, that our carnal entranchasemen (that's a hard word but I got through it!) depends on our heterogenous exertions! Bill Sculpin are our candidate, and Jack Dondee swears he is bound to shoot every man that don't vote for him! Feller Citizens—I'm going to sand my speech with quotations from Seizem the celibrated Latin cricket, when he addressed the Cathagenions and Rocky Mountain cods at the baittle of Cow Pens! Look out I'm comin—cock your rifles and be ready! Eat ye brute! As the immaculate feller said, when he got stabbed in the back in the House of Representatives!"

To this brash sanding of an Arkansas stump speech with the words of the "great Seizem" by the friend of Bill Sculpin, a raw specimen replied: "Feller Citizens, there arn't no one skeered in this crowd! I'm not afflicted like Charlie Culliver, with the disease called *E Plurubus Unum!* Tempt us fugit! by the concordat and evacuating nabob of Jerusaleum! Old Jim Grime thought he'd frighten me with his Greek! But I can put in the big licks and pile on as much agony as he ever heard of! Poe stultus! Santa Parsima Block, Island Point, Judih Lex Taglinois! Historia Sacre! and fiducet et Broadaxe! What does the fellow think of himself now? He's a traveling synagogue; but can't catch me with his high-falutin words! Vote for Tom Cressy, he's a horse, and so am I! Ecco Signum! Abinito! De jure dum spire-Hurrah for Tom Cressy."[12] Whether this speech was ever uttered matters little here. It is representative of the kind of stuff that flowed (and still does, possibly without the sandings of Seizem) from breast pounding politicians of the backwoods.

Occasionally voters took the matter of chastising candidates into their own hands and made it hot for any representative who went astray in his public activities. When Governor Duncan kicked over the Jacksonian traces in Illinois his supporters reminded him, "Now, Governor Duncan, we Jackson men took you up when you was young, poor and friendless; we put you in high office, and enabled you to make a fortune; and for all this you have departed us, and gone over to the Adams men. You was like a poor colt. We caught you up out of the thicket, fed you on the best, combed the burrs out of your mane and tail and made a fine horse of you; and now you have strayed away from your owners."[13] Western newspapers carried column upon column of queries from voters addressed to candidates asking them to declare their positions on every conceivable sort of question.[14] Hecklers were numerous, and often "free-for-all" fights occurred between embarrassingly inquisitive citizens, and harassed candidates at the speakings.

Repartee in stump speaking was a very necessary part of the art of impressing an audience of voters. Although the Hoosiers and Suckers did not enjoy the privilege of fighting three days around their polls, they did take their elections seriously. A frontiersman in one election went to log rollings, barbecues and other public meetings as a dutiful and unostentatious citizen. He rolled logs, basted meat and did anything else he could to help along the good cause. His opponent was a dandified fellow who never offered his services at any time, nor to any cause, but he continually chided his uncouth native opponent for wearing borrowed shoes and for doing other things which he considered beneath the dignity of a seeker after public office. This humiliating chiding continued until the buckskin son happened to realize that his dandified tormenter's name was Jack Bass, and that by dropping the "B" in his surname he could turn the tables. Not only was Jack B'Ass laughed off the stump, but out of the country. Marks Crume, a staunch Hoosier politician, found himself in a similar situation in 1836. Crume was a candidate for the legislature from Fayette County, and his opponent was a long, lank, lean stoop-shouldered "New Light" preacher who wore "a blue muslin gown, a queue hanging down to his waist, and his head covered with one of these old-fashioned corn-shuck hats, with a rim extending down to his shoulders." The "New Light" brother pointed the way to higher democracy by day from the stump, and called down the thunder of the Lord for a shouting huddle of parishioners by night. On the stump Crume was able to hold his own, but "New Light" meetings were closed to him.

If the reverend gentleman was to be defeated the Crumeites had to use strategy. A militia muster at Squire Conner's farm, four miles from Connersville, offered an opportunity to place the preacher at a ridiculous disadvantage. The disciple of the new dispensation had no horse to ride and friends of his opponent secured for his use a scrubby jack. With his blue gown covering the miniature beast from head to tail, and with his legs jack-knifed into a heroic letter "K" by the short stirrups, the servant of the new gospel put forth to the field of action. When he reached his destination, his mulish beast of burden took the studs and refused to go through the gate into the drill field. The preacher mauled and coaxed his long-eared servant but to no avail. Soon every militiaman was looking in his direction, and there he sat covered by his drooping hat looking over the fence, and the jackass peeping under the lower rail braying at the top of his bestial voice. This ended Crume's opposition because the preacher, sorely embarrassed by such a ridiculous introduction, withdrew from the race.[15]

No officers in the states' governments attracted more attention, or committed more asinine blunders than members of the general assemblies. One Fourth of July toastmaster, after speaking in stilted terms in which he bathed heroically and extravagantly every institution in the state from its cities to its "Fair," rendered in a tremulous voice: "Ohio *Legislature,* more deeds and fewer words."[16] This sentiment did, or should have, prevailed throughout the West. Surely the toastmaster in Ohio did not have in mind, when he pleaded for action, that vigorous member of the Ohio House of Representatives who announced that he would whip the first three men who voted for a bill to amend the charter of the city of Cincinnati.[17]

State general assemblies were the favorite "stomping" grounds for all eloquent sons who had more wind than brains. Some of the queerest specimens the backwoods could rake up were loaded onto flatboats, stagecoaches, or sent away on horseback to the state capitals to "make" laws. No state in the West could possibly exceed Kentucky in this respect. At least fifty volumes of legislative acts and journals stand today as open chapters revealing the devious ways of asserting democratic rights.

The sons of the Bluegrass became exceedingly wrought up over the foreign intimidation of Americans prior to the outbreak of the War of 1812. Leaders in the general assembly in 1807 laid all of the blame at England's feet. Henry Clay was active in this assault on Britain, and actually took part in passing a law forbidding citation of certain English statutes. Clay, later, was placed in a humorous predicament because of this taboo of British laws. He found occasion, when appearing before the house of the assembly on a special occasion, to quote the common law of England. A bearded representative of the people jumped to his feet and shouted, "Mr. Speaker, I want to know, Sir, if what that gentleman said is true? Are we all living under Old English law?" The speaker explained that the English common law was recognized as a part of the law of the land. "Well, Sir," resumed the ardent buckskin patriot, "when I remember that our fathers, and some of us fit, bled and died to free us from the English law, I don't want to be under it any longer, and I make a motion that it be repealed right away." The motion was seconded, and it was with difficulty that the learned gentlemen at the foot of the great hill at Frankfort were spared the ordeal of making asses of themselves and their state by repealing a great body of fundamental law.[18]

It might be that the editor of the *Monitor of Western America* was correct in part of his statement concerning the general history of the Kentucky legislature. He reported, "We are glad to find by the result of the election that the people of Kentucky prefer *men to horses*—human beings to brutes—as their representatives in the state legislature. A horse may neigh and snort, may be taught to follow his master, do as he is bid, and obey instructions; a horse may prance and kick, and do mischief, but rational beings only are worthy of a seat in the legislature, and we *do hope* in the *future* they will be sent there."[19] This optimistic scribe might have employed his time more profitably hoping for the millennium. In the very year in which he proclaimed freedom from the tyranny of "equine" legislators a singularly fine crop of long-eared sons tried to tear up not only the state government, but likewise threatened an invasion into the national constitution through the famous "relief laws."

Legislators of the early western states were restless creatures. In Illinois the assembly had its ups and downs. Pending before that body in 1826 was the business of electing a state treasurer. The incumbent in the office was defeated, and before members of the house could vacate their seats he had knocked down and thrashed four of the largest and strongest of the people's representatives, and the others "broke and fled" from the house.[20]

The Suckers had great trouble making up their minds what

should be the law of the state. At every meeting of the legislature the laws were changed to suit the whims of that particular crop of legislators. It was said that it was indeed a fortunate thing that the Illinois assembly did not have power to rectify the scriptures for if it had it would have been certain "to alter and amend them, so that no one could tell what was or was not the law of the state."[21] Perhaps the Sucker assemblymen should have adopted the suggestion of the Reverend Mr. Wiley and the Covenanters of Randolph County who complained that the Governor of Illinois was unbaptized and therefore was a heathen chief executive. They begged that the constitutional convention, make Jesus Christ the head of the state, and the scriptures the rule of faith and practice.[22]

Laws were transferred from Virginia and the other southern states, and from Kentucky many of them were spread throughout the western states without much fundamental change. One of the most disturbing bits of legislation ever passed in a western general assembly was the "scalp" or "bounty" law which permitted payment of rewards for wolf scalps.[23] The original laws instructed magistrates to pay bounties for scalps with few or no questions asked, but soon more scalps were appearing than there were funds with which to pay rewards. In Kentucky the honorable gentlemen of the assembly discovered that scalpers were not killing bitch wolves, but harboring them for breeding purposes. In Clay County an ingenious evader of the law exercised a rare entrepreneurial ability by maintaining wolf pens where he caught bitches and kept them for breeding. With the scalps from his domesticated pups he was highly successful in euchering a sumptuous living out of the state treasury. When laws were passed forbidding payment for wolves under six months of age, the boys learned the fine art of stretching scalplocks from weanling pups to make them appear as old varmints.[24]

More disputes and bickerings occurred over wolf scalps possibly than over the scalps which the Indians removed from the heads of early pioneers. Indiana and Illinois adopted scalp laws from Kentucky,[25] and, apparently, a generous number of Kentucky tricksters were included in the deal because the Hoosiers and Suckers were continually wrangling over the dishonesty of bounty-seekers. Time and again they changed laws to prevent swindling, but only the disappearance of wolves saved the states from eventual bankruptcy, or at least from a generous run upon the treasury.

Wolves were more plentiful in Arkansas, and the scalp law was a lucrative source of income because many of the hillbillies wandered throughout the wooded sections of that state. The old Arkansas law permitted magistrates to issue certificates of payment upon the delivery of scalps, but as wolves grew scarce the bold hunters cut a single bounty into many strips, and cut larger scalps from sheepskins. When they appeared to take the oath that they held in their hands a wolf scalp they clutched the thin strip just tightly enough to evade the law. A "wolf bill" was proposed in the house in December, 1837, which would be more lenient on the riflers of the state treasury. This law had been passed by the senate, and had come to the house where another important law, the real-estate bank bill, was pending. A long series of amendments were offered to both bills, and the good-natured Major Anthony proposed that the president of the real-estate bank sign all bounty certificates—since both involved the delicate frontier art of scalping the people. Since the president of the bank was the speaker of the house, and was a man of extremely fine sensibilities, he took as personal any disparaging remarks about his pet bill. This suggestion of Major Anthony had a bit of sneer in it. The Speaker deserted the chair, reached for his bowie knife and made straight for the wise-cracking member. Major Anthony staved off this vicious attack for a time with a chair and his bowie knife, but the Speaker being experienced in such delicate matters soon knocked Anthony's knife out of his hand, and thrust his blade to the hilt in the innocent member's breast.[26]

Interfering with the sanctity of the people's rights in Arkansas was an extremely dangerous business, and the boys from the "big bottom" cherished with genuine affection their "wolf law."

Speakers of the house in some of the other states did not stab members for their frivolities on the floor, but surely a Hoosier one would have been justified in committing mayhem upon the Honorable Mr. Marvin of Hendricks County. Mr. Marvin, whose term was about to expire, and who was not accountable for legislative blunders back home, proceeded to "come the giraffe" over a bill to reduce the assessor's pay to one dollar and fifty cents a day. His ire was up, and he bellowed: "Mr. Speaker! I second the motion of the gentleman from Carroll, I do by God! I'm for paying men damned well for their services, and not for starving them until they are as lean and hungry as starved wolves. I'm not so infernal pussillanimous as some gentlemen who haven't no guts! I'll be damned if I don't oppose some gentlemen here who are cavorting on this question like stub-tailed dogs in high rye, or a young heifer in fly time. I'm fornenst such cussed stinginess, and for the proposition of the gentleman from Carroll, who for onst is right, but by God that is rarely the case, I must admit. I hope the committee of the whole will do their duty and not act the part of damned fools. I am now done, and would say to the house, go it, go it."[27]

It was a far more docile member who appeared for his first term in the Missouri legislature. This honorable gentleman, who having been caught up by the scruff of the neck and instructed "to hit" for Jefferson City as a representative of the people, appeared at the statehouse and entered what he thought was the lower house. The members of this chamber, however, were cavorting somewhat after the manner of "stub-tailed dogs in high rye," and he ventured upstairs to the senate where he found proceedings under way in a less riotous manner. He presented his credentials to the president who in turn informed him that the room below was the house. The "green" member stood looking frightened for a moment and then replied in a timid voice, "Why I was in *that* room and thought it was a grocery [saloon]."[28]

Often there was a bit of difficulty with public servants who took their oaths of office too seriously—or, at any rate, too literally. When the Missouri legislature was organized for the first time, an honest but indiscreet colonel was given the choice plum of doorkeeper. With uplifted right arm he swore sanctimoniously "to support the constitution and to keep the doors of the house open." Upon assuming the responsibility of guaranteeing the liberties of the people, the pompous colonel threw open the double doors, disregarding the coolness of the weather, and complaints from the legislators. To all requests "to shut the doors," the colonel replied that he had sworn to keep the doors of the house open, and keep them open he would as long as there was breath in his body. Finally this faithful public servant chose to resign his office rather than be a party to the raping of constitutional authority in the sovereign state of Missouri.[29] Timothy Flint was in Missouri at the time the state government was organized, and he found a wild scramble for political positions. He thought all the evils of office-seeking in the eastern states seemed to be concentrated in this new commonwealth. When the assembly met, not only did the open doors cause confusion, but likewise the headless activities of the "gentlemen" who represented the people. A waggish member inscribed above the Speaker's chair, "Missouri, forgive them, they know not what they do."[30]

Kentucky was most notorious of all western states for its verdant statesmen. There were a few Clays, Nicholases, Marshalls and Breckinridges. Other legislators were pale imitations. Eastern counties elected loud-mouthed "yahoos" who floated to the "outside," and to Frankfort on the Kentucky River. Roads were poor, and there were few or no public conveyances to transport the "statesmen" from the upcountry. One such "honorable representative," Mullins by name, floated into Frankfort on the famous old Kentucky River packet, the *Blue Wing,* and began "looking into the situation" at once. At court day back in his beloved county, following adjournment of the assembly, he gave an accounting of his lawmaking activities in a sonorous oration which fell a little short of the manner of Clay. "Feller Citizens!" saluted the redfaced Honorable Mullins, "when you elected me to the legislature I wished that I mought have the tallest pine growed in the mountings, so that I mought strip the limbs from the same and make it into an enormous pen, and dip it in the waters of the Kaintuck River and write acrost the clouds, 'God bless the people of Estill County!'

"Arter you elected me I went down to Frankfort on the *Blue Wing* and as we wended our winding sinuosities amidst its labyrinthian meanderings, the birdlets, the batlets, and the owlets flew outen their secret hidin' places and cried out to me in loud voices: 'Sail on, Mullins, thou proud defender of thy country's liberties.'

"When I reached Frankfort, I went up into the legislatur hall and thar I spied many purty perlicues a-hangin on the ceiling to pay for which you had been shamefully robbed of by unjest taxation. When matters of small importance were before the body I lay like a bull pup a-baskin in the sunshine, with a blue-bottled fly a-ticklin of my nose; but when matters of great importance come up I riz from my seat, like the Numidian lion of the desert, shuck the dew drops from my mane, and gave three shrill shrieks for liberty."[31]

The gentlemen of the Bluegrass were always gallant. They were defenders of the "fair" of the land at all times, except when it came to the matter of granting divorces to women whose husbands had departed the domestic fold and had, in biblical terms, lain with Ethiopian women. William Littell took the gentlemen of the assembly to task in his *Festoons of Fancy*. He said, "In the realm of Kentucky there are many sons of Belial. And these men in their youth go in unto Ethiopian women, with which the land swarmeth, and beget sons and daughters, and these sons and daughters become bondmen and bondwomen."[32] These were stinging words of criticism, and some of the sensitive "Sons of Belial" were considerably up in the air over this attack. They appeared before the legislative altar with contrite hearts, but they were not brought so low as to vote for the divorce bill.

The assemblymen, however, were not to be labeled as ungal-

lant in all things. When the poor bedraggled Clarinda Alling-
ton came before them in 1804, and tearfully described her hardships of the past twelve years as a captive among the Indians, she
found sympathetic and generous listeners. Clarinda had been
captured by the Indians, and her charms had captivated a Cher-
okee chief who claimed her as his wife. Thrice she was brought
to bed with child, but she found means to escape the harsh
tyranny of her savage lover and returned with her three half-
breed children to the bar of the House of Representatives at
Frankfort, Kentucky. In order to restore this long-suffering
child of the forest to civilized life, the generous assembly, with
a collective gesture of gentleness, appropriated an annuity for
three years of sixty, fifty and forty dollars respectively. Thomas
Allen, Robert Mosby and George Thompson, "gentlemen," were
placed in charge of this forlorn ward of the state, and they were
instructed "to care for her" as long as she remained in Kentucky.[33]

Legislators of the early West were tenderhearted individuals
when a constituent approached them with a tale of woe and
despair. They would get him a divorce from a wife who had
been delivered of a mulatto baby, change his name, or slice off
a nice chunk of public land and waive the fee.[34] Poor widows,
indigent orphans, and ailing and aged patriarchs were ever uppermost in the minds of the "servants of the people." Often
legislators did foolish things for the "boys up the creek."

The representative from Monroe County, Kentucky, announced to a sympathetic assembly that Mrs. Chillian Carter,
the wife of a loyal supporter, had been delivered of triplets. This
unexpected stroke of generosity on the part of Mother Nature
placed a serious burden on poor Chillian's shoulders, but his
friend, the gentleman from Monroe, proposed to aid him. He
introduced a bill in the house which is a masterpiece of legislative drafting. "Whereas, it is represented that Mrs. Carter, wife
of Chillian Carter, of the County of Monroe, had on the eighth

day of the present month of January, three children at one birth
—one son and two daughters," and "For encouragement where-
of," the general assembly of Kentucky authorized the county
court of Monroe to appropriate "one thousand acres of vacant
and unappropriated land lying in the state of Tennessee." A
question arises at this point as to whether the gentlemen of the
Kentucky assembly were adding chaos to confusion and frus-
tration in the fruitful Chillian Carter's household. Perhaps these
statesmen-like gentlemen recalled the date of birth, January 8,
and believed that Tennesseans, remembering that this was the
anniversary of the great victory of their favorite son at Chal-
mette, would overlook this rather bold violation of their sanctity as a sovereign state.[35]

Frontier legislation was fearfully and wondrously made at
times. There were no centralized drafting bureaus, and few
private drafters who could see beyond the limits of their districts
when they prepared a bill. A Westerner who became disgusted
at the apparent conception of fundamental law on the part of
his colleagues, said they were like a profligate old pioneer who
came home after a night of debauchery and inquired of his wife
if there was any "buttermalk." "Yes," she said, "look for it in
the press." After fumbling about for a few minutes the sodden
swain again asked, "Jinsey dear, did you say the buttermalk was
in the press?" "Yes," she replied, "go look for it." At length the
hungering spouse was back, but his patronizing air had changed
to one of anger and he shouted "Jinsey! *Jinsey!* Jinsey! I say, is
the buttermalk in a crock, or is it just loose so?"[36] Many times
the western courts were placed in the position of asking the assemblies if their laws were within constitutional limitations, or if
they were "just loose so."

"Phil" of Jefferson City, Missouri, contributed the following
story of a Missourian appearing before the state legislature with
chickens for sale. If what Timothy Flint saw in the Missouri
assembly is a true account of what went on there this yarn is
not an unreasonable one.

## Selling Chickens to the Missouri Legislature

While the Legislature of Missouri was in session a few years ago a green fellow from the country came to Jefferson to sell some chickens. He had about two dozen, all of which he had tied by the legs to a string, and this being divided equally, and thrown across his horse or his shoulder, formed his mode of conveyance, leaving the fowls with their heads hanging down, with little else of them visible except their naked legs, and a promiscuous pile of outstretched wings and ruffled feathers. After several ineffectual efforts to dispose of his load, a wag, to whom he made an offer of sale, told him that he did not want chickens himself, but that perhaps he could sell them at that large, stone house over there (the capitol), that there was a man over there buying, on speculation, for the St. Louis market, and no doubt he could find a ready sale.

The delighted countryman started when his informer stopped him.

"Look here," says he, "when you get over there, go upstairs, and then turn to the left. The man stops in that large room. You will find him sitting up at the other end of the room, and now engaged with a number of fellows buying chickens. If a man at the door should stop you don't mind him. He has got chickens himself for sale, and tries to prevent other people from selling theirs. Don't mind him, but go right ahead."

Following the directions, our friend soon found himself at the door of the Hall of Representatives. To open it and enter was the work of a moment. Taking from his shoulder the string of chickens and giving them a shake to freshen them, he commenced his journey toward the speaker's chair the fowls, in the meantime, loudly expressing, from the half-formed *crow* to the harsh *quaark,* their bodily presence, and their sense of bodily pain.

"I say, Sir,"—Here he had advanced about half down the aisle, when he was seized by Major Jackson, the doorkeeper, who happened to be returning from the clerk's desk.

"What the devil are you doing here with these chickens; get out, Sir, get out," whispered the doorkeeper.

"No you don't, though, you can't come that game over me, you've got chickens yourself for sale, get out yourself, and let me sell mine. I say, Sir (in a louder tone to the Speaker), are you buying chickens here today? I've got some prime ones here."

And he held up his string and shook his fowls until their music made the walls echo.

"Let me go, Sir (to the doorkeeper), let me go, I say. Fine large chickens (to the Speaker), only six bits a dozen."

"Where's the Sergeant-at-Arms," roared the Speaker. "Take that man out."

"Now don't will you, I ain't hard to trade with, you let me go (to the doorkeeper), you've sold your chickens, now let me have a chance. I say, Sir (to the Speaker in a louder tone), are you buying chickens too?" "Go ahead," "At him again," "That's right," whispered some of the opposition members, who could command gravity enough to speak. "At him again." "He'll buy them." "He only wants you to take less—at him again."

"I say, Sir (in a louder tone to the Speaker)—cuss your pictures let me go—fairplay—two to one ain't fair (to the Speaker and Sergeant-at-Arms), let me go: I say Sir, you up there (to the Speaker), you can have 'em for six bits: won't take a cent less. Take 'em home and eat 'em myself before I'll take—Drat your hides, don't shove so hard, will you! you'll hurt them chickens, and they have had a travel of it today, anyhow. I say you, Sir, up there—"

Here the voice was lost by the closing of the door. An adjournment was moved, and carried, and the members almost frantic with mirth, rushed out to find our friend in high altercation with the doorkeeper about the meanness of selling his own chickens and letting nobody else sell his adding that "if he could just see that man up there by himself he'd be bound they could make a trade and that no man could afford to raise chickens for less than six bits."

The members bought his fowls by a pony purse, and our friend left the capital, saying, as he went down the stairs:

"Well, this is the darndest roughest place for selling chickens that ever I come across, sure."[37]

Wolf Jim was a tight specimen from upcountry Missouri who ambled down to the state capitol to get "jestice." The Wolf's famous speech was preserved in the St. Louis *Ledger,* and it is, indeed, a shrill shriek for the people.

### Wolf Jim's Speech

Mr. Speaker, I'm Wolf Jim, from one of the upper counties. I can whip the toe-nails off a grizzly b'ar, and depopulate the wolf diggin's of their inhabitants, just as fast as a skinflint, St. Louis Yankee would wiggle himself into a money corporation— therefore, I go hide, hair, and eighteen squeals agin' this invasion of extarnal rights. What, sink the liberties of the whole north-easternmost part of our country, by repudiating the bounty on them *varmint's* headdresses; and all this that the Governor's little boy, Bill, may wear ruffle shirts, and that suck-in shavin' shop, St. Louis, may keep her inhabitants chawin' up-river corn at a cheap price. Why, it's monstrus! Do you happen to know, Mr. Chairman, that they have got in that thar place a combination? You needn't look as if a wildcat had lit on you, for they have. Fire engins, steam sawmills, patent machines, two hundred lawyers, as many doctors, a shop to make more in, with a row of steamboats—all combined in an undissolved phalanx to wage an exterminating, never-ending grab-all-you-can-git warfare agin' the rights of the upper counties, and the north-easternmost part of our state, not forgetting the unalienable rights of Wolf Hollow, and its staple productions in particular.

Is this any longer to be tolerated? No, Sir! rather let us be exiled to the dark gorges of the Rocky Mountains, where corn whisky is not to be found, and where the light of civilization can't penetrate, they are so far down; rather let us submit to become lightnin' rods to the snow-headed summits of these bluffs of the Pacific, than be melted like thin cakes of ice, by the fire of this aristocratic cooking-stove.[38]

## CHAPTER VII

## WHERE THE LION ROARETH AND THE WANG DOODLE MOURNETH FOR HIS FIRST-BORN

A wrathful God kept vigilant watch over the western frontier. He was a God of tremendous force, who, in the highly descriptive words of one of his backwoods servants "toted thunder in his fist, and flung lightning from his fingers."[1] These claims of divine power were not made, however, until the beginning of the nineteenth century. The earliest frontiersmen were too busily engaged with immediate worldy matters to "fall down before a wrathful God."

Settlers at Boonesboro in 1775 held a religious meeting, and later Baptists, of a dozen strains, Presbyterians, Catholics and Methodists swarmed over the mountains to evangelize a sinful western population. But the early frontier was not truly worshipful. It was not, on the other hand, godless for it did have a deep religious feeling, a feeling which was buried beneath a covering of determined individualism. Frontiersmen appealed to God, but their appeals were direct, in their own words, and on their own terms. Once the back country was free from Indian attacks, and Westerners saw their way clear to permanent settlement, their thoughts turned to more organized Christianity.

In 1800 the spirit of the Lord began to make itself manifest upon the frontier. Beginning in Kentucky, this wave of riotous religious revivals poured over the West with an increasing fury. At Russellville, and later at Cane Ridge, in Bourbon County, there was an outpouring of the spirit which outdid anything the frontier had ever seen. Hundreds of poor wretches fell in their tracks as though they had been fired upon by a legion of crack militiamen. The Lord indeed "toted thunder in his fist, and flung lightning from his fingers." The noise of these meetings was likened to the roar of the cataclysmic Niagara. "The vast sea of human beings seemed to be agitated as if by a storm," said one observer. "I counted seven ministers, all preaching at one time, some on stumps, others in wagons, and one, the Reverend William Burke, now of Cincinnati, was standing on a tree which had fallen and lodged against another."[2]

Hardened and sinful frontiersmen experienced a change of heart and they came forth to be saved. They fell in sin, they jerked and ran and fell prostrate in the sight of God. Others treed the devil and barked mournfully in imitation of their faithful 'coon dogs until they were huddled about the altar. Some sinners became so conscious-stricken that they dropped on their knees in the aisles and began playing marbles in literal obedience of the scriptures, "Except ye be converted, and become as little children, ye cannot enter the Kingdom of heaven."[3]

An Irish preacher, named McNemar impersonated Satan by crawling on his hands and knees through the crowd, saying as he went, "I am the old serpent that tempted Eve." Brother McNemar approached a skeptical Scotchman, and announced his serpentine sinfulness. The heathen Scot raised a foot and smashed the Hibernian's crown saying, "The seed of woman shall bruise the serpent's head."[4]

Cane Ridge and its associated outpourings were the beginnings of the camp meeting in the West. From this great outpouring of the spirit, native converts flocked over the frontier to spread the gospel wholesale. Zealous preachers disavowed their former modes of life, and preached long sermons on the horrible examples of sinfulness which they had been. One of these militant servants said of his conversion that while he was at Cane Ridge he became excited, but there "being a tavern a mile off, I concluded to go and get some brandy, and see if it would not strengthen my nerves. When I arrived I was disgusted with the sight that met my eyes. Here I saw about a hundred men engaged in drunken revelry, playing cards, trad-

ing horses, quarreling and fighting. After a time I got to the
bar, and took a dram and left, feeling that I was as near hell as
I wished to be, either in this world or the one to come."[5] He
became so excited and frightened that he got on his horse and
started for home, but at the Blue Licks he was stricken down
by the Lord, and not until he decided to become a Methodist
circuit rider was his peace of mind restored.

Frontier preachers, for the most part, were curious individuals
indeed. Many were "unlarnt" for they had been called to the
service from between the handles of the plow or from other
manual labor. They drifted through the West mounted on un-
derfed nags, with their battered saddlebags thrown across the
seat of worn saddles. In these bags they carried the trinity of
the circuit: Bibles, hymnbooks and copies of *Paradise Lost*. It
was not a serene heaven which these roving evangelists held out
as a reward to their listeners, but rather it was a matter of avoid-
ing eternal destruction in a sulphurous hell. John Milton's highly imaginative lines describing an infernal pit stimulated the
faculties of the backwoods parsons and they drew with lusty
strokes pictures of destruction which were awful to behold.[6]
They led their flocks away from hell, and seldom if ever to an
attractive heaven. Celestial rewards for worldly righteousness
were only incidental in the whole exhorting process.

An English army officer likened the frontier attacks upon sin
and Satan to that of one large army advancing against another.
"The army of the church," he said, "was under the command
of Immanuel, and that of the World under Diabolus." Every
camp meeting was an attack or retreat on the part of one of
these armies. Converts were listed as deserters from the "black
army." Attacks lasted all day and all night with many generals
assuming command. Diabolus was attacked from front and
rear and infiladed from the flanks. Horse, foot and dragoons
were put to flight, and the banner of Immanuel was planted
safely atop the ramparts.[7]

Minor engagements brought the army of the holy banner out
in full force. These long-faced troopers waded into the conflict

from the beginning with intentions to wage war to the hilt. A good sister would strike up that noble hymn of battle: "Come, humble sinner, in whose breast a thousand thoughts revolve," and the saintly troops would fall into battle formation. Class meetings were turned into veritable bedlams with shouting, screaming, snorting, jerking, jumping, clapping of hands, "holy" laughing, falling down and swooning. One minister said that these "scenes beggar description." On one occasion he was a bit startled when he saw a stout brother, at whose house the meeting was being held, stand in a chair and sing hymns at the top of his voice until three o'clock in the morning. By that time the "people" had become so exhausted that few if any of them could lift their exhausted bodies from the floor.[8]

Though the soldiers were faithful and willing, frontier preachers were not halfway workers. When they brought sinners "through" they wanted them to come all the way. Ringing sermons peppered with flowery, but misused words, and violent word pictures of helpless and tormented souls pouring into the scorching maws of hell fetched the mourners in droves. Smoke, fiery tongues of flame, and sulphurous smells swirled through the camp meetings like typhoons through coast cities of the Far East. Few self-conscious sinners could withstand the rampant persuasiveness of these "hell-fire" sermons. A preacher who could not bellow like a scrub bull in a canebrake during cocklebur season had little success in the pulpit.[9] Many congregations demanded long-winded and noisy ministers. One board of stewards warned a minister, after he had used notes for his sermon, that "we don't want you—no 'Piscopalians here —no Prispatarians nother."[10]

Denominational fights were often substituted for the theme of eternal perdition. Hardshell Baptists avowed that their faith was the only route to celestial happiness in the afterlife. "My text is this:" said an orthodox foot washer, " 'On this rock will I build my church, an' the gates of hell shall not prevail against hit.' Now I'm goin' ter speak the truth terday no matter who hit hits. Ef they's ary man in this aujience thet don't agree with me, thet's his lookout, an' not mine. The question fur us to answer 'bout this tex' is this: Whut church war hit thet the Lord founded? Whut church is hit thet the gates of hell hain't agoin' ter prevail against? I'm agoin' ter answer thet question; an' I'll tell yer whut church hit is; hit's the Ole Hardshell Baptist Church; thet's whut it is."[11] These "New Lights" of the cretaceous variety condemned every other faith to eternal destruction because they attempted to "go it dry."

Gilbert Tement hurled invectives of the bitterest sort against members of the other sects. He declared them "hirelings, catterpillars, letter-learned Pharisees, hypocrites, varlets, seed of the serpent, foolish builders whom the Devil drives into the ministry, dead dogs that cannot bark, blind men possessed of the Devil, rebels, enemies of God."[12] Peter Cartwright said the Baptist exhorters yelled, "Water, water; you must follow your Lord down into the water." This courageous servant of the Lord literally "grinned" his weaker adversaries of opposing faiths out of his way. He shouted charges that "infidelity (the Baptist faith) literally quailed before the mighty power of God which was displayed among the people."[13]

Methodist and Baptist brethren sat up and argued by the hour about the saving grace of their respective faiths. The Methodists accused the Baptists of being "forty-gallon" Christians, while the Baptists chided the Wesleyan faith for its fear of water. Bascom, Axley, Mason, Finley, Cartwright, and, earlier, Asbury, challenged the free-will brethren to open debates. Some of these hoary servants even invaded meetings of opposing sects and took the ministers to task before their congregations on points of theology. Hard shells became numerous in the West, and from time to time they were called "New Lights," but it is doubtful if their doctrines were either new or enlightening. Like many of those vigilant champions of the Methodist cause they had a perfect disdain for "book larnin'" and depended upon the Lord to meet them at the pulpit with a sermon.

"Yes, bless the Lord, I are a poor, humble man—and I doesn't know a single letter in the ABC's and couldn't read a chapter

in the Bible nohow you could fix it, bless the Lord," philosophized an "inspired" clergyman to his audience. "I jist preach
like old Peter and Poll, by the spirit. Yes, we don't ax pay in
cash nor trade neither for the gospel, and aren't no Hirelin's
like them high-flowered college-larned (Presbyterians) sheepskins—but as the Lord freely gives us, we freely give our fellow
critturs."[14] Missionaries along the frontier were against accepting pay for their services. One returned a land title because he
was fond of a hymn which had a line: "No foot of land do I
possess." He said that "I had rather sing that song with a clear
conscience than own America."[15] This was a fine bit of moraliz-
ing because few of the preachers received enough salary to agon-
ize even the most tender conscience. Many of them believed that
if they accepted pay they were committing sacrilege because
they would come to think in terms of income rather than the
gospel.[16]

Backwoods sermons were clumsy at best, and they generally
took a practical turn. The ministers were keen judges of their
audiences. Some of them started the services by making a
whole series of announcements which had nothing to do with
their sermons. A Hoosier divine announced from the sacred pre-
cincts of the pulpit that a neighbor "living down the lower end
of Sugar Holler, would like to hear if anybody in this here settlement has heern or seed a stray crittur of hissin, as his hoss-beast,
a three-year-ol' black gelding, come next spring, with a switch
tail, but kinda eat off by his other colt, slipt his bridle on Hickry
Ridge last big meetin', and he ain't heern or seen nothin' of him
sense." This opened a general discussion and a brother allowed,
"The crittur didn't come over here, as he'd been heern on or
seed by some of us—but if anybody hears or sees sich a stray
we'll put him up, and let neighbor Bushwack (evidently a
made name) know about it."[17]

Preachers of the back country had a way of sizing up their
auditors and leading them one by one to a general conclusion by
using their individual interests as illustrations. Brother Merry,
seeing that he was about to lose his hearers asked in a loud tone,

"My friends and neighbors don't you all shoot the rifle in this settlement?" He then fired away with a long discourse on shooting matches as a moral stigma upon the community. Spying a jug sitting in the audience he began another tirade by assailing the vices of drinking and swearing. Before he had finished he stepped on every toe in the house. "You all know," said the overwrought parson, "how as we are going through a clearing we sometimes see a heap of ashes at an old log heap—and at first it all seems cold and dead, but when we stir it about with a piece of brush, or the end of a ramrod, up flashes sparks, and smoke, too, comes out. Well 'tis exactly so with our natural hearts. They conceal a thing like a shooting match, or when we get angry, or are determined to have money or a quarter section of land at all hazards." This was the final straw, and the native sons gave in rather than be pounded to death for the next six hours by a masterful orator who hit close home every time he introduced a new subject of attack.[18]

If preachers took an informal attitude toward their duties as shepherds of wilderness sheep, the flock was even more informal. Homes were thrown open for gatherings, and the preachers accepted such accommodations as they found. Sometimes they were forced to pile up for the night with a dozen snoring fellow communicants in the same room. To add to the discomfort of the situation there were good sisters jammed in among the flock to give rise to suspicion. The preachers were shown the courtesy of being allowed to sleep on the bed, but to the man who occupied the middle there was ample reason to doubt the genuineness of the backwoods gesture of hospitality. Cord beds sagged, and it took all the fortitude of a strict ministerial disciplining to keep a brother in the good graces of his flock.[19]

Food constituted a problem among the parishioners. Brother Finley instructed "Father" Ellis that when riding the frontier circuits he would be offered 'coons and 'possums at each meal. Brother Ellis was not disposed to accept such hospitalities, however. He avowed that he would not eat "dogs and cats." One of the first families he visited had just secured a supply of fresh meat in a fine fat bear. The circuit rider took one long look at the bear and unhorsed his hosts completely by saying "They have the very foot of a negro, and the tusks of a dog."[20]

Henry B. Bascom was more fortunate than Brother Ellis in his fare, although he visited many converts who lived from hand to mouth, and seldom had anything for a visitor. On one occasion the eloquent Bascom was engaged in pouring forth the gospel when the head of the house where he was preaching jumped up, grabbed his rifle from its rack and rushed into the front yard. In a moment there was the report of the weapon and the good brother returned it to its place on the wall and resumed his seat as calmly as if he had just "scotched" the preacher with a ringing "amen!" When the service was over, Bascom asked his host why he had rushed from the house with his rifle in hand. "Sir," replied he, "we were entirely out of meat, and I was perplexed to know what we should give you for dinner, and it was preventing me from enjoying the sermon, when the Good One sent a flock of wild turkeys this way; I happened to see them, and took my gun and killed two at a shot; my mind felt easy, and I enjoyed the last of the sermon with perfect satisfaction."[21]

Perhaps the most difficult part of preaching on the frontier was coming in contact with and dealing with drunken bullies who tried to break up meetings. Confusion was the rule in many of the meetings, and when this occurred, especially in the class meetings of the Methodist faith, outsiders became excited and caused trouble. Brother Mason said that in one of his class meetings a devout convert shouted, "Oh, there's a better time a coming, hallelujah!" This sounded off the charge, and in a few moments the room was a bedlam of shouting, screaming, jerking, crying and laughing Methodists. This uproar excited the dogs under the floor and they began barking and fighting, sounds of which could be heard for a mile. The "barbarians" in the community who were without the pale of the sect began to wonder just what went on in one of these services. Especially was it a matter of wonderment to husbands whose wives showed a fondness for attendance upon these thunderous upheavals. One deserted husband decided that the time had come when he should know in detail why his wife found these meetings so fascinating. He appeared before the door and demanded of the keeper that he be admitted, although he was not "a jiner." The doorkeeper refused to admit him unless he promised to become a communicant in the faith. "Well," snorted the excited benedict, "I won't jine your meetin', for I believe you're a set of howlin' hypocrites you won't do nohow; and you're enemies to the country and to our dimocratic government. Meetins' ought to be free anyhow. See here, friend, ain't you going to let me in?" "Can't do it; it's agin' the rules," pleaded the doorkeeper. The intruder declared that his wife was in there and that he was coming in if he had to trample on the dead body of the stubborn doorkeeper. These words set the two at each other and they fell into the midst of the shouting congregation in a bloody fist fight. Women jumped through the windows, old men rushed out the door, and strong-armed brethren tussled with the invader. Outsiders rushed in and took a free hand in the fight, and in short order the whole room was wrecked and the floor smeared with the blood of the fathers of the neighborhood.[22]

Camp meetings were among the most attractive community affairs in many sections of the West. People came from miles around and stretched tents or built cabins and lived on the grounds for two weeks' to a month's time. A complete community was organized with the "tabernacle" as the center. Here attendants combined gossiping, horse trading, courting and frolicking with shouting and "getting religion." A visitor to one of these gatherings wrote: "I was struck with surprise, my feet were for a moment involuntarily arrested, while I gazed on a preacher vociferating from a high rostrum, raised between two trees, and an agitated crowd immediately before him, that was making a loud noise, and the most singular gesticulations which can be imagined. On advancing a few paces, I discovered that the turmoil was chiefly confined within a small enclosure of about thirty feet square, in front of the orator, and that the ground occupied by the congregation was laid with felled trees for seats. A rail fence divided it in two parts, one for females, and the other for males. It was my misfortune to enter the wrong side, and I was politely informed of the mistake by a Colonel P——, of my acquaintance, who, it appeared had undertaken the duty of keeping the males apart from the females."[23]

Camp meetings not only attracted the devout, but likewise the scoffers. Pastors occasionally had to take a hand in "roaching" disturbers. Peter Cartwright did not hesitate to take the erring brethren to physical task when they invaded his meetings. On one occasion this good servant of the Lord attacked a visiting dandy and shook him considerably because he insisted upon the unusual privilege of "setting with the gals."[24] This obstreperous dandy took a keen delight in baiting the Reverend Cartwright by his persistent disobedience of the Methodist seating rules. He likewise added insult to injury by standing upon the seats and staring with frank amusement at the performance of the shouters about him. Cartwright approached him and thundered the reproof, "I mean that young man there, standing on the seats of the ladies, with a ruffled shirt on. I doubt not that shirt was borrowed." This caused a commotion, and the dandy swore he would whip the preacher. He misjudged the minister's physical courage, and the hardy old frontiersman rushed up and demanded, "Gentlemen, let me in here to this fellow." "I walked up to him," said Cartwright, "and asked him if it was me he was cursing, and going to whip." This quarreling pair retired to the woods, where the preacher reached inside of his pocket as though he had a dirk. The bully inquired, "Dam' you are you feeling for a dirk? Are you?" Brother Cartwright's threatening gesture and declaration that he *would* stick a dirk in him frightened the knight of the ruffled blouse and he beat a rapid retreat. A committee of faithful members of the congregation caught the disturber and tied him with hickory thongs to a pole and ducked him in a pond until he was almost drowned.[25]

At Rushville, Ohio, a drunken band of about twenty men invaded a Methodist camp meeting and began cavorting around like Shawnee Indians. A preacher was knocked down, and Brother Birkhammer, a short stout man, knocked the leader down and offered to take on all challengers. Before the fighting had got under way two of the drunken offenders were on the ground unconscious, and eight more were held in durance vile awaiting the arrival of the sheriff and a magistrate.[26] Sometimes, however, the congregations were not so co-operative in the business of trouncing disturbers. The ministers of a central Ohio camp meeting were faced with the problem of enforcing peace themselves, or of being driven out of the community. They caught the ruffians by the heels and dragged them one by one outside where they administered a stiff pummeling followed with orders to leave the grounds, but this affair got the preachers in bad with their timid congregation. One old brother, who lacked courage to insure peace, got up in an experience meeting and moaned, "I'm pained, I'm pained. Oh! the scenes of last night pain me—yes—the cruelty of our preachers." Another wept as he testified, "I'm pained too, I fear our meeting will do no good—our preachers—Oh! Our preachers are not as pious as they might be. I feel I can't enjoy myself here, and I must go home."[27] This mournful testimony infuriated the preachers and disheartened the brothers; they all went home.

There were gradations of preachers. Those who could only get up steam and lay the groundwork for the "power" preachers were called *eight o'clocks,* but those gospel titans who could open up the horrors of hell, and display the wonders of heaven were reserved for the eleven-o'clock period. The *eleven o'clocks* were the ones who could paint the most horrible examples of human failures which the mind of man could conceive. One of these "Sampsons of the eleventh hour" pictured to a congregation a sinful and wayward man of the community returning to his home, and just as he started in the door the Lord struck him down. In a semi-conscious state he shouted, "Oh hell! hell!

hell!" he then withered away while his religious brethren prayed over him, and then the light appeared. As he beheld the promised land within the "gates" he jumped to his feet and shouted in a strong voice, "Glory, glory, glory!" In a few moments this hardened sinner had been within both the gates of hell and heaven. Such illustrations were certain to bring a flock of mourners crowding to the bench.[28] Sometimes, however, it brought some queer specimens to their feet and they frightened away those on the road to salvation.

Brother Mason had "raised the roof" in an eleven o'clock sermon when there pranced on the scene a bumpkin with yellowish hair, light gray eyes, freckled face, dressed in a red homespun shirt, a yellow tie, a gray satinet coat with flaring skirts and large pockets, brown pants which were not within speaking distance of his waist, and feet that covered a large sector of the mourner's pen. He groaned, gnashed his teeth, prayed and pounded the benches with his fist. At length he came up and went into action shouting, "Luck at the lite! Luck at the lite! Luck at the lite! Oh! the lite I see! Luck at the lite." His old Irish mother rushed up to him and inquired, "Och, och, Jammy, ir ye takin' l'ave o' ye sinses? What do ye sa?" This started the viewing of the "lite" all over again. He shouted interminably, "Luck at the lite! Luck at the lite!" When his mother inquired where, he explained, "Just yonder, Mother do you see it? It's a bigger lite than iver I saw in Irelan'. All the bog lites, an' will-o-the-wisp lites that iver ye saw is not like the lite I see." This was an occasion when the preacher stirred up a little more "lite" than he could handle.[29]

The West produced scores of preachers who took the gospel to the doors of the frontiersmen, and among this number there are many who stand out today in the history of American churches. None is more famous than Peter Cartwright who started his preaching career in western Kentucky and later moved into Illinois. He was a man of determination and daring. He asked no odds of anybody. If he found it necessary to take the situation in hand he never hesitated. On one occasion it was said that General Andrew Jackson entered the church where Brother Cartwright was holding forth with his usual vigor, and a cautious brother nudged him and whispered that Old Hickory had just come in "now be careful what you say." This just excited the circuit rider that much more. He astonished his hearers by shouting, "Who cares for General Jackson? He'll go to hell as quick as anybody, if he don't repent!" This boldness pleased Jackson and he was reputed to have said, "Sir, give me twenty thousand such men, and I'll whip the whole world, including the Devil."

Cartwright was crude. He spoke the language of his flocks, and he knew the art of exciting them to the highest pitch, but underneath his gruff manner there was a bit of refinement. It took a cruder person to bring this side of his life out into the open. His famous yoke-mate, Brother James Axley embarrassed him on many occasions by his coarse conduct. In the year 1806, the two were holding a meeting on the Scioto Circuit, and they were invited to visit with Governor Tiffin. Brother Axley, true to the tradition of Methodist parsons, had a marked fondness for fried chicken. He took a generous helping of the golden-brown delicacy and stripped the bones in true frontier hunter style. He then whistled for the dog and threw the bone on the carpet. That night when the circuit riders had retired to their room Cartwright gave his compeer a lecture on etiquette. "Brother Axley," said he, "you surely are the most uncultivated creature I ever saw. Will you never learn any manners?" This took the Kentuckian aback, and he innocently inquired, "What have I done?" "Done," said Cartwright, "you gnawed the meat off of your chicken holding it in your fingers; then whistled for the dog, and threw your bone down on the carpet; and more than this, you talked at the Governor's table, and in the presence of Sister Tiffin, about scalding your stomach with tea and coffee."[30]

Brother Axley may have gotten off base at the Governor's table in Ohio, but he carried thunder and lightning to the door of a member of the high court in Tennessee. "Old Jimmy," as

he was called, let it be known that he would preach at Jones-
boro, and a large crowd had gathered for the treat. But a
younger preacher decidedly of the "eight-o'clock" class was "put
up" and his sermon was unduly dry and uninteresting to his
lively audience, and there was considerable frisking about and
general misconduct. When Brother Jimmy "took the floor"
he opened with a tirade against his restless listeners. He made
his attack from the negative point of view. Shaking a bony
finger before his face he began "that man sitting out yonder
behind the door, who got up and went out while the brother
was preaching, stayed out as long as he wanted to, got his
boots full of mud, came back, and stamped the mud off at the
door, making all the noise he could on purpose to disturb the
attention of the congregation, and then took his seat; that man
thinks I mean him. No wonder he does. It doesn't look as if
he had been raised in the white settlements, does it, to behave
that way at meeting? Now, my friend, I'd advise you to learn
better manners before you come to church next time. But I
don't mean him." He next attacked a girl with flowers on her
bonnet and a breast pin on her dress, but he "didn't mean her."
The sleepers and snorers came in for a scorching, but he "didn't
mean them."

Judge Hugh White sat with a "chaw" of tobacco in his
mouth, spitting all over the floor, and enjoying thoroughly the
roasting which the fiery minister was handing his recalcitrant
listeners. He was surprised, however, when the good brother
pointed to him and bellowed, "And now I reckon you want to
know who I do mean? I mean that dirty, nasty, filthy tobacco
chewer, sitting on the end of that front seat. See what he has
been about! Look at those puddles on the floor; a frog wouldn't
get into them; think of the tails of the sisters' dresses being
dragged through that muck." He "did mean" Judge White,
and the Judge did not like it either. Brother Axley was a hewer
of wood who struck to the line, and never exempted any toes
from his general tramplings.[31]

There were more enterprising and sporting clergymen on the

frontier than those preachers who used homely terms to catch the attention of backwoods listeners. As civilization moved deeper into the western country it became less attentive to spiritual matters than affairs of the world. The Reverend Blaney appreciating this fact fetched the sinners in when he advertised "The Reverend Mr. Blaney will preach next Sunday in Dempsey's Grove, at ten A.M., and at four o'clock P.M., Providence permitting. Between services, the preacher will run his sorrel mare, Julia, against any nag that can be trotted out in this region, for a purse of five hundred dollars!

"This had the desired effect. People flocked from all quarters, and the anxiety to see the singular preacher was even greater than the excitement following the challenge. He preached an elegant sermon in the morning, and after dinner he brought out his mare for the race. The purse was made up by five or six planters, and an opposing nag was produced. The preacher rode his little sorrel and won the day, amid deafening shouts, screams and yells of the delighted people. The congregation all remained for the afternoon service, and at its close, more than two hundred joined the church; some from the excitement, some from motives of sincerity, and some from the novelty of the thing, and some because the preacher—in the unrefined language of the country—was 'a damned good fellow!' "[32]

Scores of books have been written by and about preachers of every denomination, but most of these have been arguments over theological questions or the rehashing of sermons. Some have argued, as did Alexander Campbell and David Rice, for days at a time over the ordinance of Christian baptism, but few of these discussions pictured the human servants of the Lord on the frontier. These brethren were militant and they stormed and reared in their pulpits. They jumped into the middle of sin and kept the waters muddy, like that Hardshell brother who shouted: "My brethering, you'll find my tex' somers in the Bible, an' I hain't agoin ter tell yer whar; but hit's thar. Ef yer don't believe hit you jest take yer Bible an' hunt twell yer fine hit, an' you'll fine a heap more thet's good, too." They were not specific about "tex's" but they hated sin. "Saddlebag" missionaries preached sermons on subjects which ranged from the roaring of the lion and the rare biological gem the "wang doodle," to keards, quarter hosses, fiddles and foolin' with the gals. Fortunately some of these classics remain.

S. P. Avery has preserved the classic sermon which follows. Avery did not identify the source of this rousing exhortation, but it is expressive of the preaching of the West. Perhaps a sermon very similar to this one might be heard at any of the many Holiness meetings held in the backwoods today.

### WHERE THE LION ROARETH AND THE WANG DOODLE MOURNETH FOR HIS FIRST-BORN

I am an unlarnt Hardshell Baptist preacher of whom you've no doubt hearn afore, and I now appear here to expound the scriptures and pint out the narrow way which leads from a vain world to the streets of Jaroosalem; and my tex' which I shall choose for the occasion is in the leds of the Bible, somewhar between Second Chronicills and the last chapter of Timothytitus; and when you find it, you'll find it in these words: "And they shall gnaw a file, and flee unto the mountains of Hepsidam, whar the lion roareth and the wang-doodle mourneth for his first-born."

Now, my brethering, as I have before told you, I am an oneddicated man, and know nothing about grammar talk and collidge high-falutin, but I am a plane unlarnt preacher of the Gospil, what's been foreordaned and called to prepare a perverse generashun for the day of wrath—ah! "For they shall gnaw a file, and flee unto the mountains of Hepsidam, whar the lion roareth and the wang-doodle mourneth for his first-born—ah!"

My beloved brethering, the tex' says they shall gnaw a file. It does not say they may, but shall. Now, there is more than one kind of file. There's the hand-saw file, the rat-tail file, the single file, the double file and profile; but the kind spoken of here isn't one of them kind nayther, bekaws it's a figger of speech, and means going it alone and getting ukered, "for they shall gnaw a file, and flee unto the mountains of Hepsidam, whar the lion roareth and the wang-doodle mourneth for its first-born—ah!"

And now there be some here with fine close on thar backs, brass rings on thar fingers, and lard on thar har, what goes it while they're yung; and thar be others here what, as long as thar constitooshins and forty-cent whisky last, goes it blind. Thar be sisters here what, when they gets sixteen years old, bust thar tiller-ropes and goes it with a rush. But I say, my dear brethering, take care you don't find, when Gabriel blows his last trump, your hands played out, and you've got ukered—ah! "For they shall gnaw a file, and flee unto the mountains of Hepsidam, whar the lion roareth and the wang-doodle mourneth for his first-born."

Now, my brethering, "they shall flee unto the mountains of Hepsidam," but thar's more dams than Hepsidam. Thar's Rotterdam, Haddam, Amsterdam, and "Don't-care-a-dam"— the last of which, my brethering, is the worst of all, and reminds me of a sirkumstance I onst knowed in the state of Illenoy. There was a man what built him a mill on the north fork of Ager Crick, and it was a good mill and ground a sight of grain; but the man what built it was a miserable sinner, and never give anything to the church; and, my dear brethering, one night there came a dreadful storm of wind and rain, and the mountains of the great deep was broke up, and the waters rushed down and swept that man's milldam to kingdom cum, and when he woke up he found that he wasn't worth a dam—ah! "For they shall gnaw a file, and flee unto the mountains of Hepsidam, whar the lion roareth and the wang-doodle mourneth for his first-born—ah!"

Now, "What the lion roareth and the wang-doodle mourneth for his first-born—ah!" This part of my tex', my beseaching brethering, is not to be taken as it says. It don't mean the howling wilderness, what John the Hardshell Baptist fed on locusts and wild asses, but it means, my brethering, the city of New Y'Orleans, the mother of harlots and hard lots, whar corn is wuth six bits a bushel one day and nary a red the nex'; whar niggers are as thick as black bugs in spiled bacon ham, and gamblers, thieves, and pickpockets goes skiting about the streets like weasels in a barnyard; whar honest men are scarcer than hen's teeth; and whar a strange woman once took in your beluved teacher, and bamboozled him out of two hundred and twenty-seven dollars in the twinkling of a sheep's tail; but she can't do it again! Hallelujah—ah! "For they shall gnaw a file, and flee unto the mountains of Hepsidam, whar the lion roareth and the wang-doodle mourneth for this first-born—ah!"

My brethering, I am the captain of that flatboat you see tied up thar, and have got aboard of her flour, bacon, taters, and as good Monongahela whisky as ever was drunk, and am mighty apt to get a big price for them all; but what, my dear brethering, would it all be wuth if I hadn't got religion? Thar's nothing like religion, my brethering; it's better nor silver or gold gimcracks; and you can no more get to heaven without it than a jay-bird can fly without a tail—ah! Thank the Lord! I'm an oneddicated man, my brethering; but I've sarched the Scripters from Dan to Beersheba, and found Zion right side up, and hardshell religion the best kind of religion—ah! 'Tis not like the Methodists, what specks to get to heaven by hollerin' hell-fire; nor like the Univarsalists, that get on the broad gage and goes the hull hog—ah; nor like the Yewnited Brethering, that takes each other by the slack of thar breeches and hists themselves in; nor like the Katherliks, that buys threw tickets from their priests; but it may be likened unto a man what has to cross the river—ah!—and the ferryboat was gone; so he tucked up his breeches and waded acrost—ah! "For they shall gnaw a file, and flee unto the mountains of Hepsidam, whar the lion roareth and the wang-doodle mourneth for his first-born!"

Pass the hat, Brother Flint, and let every Hardshell Baptist shell out.[33]

During the 'thirties and 'forties of the nineteenth century religious sects sprang up all over the country. One of these was the Millerite sect, or the Ascensionists. They stood momentarily ready for the day of doom to arrive. Preachers of the chief Protestant denominations condemned and ridiculed their beliefs, and waggish individuals played practical jokes on them. According to C. A. P. the smart boys of Louisville helped the faithful followers of Millerism at Jeffersonville, Indiana, to bring about a partial ascension.

### A MILLERITE MIRACLE

In a little village in the state of Hoosierana in the year 1844 there was all sorts of excitement concerning the doctrines and prophecies of that arch deceiver Miller. For months the Midnight Cry, followed by the Morning Howl, and the Noonday Yell, had circulated through the village and surrounding counties, to an extent not even equaled by Dr. Duncan's celebrated Coon Speech. Men disposed of their property for little or nothing. The women were pale and ghastly from watching and praying, and in fact, the whole population, or at least those who believed in the coming ascension, looked as if they were about half over a second attack of chills and fever. There were, however, some choice spirits, (not choice in theirs, however,) who, notwithstanding the popularity of the delusion, would not enlist under the banners of the ascensionists, and among these was a wild harum-scarum blade from Down East by the name of Cabe Newham. Now Cabe was as hard a case as you would meet on a Fourth of July, in Texas, always alive with fun and sport of any and every description, and a strong disbeliever in Millerism.

The night of the third of April was the time agreed upon out west here, for the grand exhibition of ground and lofty tumbling, and about ten o'clock, of the said night, numbers of the Millerites assembled on the outskirts of the town, on a little eminence, upon which the proprietor had allowed a few trees to stand. In the crowd, and the only representative of his race present, was a free negro, by the name of Sam, about as ugly, black, woolly, and rough a descendant of Ham, as ever baked his shins over a kitchen fire.

Sam's head was small, body and arms very long, and his legs bore a remarkable resemblance to a pair of hames; in fact, put Sam on a horse, his legs clasped round its neck, his head toward the tail, and his arms clasped round the animal's hams, and at ten paces off you would swear he was an *old set of patent gearing*.

Now on the morning of the third, Cabe had, with a deal of perseverance, and more trouble, managed to throw a half inch cord over the branch of an oak, which stretched its long arms directly over the spot where the Millerites would assemble; one end he had secured to the body of the tree, and the other to a stump some distance off. About ten o'clock, when the excitement was getting about "80 lbs. to the inch," Cabe, wrapped in an old sheet, walked into the crowd, and proceeded to fasten in as secure a manner as possible, the end of the rope to the back of the belt which confined Sam's "robe"—succeeded, and "sloped," to join some of his companions who had the other end. The few stars in the sky threw a dim light over the scene, and in a few moments the voice of Sam was heard, exclaiming, "Gor Alimighty! I'se a goin' up! Whoo-o-op!" and sure enough, Sam was seen mounting into the "etheral blue"; his ascent was, however, checked when he had cleared terra firma a few feet. "Glory!" cried one, "Hallelujah!" another, and shrieks and yells, made hideous; some fainted, others prayed, and not a few dropped their robes and "slid." Now whether it was owing to the lightness of his head, or the length and weight of his heels, or both, Sam's position was not a pleasant one; the belt to which Cabe's cord was attached, was bound exactly round his center of gravity, and Sam swung like a pair of scales, head up and heels down, at the same time sweeping over the crowd like a pendulum, which motion was accelerated by his strenuous clapping of hands, and vigorous kicking. At length he became alarmed, he *wouldn't* go up, and couldn't come down! "Lor a Massy," cried he, "jist take um poor nigger to um bosom, or lef him down again, *easy, easy,* Gor Almighty! Lef him down again, please um Lord, and dis nigger will go straight to um bed. Ugh-h-h." And Sam's teeth chattered with affright, and he kicked again more vigorously than before, bringing his head directly downward and his heels up, when a woman shrieking, "Oh! Brother Sam, take me with you," sprung at his head as he swept by her, and caught him by the wool, bringing him up "all standing." "Gosh! Sister," cried Sam, "lef go um poor nigger's har." Cabe gave another pull at the rope, but the additional weight was too much, the belt gave way, and down came Sam, his bullet head taking the leader of the saints a "feeler" just between the eyes. "Gosh! is I down agin?" cried the bewildered Sam, gathering himself up. "I is, bress de Lord! but I was nearly dar, I seed de gates!" The leader wiped his overflowing proboscis, took Sam by the nap of the neck, led him to the edge of the crowd, and giving him a kick "a la posteriore," said, *"Leave! you cussed baboon, you are so damned ugly I knowed they wouldn't let you in!"*[34]

## CHAPTER VIII

## BENCH, BAR AND JURY

A MALARIA-RIDDEN native of Arkansas inquired of a traveler:
"Ar' you a lawyer?" "No I am a poor businessman," responded the stranger. "Well then I swar that's jist what I am, and I'm glad you are not a lawyer, for the lawyer is the cursedest varmint, I recon, that's about." "Where have you met with any lawyers? There are none in this part of the country." "Stranger I once lived adjyning Gasconade what runs into the Missouri and so they set off Franklin Caywnty adjyning it; and wherever they set up a cawnty you see, there the lawyers is sure to come. And so a farmer what I owed fourteen deerskins to sent a constable and tuk me and wanted me to go, and the more he wanted me to go, the more I wouldn't go, and I gave him an almighty whipping. Soon arter three fellows comed from Franklin and tuk me and hauled me to what they called the courthouse where there was a lawyer they called Judge Monson, and he fined me ten gallons (of b'ars oil) for whipping the constable. Why said I you don't mean to say you will make me pay ten gallons for whipping that ar' fellow?" "Yes I do," says he, "and that you shall see." "Then says I, I calculate I will whip you like the devil the first time I catch you in the woods. If I have to pull all the trees and b'ars in Missouri from their holes; and so the critur had me locked until one of the settlers that wanted me to do a job for him said he would pay the ten gallons; but I didn't like them practyces; I seed the country warn't agoing to be worth living in, and so I left Gasconade County and comed here, for you'll mind that wherever the lawyers and courthouses come, the other varmints, b'ars and sich, are sure to quit."[1]

The varmints and "sich" had to be on a steady move westward because no institution on the frontier became more common, or more representative of the western country than the courts. Around the courthouses, or temporary places of meeting, most of the early western society revolved. County and circuit court days were gala affairs in the community. Early in the history of the West, lawyers who were pinching pennies along the seaboard to make ends meet received word that in the new country litigation was plentiful and that lawyers were scarce. No less persons than Henry Clay and John Breckinridge of Kentucky crossed the mountains in answer to such invitations.[2] Immigrants had to run off from the eastern states and left behind them unpaid debts and their debtors were on their heels with lawyers. Land laws in the West were in a continuous muddle, and killings and lawsuits were as common as buckeyes in the fall. Land suits alone yielded sufficient revenue to support an army of gaunt Virginia barristers.[3]

The county-court system which had prevailed in the colonial states was transferred bodily to most of the western states, and this institution was involved continuously in straightening out legal entanglements which arose over every conceivable question from fornication to miry roads. When not in session as a body this court was split into four or five parts and sat as magistrate's courts. The magistrates were members of the county courts, and some of them were rare specimens who possessed a strange brand of legal knowledge. An interesting sample was one William F. Foster, who early held a judgeship in Illinois. A contemporary said that "he was a great rascal, but no one knew it then, he having been a citizen of the state only for about three weeks before he was elected. He was no lawyer, never having studied or practiced law; but he was a man of winning, polished manners and was withal a very gentlemanly swindler from some part of Virginia. It might be said of him, as it was of Sombro, 'he was the mildest mannered man that ever scuttled a ship or cut a throat, with such true breeding of a gentleman, that you never could divine his real thought.' He was believed to be a clever fellow in the American sense of the phrase, and a good-hearted soul. He was assigned to hold court on the Wabash; but being afraid of exposing his utter incompetency he never went to any of them."[4]

Court day brought the people together as no other occasion could, except a political barbecue, or a "delayed funeral." This was not because the visitors were interested in the course of justice, because most of them never went into the courtroom, nor did they know what the court had on its docket. On the court grounds they visited with their neighbors, traded horses, shot craps, drank liquor, flirted with the gals, ran horse races, listened to fiddlers, sold cattle and were beguiled by slick-tongued Yankee and Jewish peddlers into buying notions which ranged from bustles to bed cords. There were quacking hawkers who sold on a corner of the public square healing medicines which would relieve suffering humanity of all the ills in a medical dictionary, and which had been no nearer an apothecary shop than a hollow beech stump in the middle of a clearing.

Horse-trading on court day in the West constitutes a romantic chapter in American social history. Hours before sunup on court day a parade of spavined nags and drunken jockeys was on its way to the spot near the courthouse designated as "jockey-row." "Plugs," whose shoulders were shrunken from long abuse at work, were pumped up here and there with air to give them a sleek appearance. Manes, tails and fetlocks were trimmed and straightened. It was said that gunpowder and liquor would enliven the drowsiest of plugs. A pod of red pepper turned wrong-side outward over an index finger and applied generously to a nag's rectum was sufficient stimulant, at times, to make a half-drunken "sucker" trade back for a horse at sundown which he had dragged into town at sunup. Traders quibbled by the hour over boot between two horses which had less actual value than a good skinning knife. Often trades were made between persons, one of whom had scruples against exchanges which did not involve the passage of "boot," by one giving the other a swig of bad liquor.[5]

While jockeys tore up and down court grounds pacing bony chattels, and loud-mouthed patent-medicine hawkers gathered around them the lame, the halt and the blind, other visitors were busily engaged in rampant political or religious discussions, dogfights, gander pullings, and militia musters. Enough knockdown and drag-out fights occurred on court days to bloody the noses and black the eyes of one end of the county.[6]

The judges themselves were interesting specimens. A traveler in the West saw a judge riding the circuit who carried a pair of pistols across a silver trimmed saddle bow, and gave the appearance of being a dragoon officer instead of a solemn justice of the court of quarter sessions.[7] This particular gentleman of the bench was likewise a merchant and storekeeper. Western judges at times were wild boys measured by the dignified standards of English or eastern justices. A distinguished jurist of the pure frontier type was faced with a stubborn liquor question. Distillers from "down the country" had not carried quite squarely with their customers in his district and they were hauled into court on a charge of selling bad liquor. Doubtless no more pointed charge was ever read to a jury in the western country than the one this squire read to an already prejudiced panel. "Gentlemen of the jury," said the court, "pure, unadulterated liquor is a wholesome and pleasant beverage, and as far as experience of the court extends, conduces to health and longevity; but a bad article of liquor, gentlemen, or, what is worse, a drugged article, cannot be tolerated; and if dealers from below will send into this beautiful country, so blessed with smiles of a benignant Creator, such miserable quality of liquors, as the proof shows this to be, in this court, gentlemen of the jury they cannot recover."[8]

Judges, especially justices of the peace, became pompous once the mantle of office fell about their shoulders. Amid this pomposity a dull cloud of ignorance nearly always showed through. Justices never extended themselves more than when they were issuing warrants to have culprits brought in to be tried by law as they understood it. Perhaps the warrant issued by the "Honorable Court" of Jett's Creek, Breathitt County, State of Kentucky, in 1838, is the rankest of all western court commands.

The judge informed the constable that the "State of Jett's Creek, Breathitt Hi Official Magistrate Squire and Justice of the Peace, do hereby issue the following rit against Henderson Harris chargin' him with assault and battery and breach of the peace on his brutherin-law Tom Fox by name, this warrnt cuses him of kickin', bitin', and scratchin' and throwin' rocks an' doing everything that was mean and contrary to the law of Jett's Creek and aforesaid. This warrnt otherises the hi constable Mils Terry by name to go forth comin' and 'rest sed Henderson Harris and bring him to be delt with accordin' to the law of Jett's Creek aforesaid. T"is warrnt otherises the hi constable to tak him whar he ain't as wel as wher he is and bring him to be delt with accordin' to the laws of Jett's Creek and aforesaid. January 2, 1838, Jackson Terry hi constable, Magistrade and Squire and Justice of the Peace of Jett's Creek aforesaid."[9]

Such warrants did not fail to fetch prisoners to western bars, and often the hearing of their cases was based upon just about as much knowledge of the law as was exemplified in the above warrant issued by the Honorable Jackson Terry, Magistrate, Squire and Justice of the Peace. Many of the crimes, however, were of such a nature that they deserved no better treatment.

"Justice" sat in most of the western states with a "main" judge crowded in between two grinning minions who called themselves "side" judges.[10] These bowers of judgment occasionally took judicial powers in their hands and annulled the decision of the "middle" dignitary. When the court was firmly seated, leather-lunged "Dogberries" were sent outside to inform the people that it was "a-settin," or "boys, come in, our John is a-settin."[11] Sheriffs and constables seemed to have been selected because of their ability to shout halfway across the county, and to run jurors down and drag them into court. In Indiana one conscientious and efficient sheriff reported to the court that he had run down about half enough people to serve on the jury and had them tied to a tree just outside the courthouse, and that he was in pursuit of others. Once these juries were brought together, the grand jury met in one end of the courthouse, or sometimes outdoors, while the petit jury occupied the other end of the courtroom or another spot outdoors. Cases were brought before these tobacco-chewing "peers," while raucous-voiced frontier lawyers poured forth wave upon wave of oratory. Lawyers used all sorts of tricks to impress their hearers.[12]

It was said that Kentuckians were poor counselors in Indiana because they did not use the proper tactics at the psychological moments. Kentucky lawyers banked on the persuasiveness of their oratory to win cases, and waited until all the facts were in before they opened fire, while Indiana barristers opened fire the moment the first bit of evidence was offered and continued peppering witnesses and opposition council with questions. Hoosier judges were led to believe that the reason Kentucky lawyers did not make attacks as the examination of witnesses and principals in the suit progressed was that they were ignorant of the law.[13] One such case occurred in the Hoosier State in which a distinguished congressman came to grips with one of the local pettifoggers. Throughout his argument the congressman referred frequently to the "great English common law." His native opponent saw in these references the opening which he desired, and he opened his withering argument with "Gentlemen of the jury what have you to do with the common law of England? What have you to do with English law? If we are to be guided by English law at all, we want their best law, not their common law. We want as good law as Queen Victoria herself makes use of; for, gentlemen, we are sovereigns here. But we don't want no English law. United State's law is good enough for us; yes Indi-a-na law is good enough for an Indiana jury; and so I know you will convince the worthy gentleman who has come here to insult your patriotism and good sense, by attempting to influence your decision through the common law of England."[14] Not only could the bellowing pettifoggers confuse juries, but likewise judges. The judges knew so little law that often they refused to instruct juries before lawyers for fear they would give themselves away.

Sometimes the judges confused the juries, as in the case of a

Sucker jury foreman who returned to the courtroom to say, "Why, Judge, this 'ere is the difficulty. The jury wants to know whether that ar' what you told us, when we first went out, was raly the law, or whether it was only jist your notion."[15] Judges avoided instructing juries when they could. They usually delivered hypothetical charges such as, "If the jury believe from evidence that such a matter is proved, then the law is so and so." Some of these western jurists grew restless, rubbed their faces and squirmed in their seats, saying to lawyers concerned, "Why, gentlemen, the jury understands the case; they need no instructions; no doubt they will do justice between the parties." Judges wished, in many cases, to remain in good standing with their constituents which made it difficult at times to render decisions without making a large number of people mad. A fearful and anxious justice called a prisoner who had been found guilty of murder before the bar and said: "Mr. Green, the jury in their verdict say you are to be hung. Now I want you and all your friends down on Indian Creek to know that it is not I who condemns you, but it is the jury and the law. Mr. Green, the law allows you time for preparation, and so the court wants to know what time you would like to be hung." To this the prisoner replied, "May it please the court, I am ready to suffer at any time; those who kill the body have not the power to kill the soul; my preparation is made, and I am ready to suffer at any time the court may appoint." The judge then said, "Mr. Green, you must know that it is a very serious matter to be hung; it can't happen to a man more than once in his life, and you had better take all the time you can get; the court will give you until this day four weeks. Mr. Clerk, look at the almanac, and see whether this day four weeks comes on Sunday." The clerk looked at the almanac, as directed, and reported that "that day came on Thursday." The judge then said, "Mr. Green, the court gives you until this day four weeks, at which time you are to be hung." The Attorney General of Illinois had prosecuted the case, and he said, "May it please the court, on solemn occasions like the present, when the life of a human being is to be sentenced away for a crime, by an earthly tribunal, it is usual and proper for the court to pronounce a formal sentence, in which the leading features of the crime shall be brought to the recollections of the prisoner, a sense of his guilt impressed upon his conscience, and warned against the judgment of the world to come." To this the judge replied: "Oh! Mr. Turney, Mr. Green understands the whole matter as well as if I had preached to him a month. He knows he has got to be hung this day four weeks. You understand it in that way Mr. Green, don't you?" "Yes," said Mr. Green.[16]

In Kentucky an old charge read to a jury in the eastern part of the state has bobbed up frequently to embarrass judges on the benches of that region. Sometimes opposing candidates have made capital use of this charge against incumbent jurists. For informality and the conveyance of the court's actual feelings in the matter few charges can surpass this one. In this case the court understood the defendants, and he had already made up his mind before he had heard the testimony.

Wild mountaineers were in the habit of riding their mules up to church doors and hitching them to anything strong enough to prevent their breaking away and running off home. In this particular incident, however, the boys used bad judgment in the trees which they selected. "Gentlemen of the grand jury," said the impatient judge, "I have heretofore instructed you concerning the totin' of pistols, the sellin' of liquor, disturbin' religious worship and all the other crimes that infest this neighborhood, but now, gentlemen, I want to call your attention specifically to the most heinous offense that has been committed within the knowledge of this court.

"Gentlemen: The good deacons of the Piney Grove meetin' house, in the righteousness of their hearts, went down the banks of the Cumberland River and thar, with great care, selected two of the most promisin' saplin's growin' thereon and brung them back and planted them in the yard of the meetin' house, expectin' them to grow and flourish and spread grateful shade, and, gentlemen, them trees was a growin' fine to behold; and,

gentlemen, witness the pervarsity of mankind; 'long comes two
or three of them Buck boys with their hats set back on thar
heads, with red bandana handkerchiefs round their throats, and
cartridge belts around thar middles. They rode into the meetin'-
house yard and hitched their nags to them aforesaid saplin's,
and while the congregation war interested at thar worship them
nags chawed all the bark offen' them saplin's and totally destroyed 'em.

"I say to you, gentlemen of the jury, that a man that would do
the like of that, would ride a jackass into the Garden of Eden
and hitch him to the Tree of Life; indict them, gentlemen, indict them."[17]

Judges were hard-boiled when they dealt with those accomplished banditti who floated through the western country for
the purpose of leading off all stray horses. In Indiana, a judge
who had before him three horse thieves, and who had opened
the case of the first one, became doubtful of the outcome so he
ordered the court adjourned until the next day. When the
courtroom was cleared of prisoners, lawyers and visitors, the
judge instructed the sheriff to take the prisoner on trial into the
woods at midnight and administer the customary sentence of
thirty-nine well-laid lashes meted out to horse thieves. When
the case was opened the next day, and the defense counsel requested a new trial, the prisoner, understanding the possibility
of getting a double dose of the lash, jumped up and dismissed
his lawyer, and begged the court not to whip him again.[18]

In many instances when horse thieves were sentenced, the
court and spectators marched out of the courthouse to the nearest
tree to watch the ends of justice served with the cowhide. Thieves
were whipped and branded in palms and turned loose with advice to leave the country. It made no difference where these victims of justice wandered, their backs and palms always bore
testimony to their iniquitous past.[19] Occasionally judges didn't
wait to apply the slicing lash, but administered justice of a sort
on the spot, as was the case of a western judge who laid hands
on a "horseman" at the bar: "Hold up your head, you damned

'ornary pup! Look the court in the eye!" Whereupon the honorable court planted a horny judicial fist between the "'ornary pup's" eyes.[20]

Not all of the law of the land was found between the covers of lawbooks. In Versailles, Indiana, Judge John Lindsay became offended at Jim Boice, because Jim insisted on creating a disturbance in the court. Finally the fractious Judge could stand the disturbance no longer and he said, "Jim I know little about the power the law gives me to keep order in the court, but I know very well the power the Almighty has given me, and so shall you." At that moment he knocked him down and kicked him out of the door. Suspicious-looking gentlemen traveling through the country always excited the natives. If they were not careful they were likely to meet the fate of the good-looking stranger who fell into the hands of an officious Dogberry at Washington, Kentucky. He was charged with horse-stealing, and generally corrupting the morals of the young men. An unfeeling court sentenced him to a long period of hard manual labor, and he was turned over to a blacksmith to serve out his sentence. During the daytime the prisoner was locked to the anvil, and at night he was locked in jail.[21]

Unusual sentences were passed out to culprits who were dragged in by the scruff of their necks to receive sentence at the hands of roving judges. In Kentucky a murderer reasonably expected to hang if he were convicted, but farther west he hoped to escape at least with his life; however, his back would always present a corduroy effect. In the Arkansas bottoms, a traveler saw a prisoner receive twenty well-placed lashes that ruffled his bare back considerably.[22] A thief who had made away with some intimate garments belonging to a Buckeye neighbor was hauled into court, convicted and given the choice of ten lashes, or of riding in a packsaddle on his pony, while his wife, a *particeps criminis,* took the halter and led it to every door and called the occupants of the house out and cried, "This is Brannon who stole the big coat, handkerchief, and shirt."[23] Thieves along the frontier were sometimes given exceedingly entertaining applications of the United States flag, which was a lash for every stripe, and sometimes the stars were not neglected. Administrators of the ends of justice in more heinous cases appealed to the scriptures, and found the Law of Moses sufficient, which means twenty lashes on the lowers (hips) and twenty on the uppers (shoulders) administered simultaneously so the poor wretch would feel only twenty blows.[24]

Frontier justices were faced with baffling questions, which at times would have made Solomon invent a better method of settling a dispute than simply cutting a child in two. A Sucker justice was faced with the problem of answering the important question of whether a white woman could marry a negro, and he finally decided that she had "to have negro blood in her" before he could perform the ceremony. The negro's arm was slit and his lady love drank the blood, the marriage was performed and the judge "fee'd." When cases arose which could not be settled according to the laws of the states, the judges pushed the spectators into a circle and turned the plaintiff and defendant "to it" fist and skull to see which side should receive justice.[25]

Judges, lawyers, sheriffs, constables and juries were leading institutions on the frontier. They sometimes paid true homage to justice, but more often they prostituted the shy lady. A straight line between two points was not always the nearest judicial distance, because scheming pettifoggers were actively engaged in finding loopholes, and then only the Lord could turn a jury back onto the path of justice. Bellowing lawyers attracted audiences from miles around. If the court session got off to a poor start and the judge became worried over the impression it was making on his constituents, he would privately instruct the lawyers to go it full tilt in order to keep the audience in a happy frame of mind.[26] However, there were many western lawyers who did not need this prodding to enliven the proceedings of the day.

There was nothing more thrilling in the western country than a red-hot argument between two good lawyers. In 1810

James Hall was a spectator in a courtroom in the region south of the Green River in Kentucky. Hall sensed that something extraordinary was about to happen. The streets of the county town were crowded, groups of marksmen were "cutting the center for half pints; while others, who had 'the best quarter nags in all Kentucky,' were prancing them up and down the streets." Court was being held in a log schoolhouse, and when the sheriff bellowed out his summons of "Oh yes! Oh yes! Oh yes!" there was a general rush for the building. The lawyers were in hunting shirts and the jury was composed of rugged individuals who had sauntered in from the neighboring bottoms and hills. Hall said the audience which was composed of men, "some sober, some half sober, and some not sober at all— was at once awed into silence." The chief lawyer was a homely man dressed in a hunting shirt, who had no distinguishing characteristics other than bright eyes and a seeming indifference to what was going on around him. He warmed up to his subject rapidly. He spoke in short colloquial phrases at first but later burst into an eloquent argument couched in well-rounded sentences arranged in logical sequence. He bullied, pleaded, persuaded, wept before the jury beseeching justice for his client. This lawyer defended a beautiful young girl who had been wronged by a bully, the prisoner at the bar, and he made the best of his advantage in this case. Before he finished he had proclaimed his client as pure as the driven snow, a helpless woman who had been traduced, a sacred female character. The defendant was a bully, a rapist, a traducer, a menace to all sacred womanhood in the West. When the buckskin barrister had finished his eloquent tirade against the despoiler of fair frontier womanhood he rested his case, and almost without leaving their seats the jurymen voted by acclamation to convict.

Never had the people in the region south of the Green River heard such all-powering oratory. The crowd rushed from the schoolhouse stunned. Hall reported bits of the conversation of the chattering groups: one man asked, "Did you ever hear a fellow get such a skinning?" Another allowed it was "equal to any camphire!" Hall did not know who the lawyer in the hunting shirt was and inquired of a weeping backwoodsman leaning on a rifle who this orator was. Wiping the tears from his eyes the Kentuckian said it was easy to see that Hall was a stranger, "otherwise you would never have asked that question. What man in all Kentuck could ever have brung tears to my eyes by the tin full, but Joe Daviess!"[27]

Daviess was one of the keenest lawyers in the West; it was he who had brought Burr into court. He had acquitted himself nobly in this case even though all the odds, including the court itself, were against him. There were few Daviess west of the mountains however. A rampant lawyer who defended a client in a mule-stealing charge was a fine example of the other type. This raucous-voiced shyster shouted, "Gentlemen of the jury, the whole of you, there you set; you have all heard what these witnesses have said, and of course you agree with me that my client didn't steal the mule. Do you s'pose, for one second, that he would steal the mule; a low-lived mule! Damned clear of it. What does he want of a mule when he has got a bang-up pony like that tied to yon tree, what, I say in the name of General Jackson, does he want of a mule? Nothing—exactly nothing. No, gentlemen of the jury, he didn't steal the mule, he wouldn't be caught stealing one. He never wanted a mule, he never had a mule, he never would have a mule about him. He has his antipathies as well as anybody, and you couldn't hire him to take a mule.

"Jurymen, that lawyer on the other side has been trying to spread the wool over your eyes, and stuff you with the notion that my client walked off with the aforesaid animal without asking leave! But you ain't such a pack as to believe him. Listen to me, if you want to hear truth and reason—and, while you are about it, wake up that fellow who is asleep. I want him to hear it, too.

"That other lawyer says, too, that my client should be sent to prison, I'd like to see you send him at once, but it's getting toward dinnertime, and I want a horn bad, so I'll give you a closer and finish. Now you have no idea of sending my client to prison—I can see that fact sticking out. Suppose either of you was in his place—suppose for instance I was and you should attempt to judge me. Put me in a log jail without fire, where the wind was blowing in one side and out the other, and the only thing to brag of was the perfectly free circulation of air—do you suppose, I say, that I would go? I'd see you damned first!"[28]

Lawyers and judges were literate, and they have left hundreds of court yarns behind them. As they grew older on the western circuits many of them became reminiscent and have left behind valuable memoirs. The courts were scenes of many human happenings from the standpoints both of prisoners at the bar and members of the legal profession. At least a good sugar-barrel full of yarns have poured from the frontier courtrooms, and these are of the true western flavor.

Some of the early courthouses gave the impression that they were something else. A Hoosier in search of liquid fortitude mistook the Clay County "courthouse" in Illinois for a saloon, and acted accordingly in his approach to the building. Judge Huntingdon was presiding over the court, and he was so badly disturbed that he had the loud-mouthed Hoosier brought before him.

## A WESTERN COURTROOM

While holding court at Bowling Green, in the adjoining county of Clay, some years ago, in a log cabin, the Judge, Attorney, and others in the room, were startled by a succession of sharp cracks not unlike musket shots, accompanied by unearthly shouts from stentorian lungs of "Gee—woo-a—Haw, boys!" The business of the court had to be suspended, and the Judge angrily directed the Sheriff to bring in the tumultuous ox-driver. The Sheriff soon returned with a rare specimen of the genus "Hoosier," upward of six feet high, with a foxskin cap tight on his head, and tan-colored garments hanging loosely on his person; in one hand he held the cause of the explosion, in the shape of a whip as long as a fishing pole; from under his arm protruded a half section of gingerbread. He walked coolly up to the table behind which His Honor sat as if about to ask for something to drink when the Judge, putting on his severest frown said to him, "What do you mean, Sir, by yelling through the streets and disturbing the quiet and dignity of this court?" The Hoosier stared around in utter amazement, and after a pause, shouted out, *"Court*-court did you say [giving a long whistle], —H-ll! *I thought it was a Grocery!"*

The dignity of the Judge was completely unshipped . . . court adjourned and amid roars of laughter . . . the culprit was not fined for contempt, but the Board of County Commissioners of Clay County soon afterward passed an order for the erection of a courthouse that could not be mistaken for a Grocery.[29]

It was poor business on the frontier to call a "high" magistrate a liar. Magistrates oftentimes were equipped with a pair of ready fists, and knew how to use them. Here is a brief description of a courtroom, and an unusual trial which took place in it.

## WESTERN JUSTICE

The said office was a small room about twelve by fifteen feet. Across one corner of the room was a slender pine picket fence, that separated the *dignitary* from the applicants for justice (!) and the rabble of lookers-on. At a small desk thus inclosed, sat the dispenser of the mighty law. During a trial for some trivial amount, the defendant thought he was aggrieved by some remarks of the magistrate, and plumply told his honor that he believed he *lied!* Magisterial, as well as personal dignity, was of course highly offended, and the Squire told him that he must retract. The accuser said that it was his candid opinion, and he could not and would not take it back.

Quicker than the lightning's flash, the Squire was on his feet, his brass-bowed spectacles were thrown on the little desk, and in a voice of thunder he exclaimed:

*"Gentlemen, this court is adjourned five minutes, till I whip this d——d rascal!"*

Before the words were fairly out of his mouth he had leaped the little barricade, and in much less than five minutes, he gave the offender a pair of black peepers, and started a spigot of claret, to the astonishment of all the bystanders. The magistrate walked deliberately back to his little desk, adjusted his spectacles, and coolly announced that the "court was again in session."

After hearing all the evidence in the case, and giving it a very careful judicial consideration, he gave judgment in favor of the defendant, who no doubt thought it a fair offset for his two black eyes and bloody nose.[30]

Frontier judges who were ignorant of the law were hardly in a position to solve aggravating problems. This was especially true if the case involved statutory law. At such times the "courts" turned to chance for answers.

### Wet for Defendant—Dry for Plaintiff

Possibly our sage western judges suffer unjust reproach at times from conduct of some among them but, having lived in their midst, I can bear witness to the truth of the following circumstances:

A farmer residing in this region had remarked, during the sittings of the Circuit Court, a part of his cornfield to be beaten down in a regular track of ten or twelve paces in length, as if by the ranging of some animal to and fro. Anxious to detect the cause, he ensconced himself one day among the thick leaves, and observed, about the hour of adjournment, one of the judges cautiously approaching the spot. Arrived at the path, he commenced pacing it gravely up and down, with knit brow and air of cogitation and, at length, drawing a small chip from his pocket, he spat on one side of it, balanced it an instant on his finger, flipped it up in the air, and watching its descent intently, exclaimed as it fell: *"Wet* for defendant—*dry* for plaintiff." Then stooping down: "Plaintiff has it." The farmer avoided all litigation from that moment![31]

Kentuckians seldom had the disgusting experience of having to adjourn court for lack of cases. When such a thing did happen all the parties concerned were disgusted.

## A Godless Court

From a reliable source we learn that Judge Evans of the Laurel Circuit Court once held court there in years past in which there was only one case on the civil and criminal docket each. There were fifteen or twenty lawyers present with faces as long as the moral law. The case of the criminal docket was for adultery and the accused pleaded guilty, and the one on the civil docket was a plain-note case for sixty-five dollars for which no defense was offered. Court adjourned in about an hour after it had convened. The Judge was a man who swore not only off the bench, but at interesting periods on the bench. The jury had departed, but still the lawyers lingered around with black faces. "Boys this is a damned hard time," said the Judge. "Yes," replied one of the lawyers, "the whole of us have not enough money to pay our bills and leave this Godforsaken town, and we now call upon you for aid and help."

"Gentlemen," said the Judge, "the devil has got hold of this community and of course the devil is to pay. I advise you all to quit drinking, join the church, and pray to the Lord for better times, and when you next attend this court perhaps you will reap a better harvest than a moneyless adultery man, and an uncontested suit on a plain note." "So mote it be," echoed the lawyers. Each knight of the sorrowful figure then mounted his steed and shook the dust of the town off his garments and betook himself back to his own dwelling.[32]

Western courts often were clumsy affairs. In many cases there were no courthouses, and the juries had to take to the woods to sit. Especially was this true of the grand juries. The twelve "good men tried and true" who were sent out to a ravine to bring into the court indictments against the wrongdoers of a western community usually had to establish a guard to make sure that no one "snaked" up to the assembly to hear what was being said.

### "Snaking" a Jury

The Judge said that one day after having charged the grand jury, and dismissed them to their quarters in the large hollow, a tall, rawboned, live Yankee-looking man, with hat in hand, addressed him as follows:

"May it please your honor, I wish to speak to you."

"Order, Sir; what is it?"

"Judge," continued he, with the utmost gravity, "is it right for fellows to snake it in the grass?"

"How? What is that, Sir?"

"Why, you see," said the Yankee, "there's some fellows who's tarnal 'fraid the grand jury will find something agin' 'em, which they desarve, and they are snaking up to the grand jury on their bellies, in the grass, kind o' tryin' to hear what the jury are talkin' about."

"No," responded the Judge, with as much gravity as he could command, "I do not allow 'snaking.' Here, Mr. Sheriff, go station a guard around each jury's hollow, and if a man is found 'snaking,' have him brought before me, and I will cause him to be punished. Indeed, if this 'snaking' is persisted in, I shall recommend a special act to be passed making it a misdemeanor."

The fact was, the Judge said, there were at the present time, some barefooted vagrant rascals who were probably justly suspected of horse-stealing, and had "snaked it" on the grand jury, in order to find out whether the jury intended to present them; and if so to gain time by this clandestine warning, and flee the jurisdiction of the court by escaping into Missouri.[33]

Many times western judges were embarrassed by wild associates and friends who took advantage of them in the courtrooms. Occasionally the judges, however, took care of themselves by direct, if undignified, methods.

### CONTEMPT OF COURT, MINUS $4.50

A very tall and very solemn individual, further solemnized by a very broad-brimmed beaver, entered the courtroom, walked forward toward the railing and without removing his hat, sat down opposite the surprised and offended legal dignitary.

"Mr. Sheriff," said the Judge, in a severe tone, "tell that man to take off his hat."

The Sheriff walked over to the transgressor, and, remarking that the rules of the court must be observed, gently removed the broad brim from the head and deposited it in the lap of the owner.

"Why, Judge," cried the latter, in a shrill squeak of surprise, "I'm bald!" immediately replacing his covering.

The Judge had not perceived his second contempt, at the moment, having been engaged in supplying his jaw with a fresh "chew" in order to aid his ruminations, but again looking forward, the hat once more loomed upon him.

"Mr. Sheriff!" said he, with even more severity, "tell that man to take his hat off!"

The officer again waited upon the offender, and removed his beaver.

"But, Judge, I told you I was bald!" cried the man, in a tone of increased surprise at the same time, once more, with great determination, thatching himself.

The Judge was a picture to look at! "Mr. Clerk," said he, in a voice whose solemn calm was calculated, whether it did not search the soul, "enter up a fine of five dollars against Mr. C—, for refusing to take his hat off when ordered by the court!"

Mr. C— immediately "straightened himself," walked his six

feet six, surmounted by his cloud of beaver, right up to the bar, pulled from his pocket fifty cents, and squirting through his teeth a jet of tobacco juice, he spake!

"Well, Judge, here's fifty cents, which, with four dollars and a half you owed me when we quit poker last night, makes us even, I reckon!"

"Sh-a-um-a-wah-boo—oh, Mr. Sheriff, you will not suffer the court to be interrupted!" cried the Judge. Before the court had recovered its articulation, however, the "interruption" had walked out as solemnly as he had entered.[34]

## CHAPTER IX

## GENTLEMEN OF RANK

A TRAVELER making his way through any part of the West met with much the same experience of N. Parker Willis, who said that "You seldom drive up to one [a tavern] without alighting amid a group—oftener a crowd—and the titles flying from mouth to mouth soon inform you that all the judges, generals and colonels possible to the size of the population are among the company."[1]

The western country was the great spawning ground for gentlemen who desired distinguished ranks. It was a place where a man with even a limited amount of ingenuity could create his own high rank. Continuous attacks by savage Indians and obstreperous British troopers threatened frontier safety. Trans-Appalachian citizens stood in momentary readiness to fight for their protection. Every community had its militia company which drilled with regularity in the neighboring cornfields or down community roads or village streets. At the head of each of these companies marched at least three titled dignitaries who were resplendent in their brightly colored sashes and gaily plumed hats.

Local militia companies were organized without any thought of uniformity. Clothing ranged from that of the old Continental Line to the ragged, dirty and ill-fitting linsey-woolsey of the byways. Weapons were equally as diverse; one man might come armed with a flintlock, another with a modified "cap-and-ball," while others shouldered sticks instead of guns. Drills were seldom if ever conducted by a uniform manual. The commanding officers perhaps were in a quandary at times as to the whereabouts of their right and left hands. No one was so silly as to believe that drills should be conducted according to form. Independent militiamen did not always obey commands but followed the general direction of the line of march.[2]

As long as there were Indians or British in the Northwest there was a valid excuse for the arduous weekly drills of militia companies, or the militant readiness with which men of the western country held themselves. But once the slaughter at the Thames and at New Orleans was over, there remained no good reason for the maintenance of these citizen organizations. The lack of an excuse, however, was insufficient reason for disbanding militia companies. They now were social organizations to which young blades belonged principally for the purpose of marching pompously before wide-eyed feminine admirers. It was a sorry town indeed that couldn't raise a muster, and most of them boasted two companies. There were the Blues, the Grays, the Fencibles, the Old Infantry, and the Light Infantry.[3] There were enough feathered generals, bellowing majors, pompous colonels and swaggering captains to fill the woods. There must have been some privates in the ranks, but they have marched unsung out of the pages of history, leaving a hazy but persistent notion that they did exist.[4]

Militia drills were tremendously exciting affairs. A really good muster brought out more people than a court day or a log rolling, and it involved far less manual labor than the latter. Participants and spectators gathered from miles around. Candidates seeking office were on the grounds to press their causes, preachers came to exhort the assembly to "turn aside," quacks peddled their putrid remedies, gamblers entertained and fleeced the sportive, peddlers of every kind of commodity known to the West were on hand, ladies, both sullied and unsullied, came to witness the gallantries of the day. Trading, gambling, fighting and courting were as much a part of the activities of the day as standing at attention, presenting arms, and breaking ranks.[5] The frontier militia field was likewise a sporting field. Shooting at diamond-shaped targets was as a matter of course a part of the military procedure, but throwing the rail, long bullets, kicking the hat, quarter races and gander pullings were added attractions. Sometimes fatalities brought festivities to doleful endings. Such a melancholy case was that which occurred in Lexington, Kentucky, in 1813. While the Kentucky militia was in the midst of feverish preparation for its march into the Great Lakes country militia drills were held daily. The *Kentucky Gazette,* March 16, 1813, announced that "Joshua Pilcher was unfortunately shot through the head in the market house. A volunteer was discharging his rifle. It is common practice for members of the company to fire off their guns after a parade." Poor Joshua fell a victim to a curious type of accident. As a part of the drill the militiamen were supposed to ram home imaginary wads with their ramrods, and Joshua's drill mate overlooked the exceedingly important matter of removing his rod before he fired off his rifle in celebration of the end of drill.

None of the militia officers of the West were members of the Regular Army staff. They were prominent citizens who remained at home in time of peace and engaged in businesses which ranged from being tavern-keepers to judges of the local courts. They looked upon the regular army as beneath their dignity, and they believed steadfastly that that organization was composed of drunkards. They knew the story that one of St. Clair's lieutenants had a habit of marking off missing officers and soldiers as having died from drink.[6] Local militiamen were not tools to be used in foreign aggression, but they commanded their own community companies which in a sense belonged to them.[7] Often strangers thought it ludicrous to find a dignified colonel, engaged in some extremely mundane activity. It was shocking even to the yankee traveler, Charles Fenno Hoffman, to see an Illinois colonel "dressed in leather shirt and drawers driving his ox team to Galena."[8]

Wherever the Virginian influence was a factor on the frontier, there were titles compounded. At some time in its history there grew up in Virginia and the rest of the South a tradition that at least one member of each family should bring honor and dignity upon it by possessing a title.[9] Benjamin H. Latrobe observed that everybody he met was either a "captain," a "colonel," or a "general." Every house apparently was presided over by an officered head of high rank.[10] Backwoods taverns had titled Bonifaces of majority status. If a public carriage turned over with five males aboard at least four colonels and generals were injured.[11] If a steamboat sprang a leak a mob of titled passengers was threatened with extinction.

When Mrs. Trollope made her memorable voyage up from New Orleans to Cincinnati she was conscious of the dignity which surrounded her. She, however, made some rather disparaging observations of her distinguished companions. She said of her fellow passengers that "all are addressed by titles of general, colonel and major. The captains were all on deck."[12] This snobbish English visitor lamented that there was a "total want of all the usual courtesies of the table, the voracious rapidity with which the viands were seized and devoured; the strange uncouth phrases and pronunciations; the loathesome spitting, from the contamination of which it was absolutely impossible to protect our dresses; the frightful manner of feeding with their knives, till the whole enter into the mouth; and the still more frightful manner of cleaning the teeth afterward with a pocket-knife, soon forced us to feel that we were not surrounded by the generals, colonels and majors of the old world."[13] At least Mrs. Trollope was spared the rather disconcerting ordeal among her titled companions of seeing one of them deliberately lick his knife clean to discover what name plate it bore. Such action she might have seen in the lower ranks of passengers.

When the western wars were over, and the musters were held for social and political purposes only, the plumed and sword-rattling generals, the majors and the colonels somehow or other got separated from their commands. Many of them went into fields of honest endeavor such as Major Hooker of Illinois who engaged in hunting for a living. Colonel Daniel Boone saw the wars through to successful conclusions and returned to the woods for amusement and livelihood. Numerous other titled gentlemen, engaged in various and sundry activities, were to be found around every bend of the western roads. The traveler

Faux heard of a general who actually killed his own hogs and cured the meat, and of a judge who did such a worldly thing as drive his own ox team.[14]

These were not gentlemen, however, who became famous as a collective group because of an eccentric taste in clothes, and an insatiate desire for liquor. These were not gentlemen, who like that famous Kentucky general, upon wearing his dress uniform home disturbed the peaceful course of events in his house when his young son rushed in shouting, "Mama, come quick; here's a man that talks like Papa and looks like God!" The gentlemen of title were those who were out to conquer the Indian, the forest and the streams with militia companies, axes and flatboats.

Many gentlemen bearing high military titles, having little else to do, showed a marked fondness for spirituous liquors. Doubtless many of them were raised to high rank for no other reason than that they had proved themselves precocious in this instance. A traveler in crossing over the line from eastern Kentucky into Virginia was met at the door of the inn with a mint julep—or "stirrup cup" as it was called by the colonel who conducted the inn. "You look faintish, Sir," said the convivial host, "a julep, Sir, by all means; let me recommend a julep. The table will not be spread for some time yet, and we Virginians think there is nothing between a long ride and a late breakfast like a julep."[15] It must have been a colonel with a like temperament who originated the famous Kentucky breakfast which consisted of a quart of liquor, a beefsteak and a bulldog. The beefsteak lent respectability to the repast, while the faithful dog relieved the colonel of the embarrassing responsibility of burdening his stomach with solid food. The editor of the *Western Citizen* noted the fact that a western colonel attending a political convention in Cincinnati paid a breakfast bill at the St. Charles Hotel which consisted of six brandy cocktails, tea and toast.[16] He might have been the same Missouri gentleman of high rank who represented his state at the laying of the cornerstone in Henry Clay's monument in Lexington. In the round of getting himself located in a hotel, this gentleman had the extreme misfortune to lose his carpetbag. When it was found the ungenerous hotel officials demanded that he identify the contents. To the amazement of the obstinate hosts, they found that the bag contained "four bottles of whisky and two revolvers and one shirt and two collars." One of the colonel's waggish traveling companions remarked that "possibly the shirt and collars had been put in the bag simply to keep the bottles from breaking."[17]

An old story has persisted in Kentucky that early in the state's history several good judges of whisky had purchased a barrel of the choicest bourbon for a celebration of life in general. Within a short time, however, one of these exacting connoisseurs of the amber liquor discovered there was a bit of an "off" taste, but it was so faint that he could not identify it. Thus the whole company took a hand at tasting, but they could only declare that the liquor was "off" without any reason. Two colonels of the Bluegrass, who had exceedingly delicate tastes, were called for consultation in the case. Each dipped up a generous gourd of the "off" liquor and tasted it smackingly and carefully. Finally one declared that there was "a faint taste of iron." The other maintained astutely that he had discovered "the taste of leather." Since these experienced gentlemen were hopelessly deadlocked in their decision, the liquor was strained through a sieve of fine mesh, and when the last of the liquid had filtered through the strainer, and the barrel was turned bottom up, the source of the mystery tinkled down into the metal sieve—it was a tiny leather-headed harness nail!

Of his many virtues, a gentleman of title had first of all to possess courage. He had to stand his ground, and never to evacuate the field of action, even in the face of great damage to his person. Colonel Allen Oakley of the sparsely settled state of Arkansas found himself exceedingly discomfited by this strict code of honor. This gentleman stopped at a roadside tavern in the woods to spend the night. "The weather was warm, and Oakley, when he retired to bed, divested himself of all his clothes but his shirt. About midnight a terrible fuss was raised in the yard—a catamount had been rustled up, and the dogs were fighting it. After having it 'round and 'round for some time, [the dogs and catamount] got to the door, which, flying open, in popped the catamount[.] You may guess that there was no chance to make it to the door, and the colonel sought safety by climbing up the logs to what should have been the loft; but, alas, it was deficient of everything, but the cross pole. This he straddled, with the expectation of hearing, if not witnessing, the fight going on below. But like the gallant hero at Cerro Gordo he soon had painful evidence that a man can be attacked from behind as well as before. He had waked up a wasp nest, something more than a half bushel in size, and they were putting it to him in style. One hand was necessary to hold on with and the other to slap some. To come down was to incur the danger of the mad cat's teeth, and to hold on was not a bed of roses. Yet did Oakley hold on—and so did the wasps." The colonel was courageous, but his courage made it extremely difficult to proceed by horseback on the following day.[18]

●Of one thing the colonels were jealous, and that was the dignity of their rank. If levity was to be taken with their station they permitted it to come only from one of equality. An ordinary outsider could incur enmity quickly by speaking lightly of the titled gentry. A stranger in a western settlement, who having traveled a long distance with six stagecoach passengers, four of whom were colonels, discovered a box of powder and shot, and a musket on a tavern mantel whereupon he remarked "that it was the first symptom of the existence of a private I have seen in the country." This chance observation angered some of the party, and the jest might not have passed without a challenge had it not been for the quick wit of a traveling companion who entered his observant friend's name upon the tavern register as a man of distinguished title.[19] Above all things, a titled gentleman had his honor entrusted to his care, and he had to keep it from being trampled upon even in the slightest degree. He rushed into duels that made a perfect ass of him, or he got his hide thoroughly punctured for his trouble. All of this he did for the sake of preserving unscathed that ephemeral thing called "vanity."

Of the hundreds of affairs of honor in the western country, none surpassed the dispute which arose in 1801 in Bardstown, Kentucky, between Judge John Rowan of Federal Hall and Dr. James Chambers. These gentlemen and their seconds were among the most gallant young bloods in the rapidly growing Bluegrass State. They represented the professional men of their community. Rowan was a lawyer of promise who before he died participated in some of the most important lawsuits in the state. Chambers was a surgeon of reputation and his services were very necessary to his community. The dispute which led to the fatal duel began in the upstairs room of McClean's Tavern. Judge Rowan met with two or three friends at the tavern and consumed a gallon of unusually potent beer. They then went upstairs to play whist with other friends. Shortly Dr. Chambers and John Crozier appeared on the scene, and Judge Rowan invited him, Chambers, to participate in a two-handed game of *vigutun,* or *vingt-et-un,* by the fireside. •

The party playing whist paid little attention to the *vigutun* players until they arose from their chairs and started slugging each other. The open conflict between these titled gentlemen started after Judge Rowan, considerably tipsy from drinking beer, had said several times, "Damn you, Doctor, give me a card," to which the Doctor replied, "I will Mr. Rowan, as soon as I can." This dispute led to a heated discussion as to which of the players was "master of the dead languages." Judge Rowan was emphatic in his declaration that such a lowly creature as his companion at cards was not able to dispute the subject. He cast serious reflections upon the Doctor's intellectual capacities, even in the face of the latter's positive declaration that he was "master of the dead languages" instead of Judge Rowan. The tipsy lawyer, a graduate of Doctor Priestly's Classical School, was considerably provoking in his statement of "I'll be damned if you are," and the enraged Doctor retaliated with "I'll be damned if I am not." The benighted surgeon even ventured the assertion that he was the young jurist's superior in such cultural attainments, a statement which was answered with "Doctor you are inferior to me on such subjects." Judge Rowan had now become so completely incensed over what he believed to be sacrilegious questioning of his understanding of the classics that he passed the decisive fighting words between gentlemen by announcing to his antagonist, "You are a damned liar." This brought about an open fist fight, which according to such noble authority as John Lyde Wilson's *Code of Honor,* was not an act of gentlemen.[20] Doctor Chambers sent a challenge immediately saying that if an acceptance was not forthcoming he would publish the Master of Federal Hall as a coward in every newspaper in the state.

At dawn on the morning of February 3, 1801, Doctor Chambers, Judge Rowan, Major Bullock and Judge George M. Bibb turned their horses into John Crozier's meadow. Judge Bibb represented Judge Rowan as second, while Major Bullock stood second to Doctor Chambers. The principals were dressed in small clothes of the colonial era with trousers bound at the knee, and each wore a greatcoat. They dismounted and shed their topcoats. Each contestant was handed a pistol. They were placed back to back and instructed to take five paces, which placed them ten paces apart. They had agreed to turn upon a given signal, and to take deliberate aim and fire. Judge Rowan balanced his long-barreled dueling pistol on his left hand, while Doctor Chambers rested his piece on his arm above the left elbow. Upon the first fire each inquired if the other was hurt. Rowan declared in the negative, and Chambers said, "I am sorry for it." Upon the second shot Judge Rowan's ball struck his antagonist four inches below the left arm socket. Truly a Kentucky gentleman, Judge Rowan expressed the profoundest sorrow for the "accident" and offered to send his carriage immediately to convey the mortally wounded Doctor to his house.[21] This affair attracted much attention, and newspapers carried several pages of description of the duel, and numerous affidavits by the partisans of both sides.

Political discussions throughout the West grew warm, and because of debates in state legislatures which grew embarrassingly personal at times duels were frequent. Most outstanding of these political affairs of honor was the one between the rampant Federalist Humphrey Marshall and the astute Republican Henry Clay. Marshall, in 1808, actively baited Clay and his Republican colleagues in the Kentucky legislature on the actions of Jefferson, and their attitude toward the banking question in Kentucky. His remarks became so personal and inflaming that Clay stepped down out of the Speaker's chair and took charge of the debate, the Lexington lawyer challenged Marshall, and the duel was fought on the west bank of the Ohio near the city of Evansville in Indiana. Clay, a notoriously poor shot, and Marshall a "butter-fingered" marksman, were stationed facing each other at the usual polite distance of ten paces. Two shots were made from the trembling dueling pistols, and each of these honorable gentlemen were pinked in the exchange of shots. Clay was struck in the leg, and his wound was serious enough that he was kept from an exacting law practice for several days while convalescing at the home of a friend in Louisville.[22]

Gentlemen met gentlemen throughout the West. Every large gathering was almost certain to result in a series of insults and challenges. On July 4, 1819, the Franklin County, Kentucky, militia held a grand muster on Peak's Mill Road. A large assembly of people turned out to see the local company go through its fancy maneuvers. At the head of the column was the strutting General Jacob Holman, and subordinate to him was the pompous Virginian, Colonel Francis G. Waring. Both were vain officers, and both were showing off before their admiring audience. In the midst of the business of drilling, however, the strict military decorum of the august occasion was disturbed by the appearance of Waring's pet dog which trotted on the drill field to take its place affectionately at its master's heel. General Holman became so highly incensed at this breach of parade-ground discipline that he ran the beast through with his dress sword. This letting of innocent canine blood was more than the high-strung Waring could tolerate and he engaged his superior officer in a fist fight. This affair brought the grand Independence Day review to an inglorious end. Waring had fought several duels, and on the following day he challenged the dog-murdering General Holman. At sunup on July 16, the principals and their seconds pulled their horses into the beautiful woodland on Reverend Silas M. Noel's farm to settle the matter. They had agreed upon pistols at ten paces. At the count of three each contestant was to fire. If, however, one of the duelists became overanxious and jumped the count he was to be shot down by the seconds. Waring, an experienced man in such matters, received General Holman's shot in the heart and fell to the ground immediately in the throes of death. Holman was struck in the hip and was crippled for life.[23] Surely it angered the suffering General when Niles' *Weekly Register* appeared with the irreverent announcement that "a pair of dunces agreed to shoot at each other a few days ago near Frankfort, Kentucky. One was a young Virginian, the challenger, the other a printer. The first was instantly killed on the spot, and the other badly wounded."[24]

The custom of dueling followed the frontier westward. Wherever Virginians and, later, Kentuckians appeared there were certain to be affairs of honor. One of the most outstanding of these frontier duels occurred in Arkansas in 1830 between General Henry W. Conway and Robert Crittenden, a Kentuckian. These gentlemen were candidates for Congress, and they had whipped up tremendous excitement on the stump; however, they had not met face to face in debate. Their constituents became so excited over the campaign that they insistently urged the contestants to cease their long-distance cannonading and come to grips in close quarters. A date was set, and the scene was laid in the capital city of Little Rock. On the morning of the great political jousting there appeared on the

scene thousands of hunters, squatters, herdsmen, backwoodsmen
and nondescript camp followers in general. There was great
commotion with partisans cheering for Conway and Crittenden. The stage was set under the canopy of a scrub pine grove,
and when the principals appeared on the platform they were
clearly flushed with excitement. In the round of speaking,
Crittenden warned General Conway that he hoped he would
make no statements which couldn't be defended under the code
of honor. The latter became incensed, and denounced his opponent in a torrent of bitter invective. Crittenden retorted,
"Your language, General Conway, admits of only one answer,
and that, you may be sure, I will make right speedily." Arrangements were made, and a duel with pistols at the customary distance of ten paces took place. A vast throng of friends of both
contestants assembled on the field of honor to see the affair. On
the count of three, General Conway fired, cutting a button off of
Crittenden's coat. The latter took dead aim and dropped
General Conway dead in his tracks.[25]

At Little Rock, Arkansas, in the 'thirties a blustering young
blade from a near-by plantation swaggered into a tavern and
threw his coat aside exposing to public view a bowie knife and
two pistols. He announced to his audience that "I don't know
whether you are the very beginning of men or not, but I've got
3000 acres of prime land, two sugar plantations, 150 negurs, and
I reckon I can chaw up the best man in this room!" Failing to
provoke a challenge with this crowing about his standing in the
community, this landed bully tried a new tack in which he
boasted that "I've killed eleven Indians, three white men, and
seven painters: and it's my candid opinion you are all cowards."
This final immodest denouncement brought him trouble in
shoe leather because one of the company made a beeline for
him. Soon the insult was complete and a challenge was immediately forthcoming. The challenger was a doctor, and he
instructed his seconds to agree to any proposal of arms and
conditions. The house had a darkened room, and the plantation
owner proposed two pistols and a bowie knife in this room. This

plan was agreed to, and the duelists were stripped to their waists, greased with lard and placed in the dark room to butcher each other upon a given signal from the seconds on the outside. Four shots were fired, two of which took effect in the doctor's shoulder and thigh respectively. The young blade moved on the disabled physician, and would have dispatched him to a world beyond had the latter not made a final and desperate effort by which he succeeded in driving home his bowie knife to his attacker's heart. When the seconds entered the room they found the doctor bleeding to death, but holding on to his dirk which was driven to the hilt in the dead man's body.[26]

Not all of the colonels, generals, doctors, judges and majors, however, took their honor so seriously that they went around nipping breast buttons off greatcoats with blue-steel dueling pistols. There was that waggish Kentuckian who incurred the wrath of a villainous knave in Lexington in 1819. A challenge was sent, and the challenged, appreciating his distinct advantage in being able to prescribe arms and conditions, asked for three months in which to settle his estate and to do a bit of spiritual fence mending. He chose long-barreled muskets loaded with grapeshot and two balls to be fired at five paces. The impulsive challenger, thinking his opponent either an idiot or bent on suicide, agreed to drop the quarrel and leave the country.[27] In a later year, George D. Prentice excited the colonels, majors and judges to white heat anger, and he hardly knew what it was to be free from a challenge. He devised a novel way of caring for his periodical dueling problems by selecting a pair of well-filled kegs of liquor and straws. The antagonists were to face each other with might and main until one or the other went down.[28]

Next to the gentlemen of high military title, were the distinguished occupants of the generous assortment of legal benches in the West. Inheriting the legal impedimenta of state and local governments from Virginia, the West was well supplied with judicial posts. There was a series of judgeships which ranged from the country magistrate to members of the High

Court of Appeals. To become a "judge" in the western sense
of the word an individual had only to linger upon the bench
for one trial, and the title endured for life. Once a citizen became legally ornamented with a judicial title he was looked
upon by the ordinary people as approaching omnipotence and
as one who could sit in judgment over all things—even though
he didn't know a statute book from a volume of home remedies.
Nevertheless the workaday world continued entrusting its problems to these men of "high" calling. For this reason these gentlemen were often selected to judge horse races, fair exhibits and
other community contests. On one such occasion three noble
Louisville magistrates blundered into an embarrassing situation
at a country fair in the region below that city. They were asked
to judge an exhibit of fancy teams in which an ill-tempered
exhibitor was reinsman over a spanking pair of high-stepping
grays which he proclaimed winners from the start. Unfortunately for this exhibitor, his judgment was a bit premature,
for the Jefferson County jurists dissented from his opinion in
their choice of the contest winners. This rowdy, seeing that the
day was lost, rode past the judges' stand and denounced them
as a "passle of idiots" that ought to be in an academy instead of
a judges' stand. The crowd became so incensed at this uncivil
conduct that it demanded a public apology from the crude bully.
This he finally agreed to make. The grounds were cleared, and
the judges stood in the stand to receive the apology. But when
the apologetic horseman appeared before them he stood up
and said, "Gentlemen, I am greatly mortified by what has occurred, and I cannot adequately express my regret that your
conduct was such as to compel me to employ the strong language
which I uttered."[29]

Many scores of Westerners distinguished themselves from
their more insignificant neighbors by the simple trick of tack-
ing on a title to their names. A title was the mark of a gentleman, and a large number of pioneers in crude leather shirts and
drawers dreamed of the day when they would become genteel.
Too, the very nature of the western country was conducive to

the creation of hundreds of military and legal titles. Advertisements appeared frequently in dozens of western newspapers giving notice that militia musters were to be held in various communities throughout the country. First, fear of Indians and British, and then the spirit of keeping alive a sporting tradition kept the local companies marching. Except for a few Indian skirmishes, and the rather satisfying forays against the British at the Thames and New Orleans, 1813-1815, the frontier soldiers did little damage to hated foes. These armies, however, added zest and glamour to political barbecues, Independence Day speakings and public gatherings in general. Especially was it thrilling to bright-eyed maidens who gathered from the country about to see the soldiers march, and to hear them fire their muskets as a long list of toasts were drunk. The Fourth of July always fetched out the militia companies, and famous parade grounds like that at John Maxwell's spring in Kentucky resounded with the bellowing of pot-bellied commanding officers who came decked out in sashes and feathers.[30]

As the frontier began to lose some of its rawness, gentlemen of title became more conscious of their distinction as though in an effort to hold on to a certain amount of departing glory. They imported codes of honor which they committed to memory. Cases of dueling pistols became prized possessions of many proud titled gentlemen. Even beautifully decorated silver and pearl-handled bowie knives were coveted prizes. Affairs on the field of honor marked a delicate departure from the ways of the woods for the ways of the manor halls and the parlor. Always the Westerner, coming under the influence of the forests and the great expanse of western country, believed steadfastly that his creator had marked his life in the way it should be spent, and there was little that he individually could do about it. With this same implicit confidence in an all powerful Deity, the gentleman of the Ohio Valley came to believe that he "would not fail to declare himself in favor of the innocent, and cause him to be victorious over his adversary." This method of settling disputes caused much anxiety, and western legislatures spent many weary hours devising means by which the custom of dueling might be destroyed.[31]

Frontier history would lack much color without its gentlemen of title. They had a role to play and they performed it with faithfulness and precision which cannot yet be conscientiously criticized. There were a few brave souls who dared the wrath of their betters and have left accounts in comic outline of their pompous fellow citizens. The numerous stories, which have lingered long after the frontier generals, colonels and majors shed their sashes and feathers and were gathered unto their fathers, are all amusing because the central figures were adorned with titles. A titled clown was a far more interesting actor than one with no title at all.

No colonels in the whole western country were as colorful as the Kentuckians. These gentlemen were eloquent, and many times apt in political repartee. Perhaps there was no finer political farce than two full-fledged colonels campaigning against each other.

### Colonel Bobbitt vs. Colonel Garrard

"Gentlemen: If Colonel Garrard were to live a thousand years, sit every night by his nocturnal luminary and have for his teacher the most distinguished, learned, ubiquitous and extraordinary scholars of the world, he would not at the end of that time know a thousandth part as much as I know now. Indeed, he is no more to be compared to me than the flickering, unsteady and uncertain light of a tallow candle is to be compared to the burning, blazing and devouring light of the great sun of day. He is no more to be compared to me than the smallest, most infinitesimal and disgusting, emaciated insect is to the great eagle that soars aloft and wets his pinions in the weeping clouds. He is no more to be compared to me than the most insignificant, worthless and undiscernible mote that floats in the circumambient air is to be compared to that elephantostical animal denominated the Behemoth."

At this point Colonel Garrard arose amid roars of laughter and said:

"I would like for the gentleman to explain himself—I do not understand him."

Bobbitt arose on tiptoe and replied with withering sarcasm: "My God, fellow citizens, am I to be held responsible for the gentleman's ignorance?"[32]

A western colonel got himself elected to the "Sinnit." This gentleman was remarkable for his ability to care for unusually large quids of tobacco, and at raising "pints of order." While engaged in his statesmanlike activities he took unto himself a wife, but before he had lived with his bride for any length of time there was discord between the Senator and his good wife. The colonel found that everything he said was in vain, and finally he concluded that he would divorce his shrewish rib.

### IMPUDENCY, BY THUNDER!

"Pints of order" were raised in vain; order could not be restored. Unfortunately, there were two Speakers, and the house was divided in contending for the privileges of the floor; breaches were made which could not be mended, except, as the Senator thought, by the state.

Elated with his bright idea, for which he was indebted to Mr. Marcy, no doubt, he repaired at once to a lawyer of celebrity in an adjoining county, and declared his intentions to be naturalized, or, in other words, through the medium of divorce, to be restored from his unnatural state to the natural one he enjoyed prior to his unhappy marriage.

Taking down his statutes, the counsellor proceeded to state the various cases under which divorce might be obtained.

"Divorce," said the counsellor, "may be decreed when either party shall desert the other for the term of five years."

The Senator shook his head sorrowfully in the negative, sententiously remarking, "twon't do."

"Or when either of them is sentenced to the confinement to

hard labor in prison, jail, or house of correction for the term of life, or for three years or more."

"That pint don't hit the case," replied the Senator, giving his quid a roll, and making a small duck pond of the counsellor's large wooden spittoon.

"Divorce may be decreed for extreme cruelty, or utter desertion of the parties for the term of three years."

"That hits the occasion, Squire," said the Senator, "only we ain't had three years of it yet."

"Divorce may be decreed for inconstancy."

Another shake of the head.

"For impotency."

"Impudency! that's it *impudent* as thunder."[33]

Sometimes western colonels stooped so low as to do a little feuding among themselves. One of the best of the yarns told on the titled gentry of the West is that of the difficulty which arose between Colonel Crickley and Colonel Drake. In this instance Colonel Crickley got a little the best of his boasting adversary.

### Colonel Crickley's Horse

I have never been able to ascertain the origin of the quarrel between the Crickleys and the Drakes. They had lived within a mile of each other in Illinois for five years, and from the first of their acquaintance there had been a mutual feeling of dislike between the two families. Then some misunderstanding about the boundary of their respective farms revealed the latest flame, and Colonel Crickley having followed a fat buck all one afternoon and wounded him, came up to him and found old Drake and his sons cutting him up! This incident added fuel to the fire, and from that time there was nothing the two families did not do to annoy each other. They shot each other's ducks in the river, purposely mistaking them for wild ones, and then by way of retaliation, commenced killing off each other's pigs and calves.

One evening, Mr. Drake the elder was returning home with

his "pocket full of rocks," from Chicago, whither he had been
to dispose of a load of grain. Sam Barston was with him on
the wagon, and as they approached the grove which intervened
between them and Mr. Drake's house, he observed to his
companion:

"What a beautiful mark Colonel Crickley's Old Roan is over
yonder!"

"Hang it!" muttered old Drake, "so it is."

The horse was standing under some trees, about twelve rods
from the road.

Involuntarily, Drake stopped his team. He glanced furtively
around, then with a queer smile the old hunter took up his rifle
from the bottom of the wagon, and raising it to his shoulder,
drew a sight on the Colonel's horse.

"Beautiful!" muttered Drake, lowering his rifle with the air
of a man resisting a powerful temptation. "I could drop Old
Roan so easy!"

"Shoot," suggested Sam Barston, who loved fun in any shape.

"No, no, 'twouldn't do," said the old hunter, glancing cautiously around him again.

"I won't tell," said Sam.

"Wal, I won't shoot this time, anyway, tell or no tell. The
horse is too nigh. If he was fifty rods off instead of twelve so
there'd be a bare possibility of mistaking him for a deer, I'd let
fly. As it is, I'd give the Colonel five dollars for a shot."

At that moment the Colonel himself stepped from behind a
big oak, not half a dozen paces distant, and stood before Mr.
Drake.

"Well, why don't you shoot?"

The old man stammered in some confusion, "That you
Colonel? I—I was tempted to, I declare! and as I said, I'll give
you a 'V' for one pull."

"Say an 'X' and its a bargain!"

Drake felt of his rifle and looked at Old Roan.

"How much is the hoss wuth?" he muttered in Sam's ear.

"About fifty."

"Gad, Colonel, I'll do it! Here's you 'X.' "

The Colonel pocketed the money, muttering, "Hanged, if I thought you'd take me up!"

With high glee, the old hunter put a fresh cap on his rifle, stood up in his wagon, and drew a close sight on Old Roan. Sam Barston chuckled. The Colonel put his hands before his face and chuckled too.

Crack! went the rifle. The hunter tore out a horrid oath which I will not repeat. Sam was astonished. The Colonel laughed. Old Roan never stirred!

Drake stared at his rifle with a face black as Othello's.

"What's the matter with you, hey? Fus' time you ever sarved me quite such a trick, I swan!"

And Drake loaded the piece with great wrath and indignation.

"People said you'd lost your nack o' shooting," observed the Colonel, in a cutting tone of satire.

"Who said so? It's a lie!" thundered Drake. "I can shoot—"

"A horse at ten rods! ha! ha!"

Drake was livid.

"Look yere, Colonel, I can't stand that!" he began.

"Never mind, the *horse* can," sneered the Colonel. "I'll risk you."

Grinding his teeth, Drake produced another ten-dollar bill.

"Here!" he growled, "I am bound to have another shot, anyway."

"Crack away," cried the Colonel, pocketing the note.

Drake *did* crack away—with deadly aim, too—but the horse did not mind the bullet in the least. To the rage and unutterable astonishment of the hunter, Old Roan looked him right in the face, as if he rather liked the fun.

"Drake," cried Sam, "You're drunk! A horse at a dozen rods —oh, my eye!"

"Just you shut your mouth or I'll shoot you!" thundered the excited Drake. "The bullet was hollow, I'll swear. The man lies says I can't shoot! Last week I cut off a goose's head at fifty rods, and I can dew it again. By the Lord Harry, Colonel, you can laugh, but I'll bet now, thirty dollars, I can bring down Old Roan at one shot!"

The wager was readily accepted. The stake was placed in Sam's hands. Elated with the idea of winning back his two tens, and making an "X" into the bargain, Drake carefully selected a perfect ball, and even buckskin patch, and beaded his rifle.

It was now nearly dark, but the old hunter boasted of being able to shoot a bat on the wing by starlight and without hesitation, he drew a clear sight on Old Roan's head.

A minute later, Drake was driving through the grove, the most enraged, the most desperate of men. His rifle, innocent victim of his ire, lay with broken stock on the bottom of the wagon. Sam Barston was too much frightened to laugh. Meanwhile, the gratified Colonel was rolling on the ground convulsed with mirth, and Old Roan was standing undisturbed under the trees.

When Drake reached home, his two sons discovering his ill humor and the mutilated condition of the rifle stock, hastened to arouse his spirits with a piece of news, which they were sure would make him dance for joy.

"Clear out," growled the angry old man. "I don't want to hear any news; get away, or I shall knock one of you down!"

"But, Father, it's such a trick!"

"Blast you and your tricks!"

"Played off on the Colonel."

"On the Colonel?" cried the old man, beginning to be interested. "Gad, if you've played the Colonel a trick, le's hear it."

"Well, Father, Jed and I this afternoon went out for deer—"

"Hang the deer! Come to the trick."

"Couldn't find any deer, but thought we must shoot something; so Jed banged away at the Colonel's Old Roan—shot him dead!"

"Shot Old Roan?" thundered the hunter, "by the Lord Harry, Jed, did *you* shoot the Colonel's hoss?"

"I didn't do anything else."

"Devil, devil!" groaned the hunter.

"And then," pursued Jed confident the joke part of the story must please his father, "Jed and I propped the hoss up, and tied his head back with a cord, and left him standing under the trees exactly as if he was alive. Ha! Ha! Fancy the Colonel going to catch him! ho! ho! ho!—wan't it a joke?"

Old Drake's head fell upon his breast, he felt of his empty pocketbook, and looked at his broken rifle. Then in a rueful tone, he whispered to the boys, "It is a joke! But if you ever tell of it—or if you do Sam Barston—I'll skin you alive! By the Lord Harry, boys, I've been shooting at that dead horse half an hour at ten dollars a shot!"[34]

## CHAPTER X

# LIARS

THE western frontier was as full of accomplished liars as the average tavern sugar bowl was of ants. Some miasmatic influence in the great West must have infected ordinary human beings and caused them to become prevaricators of the noblest order. Frontiersmen, and those who followed immediately in their footsteps, lied with coming appetites. Like Judge Joseph G. Baldwin's lovable Ovid Bolus, Esq., the Westerners' "lying came from a greatness of soul and their comprehensiveness of mind." They embraced all subjects without distinction or partiality.[1] Perhaps "the existence of lime in the water" in certain frontier regions was responsible for the expansiveness of western imagination—an imagination which lacked nothing in width, depth and height. A good story always gains by the personal element, and especially if it is told in the first person. Pioneers knew the art of telling good stories, for like good cooks their art was not lacking in savor.

Noblest of all frontier yarns is that of the famous "long-horned elks" which grazed peacefully upon the great Kentucky prairies. An ancient Virginia gentleman came west of the mountains, and returned to his Old Dominion home to proclaim it "the greatest country in the known world." He declared "that game was more plentiful there than in any other country, and far superior in size to any other animals of the same species." The Major said that "he had seen elk, having horns upwards of twelve feet in length." Timber grew in superabundance, and "massive trees," said he, "were generally so large, and so close together, that it was with difficulty a man could pass between them." Of course this enthusiastic proponent of the great western country was queried, as thousands of good accountants have always been, by a doubting Thomas who thought he had discovered an inconsistency in certain statements. "My good fellow," said the loafing killjoy, "how do those large elks with their long horns travel about among trees standing so near each other?" This was an angle which the gentle proclaimer of Kentucky's greatness had failed to consider and for a moment he was considerably "hemmed," but finally he exclaimed, "Oh, by God, that is none of my look out."[2]

Judge Thomas C. Haliburton laid the foundation for what was perhaps the tallest story that ever floated into the western country aboard a flatboat. Captain Scott, of New England birth, was the storm center of the original yarn, but later highly imaginative native sons trimmed it down to fit their local needs. Two passengers aboard a river boat fell to arguing as to which state produced the best marksmen, Kentucky or Tennessee. Ol' Kaintuck had always accepted the honor of being the best shot on "airth," as a sort of distinction *ex cathedra*. Her native sons were jealous of this laurel which held the maternal tresses closely bound to Mother Kaintuck's head. They would not tolerate, gently at least, any disparaging remarks about their handiness with a rifle. This was especially true if the taunt came from such an uncouth source as a "red-necked" Tennessean. The lanky and sunburned son of the bottoms of the Volunteer State said "he would turn his back to no man in killing racoons," and declared that he "had repeatedly shot fifty a day." This was the cue, and the Kentucky red horse was on fire. He belittled with a vengeance the Tennessean's amateurish holocaust among the ringtails by casually asking, "What o' that? I make nothing of killing a hundred 'coon a day, or'nary luck!" "Do you know Captain Scott of our state?" asked a Tennessee bystander. "He now is something like a shot. A hundred 'coon!—why he never pints at one without hitting him. T'other day he leveled at an old un, in a high tree. The varmint looked at him a minute, and then bawled out. "Halloa, Cap'n Scott! Is that you?" "Yes," was the reply. "Well, don't shoot!" says he, "it's no use! Hold on; I'll come down—I give in!"[3] This story grew considerably as it spread across the frontier. In fact, Captain Scott's 'coon became Major Harralson's deer.

Major Harralson, of Arkansas, was a crack shot, whose pride of trophies far exceeded his fondness for venison steak. On one particular occasion the Major determined that he should add a fine bucktail to his already large collection. He soon discovered "a long lean, lank-sided buck quietly feeding on the crest of the hill. To cock the gun, bring it into position, and put a finger upon the trigger, to an old sportsman, like the Major, was the work of a moment. The deer heard the click, and turned round —and would you believe it?—with the greatest coolness, said he: 'Is that you Harralson?' 'Yes sirree,' replied the Major. 'You ain't going to kill me out of season are you?' 'Oh damn you, I don't want your meat; it's only your tail I'm after.' 'Oh, if that's all, you might as well cut it off at once!'" Whereupon, with equal coolness the major outs with his jackknife, and neatly took off the point of the tail, and thereupon the respective parties resumed their several occupations.[4]

The backwoodsmen had ready answers for all questions. They were quick to size up smart alecks and greenhorns and give them as good answers in exchange for the questions they asked. Captain Basil Hall said to a native of the back country during a storm, "Why, you have heavy thunder here." "Well, yes," replied the natural son of the woods, "we do considering the number of inhabitants." Ribald joking was a favorite pastime between stagecoach travelers, bullying flatboatmen and settlers along the way. A garrulous stagecoach passenger yelled to a man fencing a field, "I say, mister, what are you fencing that pasture for? It would take forty acres on't to starve a middle-sized cow." "Jesso," responded the wise boy building the fence, "and I'm fencin' of it to keep our cattle aout."[5]

No subject in the western country provoked so much unreasonable lying as fertile land. Kentuckians, Hoosiers, Suckers, Razorbacks and what not boasted about their fertile lands, even though they were standing on soil which wouldn't sprout peas. Throughout the frontier it was said that soil was so fertile that farmers planted "a spike at night and harvested crowbars in the morning."[6] A Hoosier declared to a Yankee, "Why our soil is so rich—why, you never seed anything so tarnal rich in you life; why, how d'ye suppose we make our candles, ha? We dip them in mud puddles." Making certain that he did not understate the virtues of Indiana bottom land, the native continued, "Well, old Yankee, I'll just tell you all about it. If a farmer in our country plants his ground in corn and takes first-rate care of it, he'll get a hundred bushels to the acre, if he takes middlin' care of it he'll get seventy-five bushels to the acre, and if he don't plant at all he'll get fifty. The beets grow so large that it takes three yokes of oxen to pull up a full-sized one, and it leaves a hole so large that I once knew a family of five children who all tumbled into one before it got filled up, and the earth caved in upon them and they perished."[7]

T. B. Thorpe, in his *Big Bear of Arkansas,* has the Big Bear tell the famous frontier story concerning the fertility of western virgin land. As a squatter, desiring to move on, the "Bear" was in the act of trying to sell his holdings, and to a prospective customer he exclaimed, "Then look at my land—the government ain't got another such a piece to dispose of. Such timber, and such bottom land! Why, you can't preserve anything natural you plant in it, unless you pick it young; things thar will grow out of shape so quick. I once planted in those diggin's a few potatoes and beets; they took fine start, and after that an ox team couldn't have kept them from growing. About that time, I went off to old Kentuck on bisiness, and did not hear from them things for three months, when I accidentally stumbled on a fellow who had stopped at my place, with an idea of buying me out. 'How did you like things?' said I. 'Pretty well,' said he; 'the cabin is convenient, and the timber land is good; but the bottom ain't worth the first red cent.' 'Why?' said I. 'Cause it's full of cedar stumps and Indian mounds,' said he, 'and it can't be cleared.' 'Lord!' said I, 'them ar cedar stumps is beets, and them ar Indian mounds ar 'tater hills!' "[8]

Travelers through the West marveled at the tall talk of the

natives, and some of them took their verbal jousting seriously. Even so accurate a scientist as was John J. Audubon sometimes talked in extraordinarily tall terms. He claimed that he had seen a rattlesnake jumping from limb to limb in a treetop in pursuit of a gray squirrel. In discussing certain aspects of wild life in western America before British scientists he was denounced as a highly imaginative creature whose word was of no value. "Sir," said one of the scientific Britons, "this is really too much even for us Englishmen to swallow, whose gullets are known to be the largest, the widest, and the most elastic in the world."⁹ This perhaps was a true statement regarding the Englishman's gullibility, but among the journals left by the Anglo-tourists there is a remarkable absence of the expansive story.

It remained for Americans like Flint and Baird to discover and record the charming essence of American exaggeration. Baird published what is doubtless the most understanding explanation of the elastic quality of accounts of actual situations. "The people," said he, "of the West live amidst the elements of greatness. The lofty mountains on each side of the valley, the extensive inland seas on the north, the immense forests and prairies, and mighty rivers"—all had an important bearing upon the western conversation. This traveler explained that "these external influences are not important of themselves, except to excite the imagination and to supply striking and appropriate similes, metaphors and language of wonder."¹⁰

George D. Prentice of the Louisville *Journal* was a first-rate promoter of tall literature of the West. One of his best contributions was the famous story of John Champion's hogs. Prentice said that in the very early days many hogs were driven from Madison and other counties to the hill county of Estill in Kentucky. The people of Estill became much wrought up over the injustice being done them by their neighboring hog raisers and swore vengeance on the trespassers. The offended citizens of "bloody" Estill recalled that hogs had a great fear of bears and that if one of the varmints came near a drove of hogs the "porkers" left the woods immediately. Champion had a razorback sow which had mothered generation upon generation of long-snouted tushers, and she had made so many "mast" hunting trips to Estill that she had every cup oak tree located by memory. This hoary old female assumed the role of matriarch over the drove. She was caught up by the scheming and offended citizens of the neighborhood and sewn into a bear's skin. Prentice, in the style of a gloating native, said, "I tolled them up, and caught a good runner, and sewed her up in a bear's skin and turned her loose, when she ran after the rest, they flew from the supposed bear. The last that was seen of them was at Bassett's Creek, near forty miles from my house, only two being alive—one running from his fellow sewed in a bear's skin, and she was trying to catch the other—the rest were found dead in the road, having literally run themselves to death."[11]

Animal activities formed the basis for an excellent frontier tale. The antics of the common gray squirrel are subjects for dozens of yarns. One of these is as old as the famous Long-Horned Elk story. In a mountain community a colony of gray squirrels became particularly pestiferous in their raiding of a cornfield. They were ingenious creatures, however, because they had learned that only one side of the river was safe. Unfortunately for them the cornfield was not on the safe side and in order to harvest their share of the crop they had to use considerable strategy in crossing the river. The owner of the cornfield said, "I once had a hundred-acre river-bottom farm as fine as a crow ever flew over. One year I raised an enormous crop of corn. After the corn had ripened, I noticed on the side adjoining the river that a large quantity had disappeared. So I concluded to watch and see who was stealing my corn. I concealed myself the following morning, early, in a small thicket that bordered the river. I had not been there long before I saw a number of objects start from the opposite bank. For a time I could not discover what they were, but as they came closer, I discovered they were squirrels—about a hundred of them—each seated on a shingle and propelling it with his tail. When they reached the bank they left their shingles in a little cove and went out in the field. Presently, each one returned with an ear of corn, and, mounting his shingle propelled it to the opposite side of the river. The next day, in company with a dozen expert wood choppers, we cut down every hollow tree on the side where the squirrels landed, and found four hundred barrels of corn, besides killing many of the squirrels, indeed we lived on squirrels for several weeks."[12] This story belongs absolutely to the Ohio Valley frontier, but it has never been localized. Some versions have the squirrels crossing back and forth over the Ohio River from Kentucky to Indiana.

Practical jokes often reached the tall stage. Again Audubon figured as a master of the art of deception. He told Constantine Rafinesque, a temperamental French botanist, exciting stories about the queer fishes which he had found in the Ohio. They were outlandish combinations of colors, shapes and habits. His prize piscatorial curiosity, however, was the vicious "Jack-Devil-Diamond" fish. This impregnable monster grew remarkable stone-diamond shaped scales set in oblique rows, and when dried they would strike fire after the fashion of flint and steel.[13] To add more confusion to Rafinesque's disturbed state of mind, Audubon took him bear hunting and virtually frightened him to death in the midst of a small canebrake. Audubon led his baffled charge 'round and 'round, finally pretending that he was hopelessly lost.[14]

At Louisville, young blades, following the noble lead of Audubon, produced a wonderful and rare botanical specimen known as the "rat-tail-Niger" geranium. There was in the falls city a geranium fancier who immediately coveted the strange specimen, and by clever jockeying he was at last made recipient of the plant. Accompanying this precious Nigerian plant the Louisville bloods gave unusual directions for its care. Its stem was shriveled and generally it appeared to be much worse for wear. By following the directions, however, said the wags, it could be revived. The plant was hardy and it needed much hot sunshine and an abundance of water. Almost immediately the carefully nurtured geranium sent forth a fragrance, which was as unlike that of the ordinary garden variety "American" geranium as a "Devil-Jack-Diamond" fish is to a channel cat. Each day the fragrance became more noticeable and more nauseating, but with an increasing fragrance there was a disheartening shriveling of the stem. Upon closer examination of the structure and growing habits of this botanical rarity it was found to be an oversized gray rat planted in the dirt with its tail tied to a stick.[15]

The modern age rang down the curtain on the tall story of the frontier, but the old age passed as it had endured—with vigor, imagination and downright cussedness. Surely it was in profound appreciation of the changing times that P. Stretcher of Roaring Rapids, Kentucky, wrote the editor of the *Spirit of the Times* in July, 1843, giving an account of his experience with the famous "Essential Oil."[16] "I am an engineer on the Salt River Railroad," said Mr. Stretcher, "and I was proceeding with a train of cars from Skunksborough to this place, when the engine suddenly stopped. On examination, I found that the wheels wanted greasing. This seemed unlucky, as I was unprovided with the article, but remembering that I had a vial of Essential Oil in my pocket, I drew it out and annointed the hubs: instantly the cars were off, at the rate of one hundred and fifty miles per hour; being left alone in the world, I swallowed the rest of the oil, started on foot and arrived at the station just two and one-half seconds later than the train. While the cars were passing at this unparalleled rate, a Negro attempted to cross the track, two miles in advance; ere he had effected his object, the train was upon him. The front wheels of the engine ground him to atoms, but as the hinder one passed a drop of oil oozed from the hubs and fell upon him. He instantly rose restored and sound in wind and limb as before. So instantaneous was the whole affair that the pain, though excruciating, lasted but the twenty-second part of a second."

The frontier produced hundreds of tales and many of these have been preserved with body and soul intact. The tale in the raw is far better than one in the abstract, even though the original "teller" often wandered through a forest of verbiage in the telling. In a sense, all the frontier accounts of personal exploits were taller than the facts merited. Some, however, were more imaginative than others, and those which follow are selected because of their particular brands of imagination.

Here is an assortment of the frontiersman's own accounts of how he fit, fought, bled and died in the Old West. As one of the native sons would have said: "Stranger, this is but a suck," but it is a "suck" through the middle. The frontier was reminiscent of all of its doings from a native slinging a tiger wrong side out to the coming of industry at Cincinnati where a strolling lady's dog was converted instantaneously into "seventy-five links of fresh sausage, and a beautiful black woolly muff."

Of course there never were any tigers on the American frontier, but such a minor detail did not necessarily keep a good liar from being entertaining. "Thunder" is the authority for the following peculiar piece of western literature. It is little wonder that varmints soon disappeared with such hardy huntsmen as the hero of the tiger story waging war against them.

### FIGHTING THE TIGER

Well some time 'long in the month of July, Sal came to me one day, and says to me—says she—"Joe, I want some b'ar meat, and I guess you had better cut right out and get me some." Now, you recollect, fellers, that Sal was sorter sick about that time, and used to take the darnedest crankiest kind of notions in her head that ever I heard of. But, however, I slung "Old Bellzy" over my shoulder, and set out in full chase after the only b'ar that we had heard of in that neck of the woods during the summer. A long, and a hot, and a wearisome tramp I had; but luck was with me, and I finally brought "Old Bellzy" to a level on him, and just laid him out as slick as ever you saw a 'coon lay out a dog. Little time elapsed before he was regularly cleaned, while I made a break for home, as I was tired, hot and hungry. The tramp was a long one; the load none of the lightest, and I soon grew faint and sick under the heat of the sun. Casting about for a spot upon which to rest until the cool of the evening, I soon found a quiet nook under the shadow of a cluster of vines to our special liking. Hanging my game to the branch of a neighboring tree, and resting my gun by its side, I retired to this inviting spot, and was quickly in a land where uneasiness is not felt. How long I slept it is impossible to say; but the nap generally was a sweet and refreshing one, and might have lasted much longer, if I had not been disturbed by a slimy and compressing sensation about my throat, together with a feeling that something was passing over my face which was not very pleasant to me. I was not thoroughly disturbed; yet I felt my situation becoming more and more unpleasant, and, in a dreaming listlessness, opened my eyes to see what was going on, when—mercy me! I found an enormous snake (well-known in that region as the "Racer,") had wound himself about my neck, and was bobbying his nasty head back and forth upon my face, while his horrible tongue was playing like lightning upon my features! With a yell of horror, I sprung to my feet! Fortunately, my presence of mind did not leave me, and I bethought myself at once of my knife. Quietly drawing it from my sheath I managed to pass it between my throat and the snake, until I was sure that its point had reached beyond his widest fold; then, with a sudden movement, turned the back to my skin, the blade to my enemy, and, with a vigorous thrust of my wrist, he was laying powerless around my feet. Before I had time to recover from my alarm, I looked, and mercy again! I found a grander horror upon me! Drawn by the scent of blood, a tiger had found my game, during my sleep, and was rampant and raging over his prey. Never shall I forget the growl which he gave me when he first saw me. There he was, rearing upon the game before him, his eyes like balls of fire, waiting only for me to move to spring upon and tear me limb from limb. My brain was on fire; I saw but one hope, and that was to recover the knife, which in my first surprise I had let drop. I made one effort to secure it, but my enemy kept too close a watch upon me, and darted upon

me before I could reach it. As he came, with a thundering roar
and flaming eyes, I gave myself up for lost; blindly I closed my
fist and made a pass as he reared upon me. Fortunately my arm
passed directly into his throat as he ripped my clothes in threads
with his iron paws, I kept shoving my fist on—on—on, until it
was through and through by thunder! Quick as lightning I
seized his tail, ris upon my feet, gave a hearty jerk, and turned
the tarnal beast clean inside out! Strangers, I thought I should
aflumized right on the spot; but I got over it, and feel none
the worse for "fighting the tiger."

Who'll drink?[17]

Ben Snaggletree was a real half-horse half-alligator riverman
who could pull himself out of most any situation, but the account
which is given here is of a tight squeeze in which the snag
leaned heavily upon a passing catfish.

### BEN SNAGGLETREE'S CATFISH STORY

Ben was an ol' Mississip' roarer—none of your half and half,
but just as native to the element as if he had been born in a
broadhorn. He said that he had been *fotched* up on the river's
brink, and "knew a snappin' *turtle* from a *snag* without larnin'."

"One night," said Ben, "about as dark as the face of Cain, and
as unruly as if the elements had been untied and let loose from
their great captain's command, I was on the old Mississippi;
it was, in short, a night ugly enough to make any natural born
Christian think of his prayers, and a few converted saints trem-
ble—I walked out upon the steamboat 'guard' to cool off from
the effects of considerable liquor doin's, participated in during
the day, but had scarcely reached the side of the boat when she
struck a snag, and made a lurch throwing me about six feet into
the *drink*. I was sufficiently cool, stranger, when I came to the
surface, but I had nigh in a short time set the Mississippi a *bilin'*.
My carcass grew so hot with wrath at observing the old boat
wending her way upstream, unhurt, while I, solitary, unobserved

and alone, was floating on the old father of waters. I swam to the head of a small island some distance below where we struck, and no sooner touched ground than I made an effort to stand erect. You may judge of my horror on discovering my landing place to be a Mississippi *mud-bar,* and about as firm as quicksand, into which I sunk about three feet in a moment.

"All was dark as a stack of black cats—no object visible save the lights of the receding boat—no sound smote upon the ear but the lessening blow of the 'scape pipe' and the splashing of the surrounding waters;—the first sounded like the farewell voice of hope, while the latter, in its splashing and purling, was like the jabbering of evil spirits, exulting over the entrapped victim.

"I attempted to struggle, but that sunk me faster. I cried out, but fancied that, too, forced me deeper into my yielding grave; ere daylight dawned I felt sure of being *out of sight,* and horrid thought of thus sinking into eternity through a *mud-gate,* made every hair stand 'on its own hook,' and forced my heart to patter against my ribs like a trip-hammer. I had been in many a scrape, but I considered this the nastiest, and made up my mind that the ball of yarn allotted to me was about being spun out—my cake was all *mud!* I promised old Mississippi, if permitted to escape this time, I would *lick* anythin' human that said a word agin' her; but it was no use—she was sure of me now, and, like old 'bare bones' to an expiring African, she held on, and deeper and deeper I sunk. In a short time I was forced to elevate my chin to keep out of my mouth an over-supply of temperance liquid, which was flowing so coaxingly about my lips. My eye-balls were starin', my teeth set, and hope had wasted to a misty shadow, when something touched me like a floating solid; I instantly grasped it—it slid through my hands—*all but the tail*—which I clung to with a grip of *iron.*

"I soon discovered I had made captive of a mammoth *catty,* huge enough to be the partriarch of his tribe, and a set of resolutions was quickly adopted in my mind, that he couldn't travel further without company. A desperate start and vigorous wiggle to escape was made by my friend the catty, but there was six feet in length of *desperation* attached to his extremity that could neither be coaxed or shook off. Soon succeeded another start, and out I came like a cork from a bottle. Off started the fish, like a comet, and after him I went, a *muddy spark* at the end of his tail. By a dexterous twist of his rudder, I succeeded in keeping him on the surface, and steered him to a solid landing, where I set him loose, and we shook ourselves, mutually pleased at parting company."

"That will do, Ben," said we, "all but the *tail*."

"Tail and all, or none!" said Ben, so here you have it. Ben swears he'll father it himself.[18]

During the 'thirties and 'forties the East was very much concerned about public lands in the West. Especially was this true among those Easterners who felt that they might be subjected to exploitation by the industrialists who were rapidly gaining a foothold in New England. Land scouts were sent to the frontier by congregations and communities to secure information and to report back to their sponsors. This was the case of the Parish of Thistleton which sent Squire Cushman to the West as its agent. When the Squire returned, a parish meeting was called, and an anxious congregation awaited his report.

## SQUIRE CUSHMAN'S TRAVELS OUT WEST

At the appointed time, the Squire was found occupying the pulpit in company with the elder, who, after having made a prayer, introduced "Brother Cushman," as one who would favor them with an account of the moral condition of the people in the western states.

So far it was all right; but it was a different thing to face an audience as a lecturer, than the Squire had anticipated. Thus, after many preliminary "hems" and "haws," the Squire commenced his lecture, which savored more of natural scenery than moral philosophy.

The Squire was soon in the middle of an oak forest. Said he:

"Friends and neighbors, the state of Ohio is noted for its oak forests. I have traveled for fifty miles through one of these tracts of wood—the growth of centuries—splendid wood, a hundred and sixty cords to the acre—to say the least! Old oaks, a hundred and twenty feet in height, and as straight as arrows."

This description was exciting to an old wood chopper who sat in one of the front pews, and forgetting the sanctity of the place, and the time, he was on his feet in a moment with the following queries:

"I say, Squire, can you tell a fellow what kinds of wood are the thickest in Ohio? and what a fellow like me would get a cord for chopping that 'ere wood?"

"As to that," said the Squire, "the growth of wood in the regions I have traveled consisted of beech, birch and maple; but principally of fir, spruce and hemlock. And as to wood chopping, a fellow couldn't earn his salt at the business."

The old elder was getting uneasy; already satisfied that the Squire's reckless manner of going into wood lots savored but little of morality. Thus, he suggested in a whisper to the Squire, that probably the audience would like to hear of the spiritual wants of the people in the regions he had traveled.

"Yes, yes, Brother," said the Squire, "I am coming to that presently."

Continuing his lecture, he said: "One great evil noticed in traveling 'Out West,' especially in Illinois, is the want of good water. That procurable being, at best, of an indifferent quality. One thing to attract the notice of a stranger is the astonishing depth of the few wells the people have already sunk. Why! I recollect of coming upon a gang at work one day in sinking a well, and made the inquiry of the head workman of how deep they had gone into the earth, and for the answer, as near as I can recollect, was to this effect:

"They had been digging for water for three weeks; but it was a doubtful thing how far they had gone down; 'but,' said the workman, 'I can tell you this much—we commenced four days ago to draw up the old man's son at the bottom, and kept on drawing until yesterday morning, when hearing no tidings of him, we sent the old man down a day's journey to report progress, and I tell you what 'tis stranger, we 'spect to have a report from him every moment.'

"I waited a couple of hours, and had the satisfaction of shaking hands with the proprietor, and hearing his report to this effect: Having descended to an immense depth, he yelled out to his son below him, and wished to know what luck he had in finding water, etc.; and received for an answer that he had not found a drop of water, *but it began to look decidedly moist round the edges of the "sile" when he left the bottom!*

"As my time was too precious to await the appearance of the proprietor's son, I pursued my way to an adjoining town, and put up for the night.

"A week elapsed 'ere I heard anything farther from *that well*. Being in *Chicago* at the expiration of that time, I, one morning, took up one of the daily papers and read of a singular freak in that well, reported by the owner in person.

"By that account, it would seem that the proprietor's son arrived at the top of the well the day after I left it; but no inducement held out by the father could tempt him into the well again. By his account, it was absolutely dangerous working at the bottom; the stones and gravel when loosened, were constantly rising and striking him in the head! And then, such horrid noises as issued from the solid earth—it was too much for him, at that depth! The old man being somewhat irritated at his son's obstinacy, or want of courage to descend the well again, vowed by all the heathen gods that he would see the bottom, and *dig through,* if he couldn't find water in any other manner.

"The old man having reached the bottom, commenced a furious onslaught on the *'moist sile'* with *crow* and pick. And said he: 'Don't think I had struck but a couple of blows, ere the next thing I was aware of, I was on *"terry-firmy"* having been blown clean out through that shaft seated in a tub—*by an explosion of gas!* And what's more, there wasn't a hair on me damaged in the least; but the discharge of sand and stones had killed seven of the workmen, and the *gas* had blown my son and the windlass all to flitters.' "

"Gracious! For mercy sake, 'Brother' Cushman," said the old elder, and rising and patting the lecturer on the shoulder, "do tell the audience something about the spiritual wants of the people, and what they thought of our colporteurs in those regions!"

"Oh, yes," said the Squire, getting somewhat nettled. "Ahem! —well, the fact is just this—the truth must out: *they didn't think much of 'em, any way; but called 'em a lazy set of Yankee wolves in sheep's pelts!* And that's about all I hear them say as to spiritual matters."

The old elder hastily arose and uttered a benediction, and the audience dispersed, well satisfied in having heard the last of Squire Cushman's Moral Lectures.[19]

Uncle Billy, a wild Kentuckian, who moved on west with the frontier entertained the boys with his tall tale of how he "fit" Arthur Levenribs. The effectiveness of his story was always measured by the amount of liquor which he had consumed. When he appeared in a grocery, or saloon, the boys treated him freely and begged him to tell them about his famous fight.

## How Uncle Billy Drove Center

When I first came out from the *Kaintuck* purchase, it was sparsely settled about here, and the first fall arter I come out, we got out of whisky; not a man in the neighborhood had a drop. What to do, we did not know. But just afore Christmas, a fellow moved out from North *Calliner;* and, 'mongst his baggage, he managed to scrape up about a gallon of whisky. Now, if I was to tell you what that whisky was wuth, thar and then, you'd swar 'twas a lie; but, dog my cat, if I don't believe it was wuth a gallon of dollars.

Well, the furst I knowed of its being in the country, was one of my neighbors come over, and told me that thar was to be a shootin' match up at old Step-and-fetch-it's grocery, the next

Saturday, for that New-comer's gallon of whisky. I told him he mout jest count me thar, for I was agoing, and I was abound to tote off that roastin'-ear juice. Thar was only one fellow in the purchase, who could hold a candle to me a shootin' with a rifle, and that was a tremenjus, great big long-legged, rawboned, *lanky-bully* fellow, what was always called Arthur Levenribs. He and I had shot together several times, and I had always managed to make him come out second best. But he had sworn that he would beat me, if he had to shoot agin' me 'till Gabriel toots his horn.

Well, Saturday come, and, with my old rifle in number one order, I started for the grocery. There was about thirty fellows thar, all with thar rifles in apple-pie order, and all a hankering to git a shoot for that gallon of whisky. 'Twarnt long afore the shootin' commenced. I was about the fust one to shoot, and, as usual, I drew center. Everybody had shot except Levenribs, and nobody had teched my shot yit, but when Levenribs come to shoot, he put his ball in the same hole mine had made. So him and me had to shoot agin. We shot a second time, and both plummed the center agin; and we kept shootin', and 'twas the same thing every time. The crowd began to get awfully excited, for thar was fourteen on my side and fourteen on his'n, and they was a hollerin' and takin' on at a terrible rate, and bettin' everything they could raise. One fellow on t'other side, swore he'd risk one head of horse on his man, and every one of my men that could raise a critter, took him up afore he had the words out of his mouth. By-and-by, I seed that Levenribs was beginning to get a little worried, and then I knowed I'd git him, though 'twas as much as I could do to keep cool myself. Well, we had shot more than forty shots apiece, and, at last, Levenribs missed center just about the width of a har, and such hollerin' and caperin' as my boys done, you never seed the like, for they knew I was going to settle the thing right off. I walked up to the shootin' place, and jist as I was a raisin' my gun to my face, she accidentally went off, a thing she never did before or since. "I call that shoot," said I, as quick as I could and before the ball was fairly out of my rifle. "No you don't," says Levenribs, and the boys on both sides took it up. *My* side a swearin' I should take it back, and 'tother side swarin' I *shouldn't,* and that the whisky belonged to Levenribs. Every fellow on both sides done his best at hollerin' and swarin', for they all had bet on it; but, in a few minutes, one of my friends come and told me that my ball had struck a rock, about half way between me and the target, and had glanced and knocked out the center.

"Hello!" says I, "I won't call that shoot; let's go and see whar my bullet hit." And when 'tother side found out that my bullet had glanced and beat 'em, they jest niled, and swore as they wouldn't let me call it when I wanted to, that now it should count, and I should shoot it over. And, after *jowering* a while, every fellow pitched into his man, and thar was fifteen pair of men fighting at once. I, of course, had locked horns with Levenribs, and when all the rest was done, he and I was jest a gittin' in a good way. We commenced fighting about ten o'clock in the morning, and fit like all wrath till sundown. I begun to git awful tired, and was afraid that if Levenribs didn't soon giv' in, that I must; and while I was thinking what I had best do, my old woman, who had heard what was goin' on, came a tearin', and as soon as she got within hollerin' distance she begun: *"Hooraw,* my Bill!" As soon as I heard her, I knew that if I got whipped, she would think she had just cause and provocation to leave my bed and board, as the sayin' is. So, I made up my mind to whip that fellow, or die, right thar. So, I gathered all the little strength I had, and I socked my thumb in his eye, and, with my fingers took a twist on his *snot-box,* and with the other hand, I caught his ear in my mouth, gin his head a flirt, and *out came his ear by the roots!* I then flapped his head over, and caught his other ear in my mouth, and jerked it out in the same way, and it made a hole in his head that I could have rammed my fist through, and I was just agoin' to do it, when he hollered: "Nuff!" My old woman then jumped up on a stump, and hollered out: "If any feller in this here crowd says that ain't Bill Hardyarn's whisky, jest let him trot his wife out, and I'll use her a darned sight wuss than my old man has done Arth Levenribs, and if he's got no wife, I'll put him through!" But none of 'em dared to take her up, and after comparing notes a while, every fellow started for home, thinking he had seen a fight as was a fight.

"Boys, I won that whisky; but it was right expensive!"

"But what did he do for you, Uncle Bill?" said one of the listeners.

"Well, that's changing the subject," said Uncle Bill, "but to tell the truth, boys, he did take off some sign, if you call my har any; and next day some of us went to the place, and picked up a two bushel basket even full of ears, noses and eyes, that had been bit off and gouged out in the fuss."

"A pretty good pile, Uncle Billy, to come off of thirty men," said one of the boys, and the look of surprise that the crowd, particularly the hero, gave him, told plainer than words could, that it was rather unpopular to doubt anything that Uncle Billy told concerning himself.[20]

CHAPTER XI

## QUARTER HOSSES

TRAVELING through Kentucky at an early date François Michaux
remarked that "they (Kentuckians) meet often in taverns, particularly during the sitting of the courts of justice, when they
pass whole days in them. Horses and lawsuits are the usual subjects of conversation. When a traveler arrives, his horse is valued
as soon as they can perceive him."[1] Horses to frontier Westerners constituted the most fascinating subject of conversation and
speculation. Racing in the early West was the most vigorous of
frontier sports. James Hall wrote a rather unfavorable account
of life about the race tracks. He left the definite impression that
the throng which gathered around the judges' stand in a quarter
race was no place for a timid or modest soul. "I went out to the
race course," wrote the punctilious Hall, "as the spring race
meeting was going on, and saw one or two heats run in very
good time. There was but a small attendance, either of beauty
or fashion, and I did not stay long enough to avail myself of the
opportunity which such a scene offers for making observations
on the more rough and unpolished portion of society; indeed,
the swearing of some of the lower orders in the West, especially
among the horse traders and gamblers, would shock ears ac-
customed to the language of Billingsgate or a London gin shop,
so full is it of blasphemy; and uttered in a deliberate and determinate tone, such as to induce the belief that the speaker really
wishes the fulfillment of the curses which he imprecates. I have
heard the vulgar oaths of many countries, as the French, the
English, the Irish, and Scotch (which three last have different
safety valves of wrath), the Dutch, the German, the Italian, and
the Portuguese: of course, they are all vulgar, all more or less
blasphemous and disgusting to the ear; but I never heard them

224

so offensive or so slowly and deliberately uttered, as in the mouths of the western and southwestern Americans."[2]

Hall was an unusually sensitive Briton, and perhaps the crowd which he saw at the race course was not so profane as he believed it to be. Other observers, however, have left accounts which indicate that racing fans of the early nineteenth century were profane individuals. James Flint found a milling throng in a Lexington tavern talking and swearing about horse racing.[3] A Kentuckian said in an article to the Kentucky *Gazette* that the remainder of the Union had the impression that "horse jockeying and tippling is [our] chief employment."[4]

Horse racing in the trans-Appalachian region dates back to the arrival of the first white man west of the mountains. When Daniel Boone and his long hunting companions deserted their homes in the eastern piedmont for Kentucky they brought with them horses, and, no doubt, they broke the tedium of long months in the wilderness with an occasional match race. It would be safe to say that wherever there were two horses and riders in the western country there were races. At Boonesboro, the assembly called in the summer of 1775 by Richard Henderson to discuss the fundamental questions before the settlements in Kentucky, adopted resolutions to encourage the breeding of horses.[5]

By 1800 all the western settlements knew what it was to have quarter racing at regular intervals. Originally horses were lined up at a post, and were run over a distance of approximately a quarter of a mile. This gave the sport its name, and any contest was called a "quarter race." Even wedding parties were made more exciting by horsemen choosing sides and running "quarter hosses" through the woods for the bottle. This sport required excellent horsemanship because the rider not only had to keep his mount spurred into the lead, but he had to watch for logs, stumpholes and low swinging vines at the same time. Many a nag went home with a drawn tendon, and a rider considerably "ruffled up" because of a bottle-race accident.[6]

Quarter races were organized and run at any time and place

where there were as many as two horses that could run, and two riders who were willing to ride them. No pedigree was necessary, and few of the people watching the races, according to contemporary observers, knew a pedigree from a starting stall. Kentuckians, however, began importing fine horses from Virginia and England at an early date. Western blood lines were in process of building long before the settlements of the frontier were past danger from Indian attacks. The first issues of the frontier newspaper, the Kentucky *Gazette,* carried notices of stud horses which were standing at Bluegrass farms.[7] Not only did the press announce to the public that certain breeders had blooded studs, the services of which could be had upon payment of nominal fees, but the city fathers were forced to take official cognizance of the breeding industry. Horsemen of the Bluegrass were bold citizens and they placed their horse-breeding activities above the public modesty. Trustees of the town of Lexington were called upon to step into the breach and stop certain indiscretions of the horsemen. At a meeting, held April 2, 1798, the trustees resolved "that it be the duty of John Arthur to bring suit against persons for shewing stud horses out of [the] bounds allotted by the trustees."[8] That is, some of the breeders were not careful about where they "stood" their stallions, and were shewing them in the sacred bounds of Cheapside and before the public gaze. So flagrant was this practice in the Bluegrass that the general assembly was called upon to take action against such social indecencies.[9]

Eight years before the solemn and publicly moral trustees of the town of Lexington were resolving that Marshall John Arthur should take the law in his hands and curtail horse-breeding activities on court square, the sporting general assembly, at its first session, passed the parent "horse act" of the western country. This legislation provided for the "improvement of the breed of horses." It recognized the fact that many Kentuckians were keeping blooded brood mares of high grade, and that "stoned" horses were running at large. These animals were a distinct detriment to the pioneer blood-stock industry, and the legislature provided that any person who caught a mature stallion running at large was to geld him. When the owner appeared to claim his animal, the person gelding the stallion was entitled to collect damages, and a special fee for castration. This law was the source of many lawsuits, and not a few cutting scrapes, but it did protect the prospective breeding of good race horses in the West.[10] As other western states were organized they adopted the Kentucky law as a basis for encouraging an improved breed of horses.[11]

Before the racing industry was organized, quarter races were popular everywhere. A rugged country, however, was ill-suited to any kind of a race except after the bottle. No courses were opened to the sporting bloods, and they were forced to utilize streets of backwoods villages, and public highways. Again city fathers and state legislators were forced to step in and forbid such indiscretions. They levied fines of five dollars against such owners as were so inconsiderate of public safety as to run a horse race in a public thoroughfare. One board of trustees resolved that it was their duty to recover "the fines for firing guns and for running horses within the bounds of the in-lots."[12]

Since Kentucky was the first state to organize in the West, and its Bluegrass pasturelands were conducive to the production of horses, that state, of course, was the first to deal with problems arising from the sport of horse racing. Charters granted by the general assembly creating towns generally required in "Section 7" that "any person who shall be guilty of running or racing horses in the streets or alleys and highways of said town . . . shall forfeit and pay for every offence, the sum of five dollars, to be sued for by said trustees. . . ."[13] Lexington attempted to solve the problem as early as 1789 by opening a four-mile association track. This early course took in a part of the street system of the town, and it was novel in that it crossed two hills which took the horses completely out of sight of the spectators.

Running horses in public roads and down streets was indeed a dangerous pastime. This fact was clearly demonstrated in one western village where two groups organized quarter races to be run down main street, but the starts were made from opposite ends. By a strange coincidence neither side knew of the other's intentions and the races were started at approximately the same time, and the contestants met head-on midway of the town. It was only by good horsemanship that the riders and horses were saved from complete destruction.[14] Naturally pedestrians were of no consequence in the face of an important quarter race.

This sporting indiscretion was committed repeatedly in spite of sections in town charters prohibiting it. Village officials were unable, or unwilling, to stop racing in their streets, and too often sheriffs and constables were participants in races along the highways. State legislatures were forced to make special issues of this infraction of local laws. In 1821 the Kentucky lawmakers declared that "Whereas, it is represented to the General Assembly of the Commonwealth of Kentucky, that divers citizens are in the habit of assembling themselves together on the public highways, for the purpose of running horses, which tends greatly to the annoyance of many of the good people thereof, and frequently tends to the disturbance of travelers"; therefore the legislators attempted to set up an effective check of this frolicsome pastime. This law forbade anybody in the state of Kentucky to run horses either in practising for a race or running a race under a penalty of ten dollars.[15] A ten-dollar fine, however, was not an unusually stiff rate of rent for horsemen who were unable to afford private courses, or who were too far removed from association tracks.

The legislators at Frankfort might have had in mind that famous race between the swift-footed mule Jenny and the famous pony Spunky. They were matched in a race from Lexington to Frankfort and return. Their owners, Doctor Claiborne and Doctor Champney, matched their mounts in this long-distance race and placed large sums of money upon each of them. The horse and mule covered the distance to Frankfort in quick time in spite of muddy roads, but on the return, between Versailles and Lexington, Doctor Champney claimed that the clumsy Jenny had fouled the fleet Spunky, and she was drawn up lame. This led to a bitter quarrel between the learned physicians which caused bitter reverberations in the public press. John Bradford, editor of the Kentucky *Gazette,* denounced these sportsmen as scoundrels, and declared the race ridiculous. A righteous community became so indignant at the incessant quarreling between the Doctors that they were forced to pack up their pill bags, saddle their mounts and flee the Bluegrass, leaving the great race to Frankfort and back an unsettled question.[16]

Four years later the modest owner of the famous stud Dare Devil used a full column of precious space in the Kentucky *Gazette* to tell owners of brood mares about his stallion's unusual accomplishments. Dare Devil had shown his heels to fast competition on many occasions, but never was his performance more sensational than on the Lexington track late in 1798. Despite this course's many contours, the indomitable "iron" stud negotiated it with honor to himself and his owner. If the modest advertisement of the owner, Colonel Burrows, is to be accepted at face value, Dare Devil still holds a record of a sort in frontier turf annals. He had only a modest pedigree, but breeding was nothing in the face of his unique stamina. In March of 1797 he won the Jockey Club purse at Lexington; in the fall of '98 he distanced the popular stallion Weazle in a four-heat, four-mile race. His prime performance, however, took place at Frankfort and Lexington later that year. On succeeding days he distanced strong competition at Frankfort in the afternoon and was ridden to Lexington next morning, traveling in mud that was thigh deep most of the way. He arrived in Lexington at twelve o'clock with balls of Franklin and Woodford County mud dangling from his fetlocks, and before his handlers had time to wash him off and rub him down, the famous stud was called to the post to match his speed against a fast fresh field of blooded entrants. The Lexington course was a crude oval, and at one point near the stretch it made such an abrupt turn that a ragged board fence had been constructed to warn jockeys to pull their mounts around sharply. When Dare Devil reached this board fence, carrying his two hundred pound jockey, he flew the course and jumped the board fence, with all the grace of a pedigreed hunter. His rider pulled him back to the fence, cleared it a second time and entered the stretch to go home and past the judges' stand full ahead of his fleet competitors.[17]

Dare Devil's owner was an exceedingly modest man, and stated in his advertisement that his powerful horse had won many other exciting races, but since he was hazy about the exact details he did not care to make them public because his prospective clients would think him guilty of exaggeration. In this same year that Dare Devil cleared the wall at the Lexington course, the fast-flying Gray Squirrel started in a feature race at the Nicholasville track where he won the first heat in sensational time, and was well ahead of his field in the second lap when he ran against a stump and fell down, throwing his rider and losing the contest. His owner, however, assured prospective customers that he was a fast and worthy stud, and that his services were available for thirty dollars per mare.[18]

As rugged as western life was in general, commentators found that horse racing had influenced it for the worse. In Virginia Benjamin H. Latrobe attended a race meet at which he found a boisterous crowd shouting, swearing and carousing generally.[19] His experience coincides with that of Charles A. Murray who, a few years later, attended a meeting at a western course where he found conditions identical with those described by the architect in Virginia. Wherever a considerable number of people became interested in horses and horse racing, traders and gamblers were always found trying to catch suckers and greenhorns. Murray, like his fellow Englishman Hall, found everybody drunk and cavorting around like men possessed of devils. He heard profanity, which would have shocked the lustiest of foreign blackguards. The oaths which he was forced to hear were uttered in the slow and deliberate manner of frontier western and southwestern Americans.[20]

Native observers were quick to sense the moral effects of horse racing. H. M. Brackenridge on one occasion found the business section of Pittsburgh deserted, and the race course crowded daily with people. Inside the course there were booths of petty merchants selling everything imaginable. Fist fights occurred frequently. Dogs barked incessantly and nipped the heels of strangers, and fiddlers appeared with battered instruments to add to the noise and pandemonium. Betting ran riot, and the cry "To Horse! To Horse!" was the signal for a general shout that would have completely outdone a whole tribe of Shawnee warriors. [21] So notorious were the western race courses and the crowds gathered about them that the hoary old river geographer and navigator, Zadoc Cramer, had to comment adversely on the evils of quarter horses. "We are sorry," wrote the learned riverman Cramer, "to acknowledge that horse racing, contrary to the express law of this state, has been practiced."[22] He declared that it was both dangerous and wicked.

Perhaps the territorial legislature of Indiana would have agreed without reservation with the moral attitude of Cramer that horse racing was "dangerous and wicked." This body, with faces as long as the "moral law" itself declared itself on public morals. Since there was a lengthy category of immoral practices in the wild country of Indiana, horse racing was not to enjoy the sole brunt of attack. The assembly resolved that "Whereas, among our American fellow citizens there are many who, likewise, men and women, drink overmuch whiskey—even running for the bottle at weddings—use profane language, indulge in brutal fighting and in horse and foot racing and all kinds of gaming for money, and even take each other's lives in duels, and otherwise, in their habits of exaggerated and unbridled individuality and independence are forgetful of their social duties, and whereas all these sinners, French and American and Godless Indians, pay no regard to the Sabbath!"[23] All of these evils went with a sporting West. So long as there was the type of competition which was offered in a horse race there was of course cause for quarrels and duels on every hand. Liquor, gambling and general debauchery accounted for the profanity which visitors saw and heard about the race stands.

Horse racing, however, was not confined to the laity alone. Brother J. B. Finley reported a "painful" incident which occurred among a Methodist flock. A brother, and a trusted class leader departed the straight and narrow path by going to a horse race where he became gloriously intoxicated and uttered with perfect abandonment profane words which indicated a total depravity of mind. Soon after this good brother's total moral dissipations at the race grounds, he was taken sick and almost died. While he was delirious and wrestling with what promised to be a fatal disease he made a solemn vow to the Lord that if he would spare his life he would return to his duties as class leader, and would not indulge his base nature in worldly pleasures. "The Lord heard his vows," wrote the minister; "he was cured." Before the penitent Methodist could enjoy the fruits of a reformed life, however, temptation was placed in his path in the form of a corn shucking. He could not resist the urge to go, and he repudiated his vows when the gourd was passed. After a few sucks at the gourd the sacred vows were forgotten, and the class leader was "overseas." He was placed upon a bed to sleep off his drunken stupor, but when it became necessary to move him aside to make room for the dance it was found that he had died. Horse racing had led him astray, and the breaking of his promise "to do better" was his earthly end.[24]

Once in a while the spirit of racing entered a frontier pulpit and corrupted a servant of the Word. The Reverend Hardy M. Cryer of Sumner County, Tennessee, displeased his board of elders by participating in such a godless sport as running a quarter horse. This sporting divine was called before his brethren who raised the moral issue of the inconsistency of fox hunting, horse racing and preaching. Brother Cryer was guilty, and there was nothing which he could say or deny that would improve his standing with the board of enraged elders. He saw that the quickest way out was to plead guilty and put the burden of solving his problems squarely upon the shoulders of his accusers. "It's true, gentlemen," pleaded the minister, "Tom Watson and I do own Jake Creath together—and it's not a bad horse either—

when he starts he wins. Old man Watson trains and runs him at his own expense—I get half of the winnings, and because I allow my half of the horse to run when Colonel Watson's half goes. If you will provide a way for my half to remain in the stable during the race I am perfectly willing to retire from the turf."[25] As wise as elders were supposed to be in Tennessee this was too difficult a problem for them to solve. They voted rather than tax their brains to allow the horse-racing parson to depart from the canons of the faith and indulge himself in an occasional horse race with his half of the famous quarter miler Jake Creath.

Early in the history of the West, mineral springs became prominent as refuges of health and sports. These "health" resorts were crowded throughout most of the pleasant months of the year with "invalids" from the southern and western states. These decrepit individuals rushed to the springs in Kentucky and western Virginia in order to restore emaciated bodies and spirits. Olympia, Blue Licks, Drennon's, Graham's, Crab Orchard and Cerulean Springs in Kentucky and White Sulphur Springs in Virginia were famous gathering places for sportsmen of the early period in the West. Here gamblers, preachers, black-legs, statesmen, and ladies gathered for a gay social season. Although most of the springs boasted, as the promoters of the Olympian resort, that the waters cured all ailments and that there was a salubrity of climate and scenery, the real attractions were gambling, horse racing and fox hunting.[26] Fortescue Cuming met three young men at Talbott's Tavern near Chillicothe, Ohio, who were returning from the Olympian Springs. Their conversation failed to intimate that they had "taken the waters," but they did have much to say on the subject of "cards, billards and horse jockeying, etc."[27] A critic writing an account of the life about this particular spring in 1805 was specific in pointing out the evil practices which he found there, and one of them was horse racing.[28]

Gathered about the western springs and taverns were generals, colonels and majors who found nothing more entertaining than heated discussions of pedigrees, time, and methods of riding horses to the best advantage. There were pompous Tennesseans who loudly proclaimed the glories of such horses as Medley who stood stud in their state for more than twenty years,[29] or of Angora, Lucretia, Betsey Malone and Hibernia. Kentuckians were loud in their praise of such worthy sires as Lamp Lighter, Dare Devil, Gray Squirrel, Woodpecker, Buck Elk, Peacemaker, Muckle John, Eclipse, Rodolph and Buzzard.[30] This eternal boasting about the prowess of the horses of the two states led to a feud between their breeders. There was nothing more humiliating to a Kentuckian than to have his horse defeated by a lowly Tennessee-bred competitor, but this often happened. There was likewise a feud between Kentucky and Ohio breeders.

General Andrew Jackson of Tennessee made it hot for Kentuckians—even for the get of Clay's Buzzard—and his famous horses won for his Hermitage stud many a fine piece of plate at the Tennessee-Kentucky meets. By 1836 the Kentuckians were decidedly the underdogs in their "hoss feuding" with Tennessee. The year before they were badly humiliated when three Tennesseans showed their heels to slower Kentucky competitors in three out of four races run at the Oakland course, Louisville. Lucretia, Betsey Malone and Hibernia had lifted the silver trophies from a strong Kentucky field in clear decisions. Competition was strong, and sporting papers carried challenges from the horsemen from both sides of the Cumberland River. The Kentucky owner of Rodolph placed him at the mercy of the world, and promised to meet all comers with a none too subtle hint that he hoped the acceptance would come from Tennessee. A Tennessee breeder accepted the extravagant challenge and pledged himself to send his fast Angora into the field to settle the issue of the states. These horses were matched to run a four-heat race over a four-mile course. Betting was heavy, and the crowd was boisterous and, perhaps, in the words of Charles Murray or James Hall, oaths were uttered in such deliberate and determinate tone as to induce the belief that the speaker really wished the fulfillment of the curses which they imprecated. Bantering of a good-natured sort took place between the spectators on both sides. When the drum tapped and the two horses were turned loose down the stretch, Tennessee partisans shouted, "Where are you Kentuck?" "She is nowhere," yelled a by-stander, "except where she always was and ever will be—behind Tennessee!" "Never mind," challenged a red horse, "If Tennessee beats Ol' Kentucky I'll bet two to one that the mare's tail drops off at the judges' stand." Rodolph redeemed the honor of Old Kentucky, and in three heats he defeated without question the "flying" Angora of Tennessee.[31]

At a Bath County, Kentucky, course near the Olympia Springs a match was held between a Kentucky filly and a long-legged Ohio gelding. The jockey riding the filly was a farm boy who had drifted down to the path on Saturday afternoon to see what all the excitement was about. When he came on the ground the Kentucky challenger asked him to ride his horse for him in the contest. Backers of the gelding had most of the money, and from all appearances, most of the horsepower. The gelding was a large fine animal that could outstep the pony at any time. It was agreed that the horses should go 440 yards. This was a long run for a light horse, and even the jockey was on the verge of betting a small amount on the challenging horse when his employers pulled him aside to give him instructions, and to "fix" him for his ride. The boy's pants were stripped off, and his shirt-tail was fastened securely between his legs. At the start the Buck-eye contestant jumped fifty feet in the lead, at the turn they were even, and as they returned toward the stand the gelding's rider let his reins out for him to sail home easily ahead of the pony, but at this instant the trouserless jockey arose from his seat and allowed his shirttail to balloon in the gelding's face. This was the finish of the boys from over the Ohio. Their entrant became so frightened at the sudden flirtation of cloth in the air before him that he took to the woods in a run-away. The race, judged by Kentuckians, was declared fair, and one of the referees said that if the Ohioans wished to fight it out "he was in for two chances."[32]

As the West became more developed there were fewer Saturday afternoon quarter races between plow horses and plowboy riders. State and town laws became stricter in forbidding quarter matches on public thoroughfares. Horse racing soon became an organized sport, the first in the West, and it was confined after this to association tracks. Likewise, the breeding of thoroughbred horses from imported stallions took the sport financially out of the reach of the average individual who had indulged in racing in an earlier period. Nevertheless this element was not left without a competitive interest. Cockfighting, or cocking, was the poor man's substitute for the costlier sports. He satisfied his desires to be a gentleman by breeding a less expensive animal and sending it into battle with a neighbor's entry. The story of cockfighting in the frontier is not a written one. Perhaps many of the cages of chickens which were floated into the western country aboard flatboats, or were hauled overland on packhorses were of the same breed. Cocking is one of the oldest sports of man, and it was practiced freely on the frontier. Occasionally preachers railed out at members of their congregations who paid more attention to the sharpness of gaff points than the scriptures. This was a sport which was never brought out into the open because of a fear of criticism. Cockfighting, unlike quarter racing, was almost certain to result in the death of one or both of the contestants.

Most of the cockfighting was done under cover of darkness. Pits were located in secluded spots, and only the select were admitted to the ring. Under the blaze of torches many a cock rammed a gaff home to mortally wound an antagonist, and his owner slipped him under a coat and sneaked off home half-ashamed of his bloody victory.

Patrons of the race courses also divided their interest between hunting and cocking. Sportsmen writing in the *Spirit of the Times* and the *American Turf Register and Sporting Magazine* make frequent mention of these side interests. None of them were quite so open in their treatments of cockfighting, however, as was that Hoosier who landed his flatboat in the neighborhood of a small Mississippi River town in Louisiana. Before he could get ashore "a chap with a face whiskered up like a prairie dog" challenged him to fight one of his cocks against a native specimen. The Hoosier agreed and put up a nice cash stake. While he had his back turned arranging for the contest, the whiskered blackleg "doctored" his bird, and when the cocks were pitted the Hoosier's rooster ducked his head and ran into the weeds to vomit. This was too much for the Indiana backwoodsman and he called on a lawyer to help recover his money. In the squire's office there were rows of lawbooks, and the boatman was sure that in at least one of them there would be a statute regulating cockfighting. The lawyer heard his story through and refused to take his case. This was too much for the Hoosier to comprehend. He questioned the lawyer as to whether "he was a sure enough squire?" When he was assured that he was conversing with a learned and real limb of the law, the Hoosier boatman requested him to read aloud the laws of Louisiana on cockfighting. He was informed that out of all the books on the shelf there was not a single law relating to the bloody business of fighting cocks. Never before had the Hoosier seen such an obstinate squire. He clapped his hat on his head and strode out of the office muttering "that a squire that did not know the laws of cockfighting, in his opinion, was distinctly a damned fool."[33]

Cockfighting still persists in the West under the cover of darkness, and in tobacco and cattle barns. But "quarter hosses" no longer wade through mud up to their knees from Frankfort to Lexington and run races the same afternoon carrying two hundred pound jockeys. Nor do the fine-bred descendants of the hardy old giants of the early nineteenth century tax their muscles and wind on four-mile tracks in three and four-heat races. The famous stud Botherem, owned by the boasting Colonel Searcy, must have been among the last of the old rough-and-ready-pioneer quarter horses. Botherem had galloped home ahead of many a fast competitor to bestow honor and shiny plate upon his owner and master Colonel Searcy. But like the Colonel the time came when Botherem was not so young as he once was, and the wind and limb of the faithful stallion failed him. Colonel

Searcy was unable to understand, however, that Botherem's turf days were over, and that he should be given a task no more arduous than switching flies. Failing to understand this, he entered the veteran of many a lucky race in a mile run against a field of young horses. When the tape was dropped, and the field got away Botherem was behind, at the half post he had fallen considerably behind, and at the three-quarter mark he was even cleared of his competitors' dust. Nevertheless the Searcy colors had always triumphed when they were tied to Botherem's saddle, and the Colonel kept yelling, "Hurrah for Botherem! Hurrah for Botherem!" Realizing at last that he could no longer pretend that his horse would finish in the money, Colonel Searcy began shouting, "Rise, my hell-roaring Botherem! Yonder he comes, drivin' em all before him!"[34]

## CHAPTER XII

## *KEARDS*

FRONTIERSMEN were gamblers, whether at cards, dice, A. B. C., E. O. tables, or just living. Every time they passed beyond the shadows of their dwellings they ran a good chance of losing their stakes and their lives. Taking chances became second nature with immigrants, and when they moved westward they brought with them not only useful fruit and grain seeds for their fields, but likewise a plentiful supply of seeds of vice. Loo, brag, old sledge, all fours, whist, poker and dice diverted troubled minds from disturbing business at hand. Historians have pointed many times to the fact that these immigrants made the first civilizing advances in the West. In Kentucky the beginnings of social adjustment were made.

A discreet Kentucky legislature, of which Henry Clay was a member, held its collective tongue-in-cheek and in 1804 placed upon the statute books "An Act effectually to suppress the practice of gaming."[1] This was the legal precedent in the West for legislative frowning upon the vice of gambling. Westerners reacted in an interesting manner toward their "blue laws." The crafty hand of Henry Clay is clearly visible in the phraseology of the Kentucky law. This law applied only to the banking games such as E. O. and A. B. C. and, later, faro. At none of these was young Clay a master, but at cards he was the pride of the community. Moral forces which had campaigned for anti-gambling legislation were only half-satisfied in this clever law, because Clay and his fellow legislators had resorted to the coney-catching practice of dealing them hands in the language of western gamblers, "up from the lap," from "behind the knee," and by neglecting cards and dice. In later years a more profligate trick was played upon the moral forces of Arkansas when a dutiful general assembly unanimously enacted an anti-gambling law, and celebrated its successful passage on the following Sunday with a big crap-shooting holiday.[2]

At Lexington in Ol' Kentuck, Clay enjoyed his game of poker. At the close of a game one evening it was found that Clay had won $40,000 from John Bradford. The next day they met free from the excitement of the play, when Bradford asked Clay what he was going to do about the debt because the sale of his property would not pay half of it. Clay was quick to see the humor in the situation and said to Bradford, "Oh, give me your note for $500 and let the balance go." A few nights later Clay and Bradford were again engaged in a game when fickle fortune favored Bradford. Clay lost $60,000. Later when Clay met Bradford he asked what he intended doing, and Bradford said, "Oh, give me back that note which I gave you the other day for $500 and we will call it square."

Westerners frequented the mineral springs where they pitted their card-playing ability against all comers. At first they were forced to exercise their craftiness among themselves, but after the War of 1812 pompous cotton planters from the South migrated northward during the war months to dodge malaria, buy horses, mules, slaves and to marry off sons and daughters. They indulged their gambling instincts freely at every game known in the country. While wealthier Westerners and Southerners sat long hours at the tables, smoking "segars," drinking juleps and figuring out hands, their less fortunate brethren were indulging themselves at cards and dice on a smaller scale and among less pretentious surroundings.[3]

Up and down western rivers flat and keelboatmen gambled with snags, sandbars, currents and boat-wreckers. They played for relaxation at games of chance. Long hours of slowly floating southward were conducive to gambling, and the profitable produce market at New Orleans supplied money which was a necessity in successful games. All the way down the river, boatmen came in contact with professional gamblers. Especially was this true at Marietta, Wheeling, Cincinnati, Louisville,

Memphis, Natchez and New Orleans. These towns were breeding centers for "gentlemen" who lived by the art of frisking desirable cards up from their laps, or down from their sleeves.

Especially did Presbyterian, Baptist and Methodist ministers damn the practice of casting lots, yet they begged congregations to support lotteries to build church houses.[4] Hundreds of backwoods ministers railed against gambling practices and painted pictures of gambling hells, which, in their homely way, were superior allegory. Many of the early divines fetched sinners stumbling to the mourners' bench, and amid frame-racking sobs they begged forgiveness for debaucheries committed at the "table." Listeners shivered in their seats as charging emissaries of the Word conjured up pictures of voracious beasts stuffing their foul maws with cussers and gamblers. Starving and emaciated children administering to a dying mother, while a drunken and demoralized father shambled in from a game, was pictured as an extreme unction to soften sinners.

In experience meetings many of these transient fathers declared themselves as once having been addicts of the pasteboard and the table. James Finley blazed the way to salvation by describing to a wide-mouthed audience how he had narrowly escaped hell and financial distress by giving up gambling.[5] It was in Kentucky that the wrath of the Lord fell upon Finley, and he, like Balaam's ass, was turned aside and saved. So vivid were the moral tirades against the vice of gambling that it was soon associated with cockfighting, gander pulling, bearbaiting, quarter racing and gouging. The gentlemen of the table were often looked upon as a part of the banditti in general which infested the West. Frightening ministerial portraiture, ominous fist shaking, and fearful warnings, however, pulled few hardened frontier sons back from the brink of perdition. So long as western frontiersmen had to take chances with rugged environmental influences in the Ohio and Mississippi valleys, they continued to take chances on a turn of the cards or a roll of the dice.

True to evangelistic predictions, a wrathful Lord called down vengeance upon the West at 2:15 A.M. on December 16, 1811. He shook the Ohio and Mississippi regions like a ba'r dog would a cub. The surface of the earth moved in rolls, and houses and other structures tossed about like drunken flatboatmen. At Louisville, blasé gamblers were defiant; while the earth trembled as though in the throes of labor, they kept at their games until someone with a sense of propriety rushed in and said, "Gentlemen, how can you be engaged in this way when the world is so near its end?" The tables were finally deserted, and one of the gamblers philosophized, "What a pity that so beautiful a world should thus be destroyed!"[6] The reckless gamblers who stood in the streets of Louisville on the early morning of December 16, 1811, waiting for the world to fly to bits and send them flying into space, little knew that the steamboat which had drifted over the falls a few months before marked a new era in western gambling.

The western steamboat boosted gambling, both legitimate and illegitimate, to undreamed heights. Western taverns had been famous centers for gaming; in these were located tables and other facilities for every game then in vogue. Just as aristocrats and squatters transferred less urbane institutions over the mountains, tavern-keepers aped their coastal ancestors. Traveling through Virginia, Benjamin H. Latrobe found the tavern common rooms crowded with gamblers at all times. Isaac Weld saw drunken rowdies crowding into common rooms to play at loo, brag, whist, poker, faro, hazards and billiards. Travelers through the West sometimes remarked upon gambling in common rooms, but often it was such an ordinary thing that they failed to mention it. Perhaps a common room in which no gambling occurred would have elicited much more comment. Tavern-keepers posted requests that their patrons refrain from gambling in the bedrooms.[7] After 1817, the tavern common rooms gave way to the steamboat social rooms, and by 1820 the steamboat age was well advanced.

Steamboats plying western waters were constructed with a view to encouraging gaming. Social rooms were planned as the focal compartment of the boat. These halls were built, so said the owners, for general social intercourse, but few were used as such. Early travelers met long-fingered sharpers who had no visible means of support other than their crafty ability at coney-catching. Cards and banking games were favorites of the sharpers. Among the banking games were chuck-a-luck, *vingt-et-un* and faro. Strangers boarding steamboats with boxes under their arms were pestered to death by prospective clients who begged them to get out "their tools and set up."[8] Soon special terms came into existence to describe the various elements of the game: "gulls" or "coneys" were greenhorns who were enticed into games by the "cappers" or coney-catchers who played around the dealers and "throwers." Catching gulls and coneys was a fine art. The capper played green and got into the good graces of the green 'un by asking his advice, or by offering to split pots with him.

Once a gull was inveigled into "lighting" he was quickly cleaned of his cash by slick-tongued cheats who knew a whole category of tricks. Among these deceptive devices were "stock-ining," "hold-outs," "iteming-out," dealing "large hands," and "raising hands."[9] Gulls were often given good runs of cards from the bottom of the pile to break down their caution. Once green gamblers were in the game "whole-hog," the sharpers proceeded to pluck them of their fine feathering by tricky dealing, or by iteming-out their hands. A capper stood back from the tables and twirled out signals with a walking cane, blew significant smoke-rings, or "fingered" signals. If the green ones were docile, dealers played them along, winning and losing, so that their interest reached the highest peak near a wood-yard. Tricky dealers then dealt "heavy hands" which caused gulls to stake their piles, and of course the dealers raised bigger hands and stripped their victims in quick order and left the boats.[10]

Hundreds of gentlemen of chance traveled on the western waters. There were such cultured practitioners as thimble-riggers, dice-coggers, trigger-wheel players, strop-players, and three-card monte-throwers. No gull ever indulged in one of these games without getting his down plucked good and plenty. The gods, and they were evil ones, were against him because every device and card was controlled by the operators.

Tricky gamblers patronized that fine craftsman, Monsieur E. M. Grandine, 41 Liberty Street, New York, who advertised, with evident vanity, among a selected clientele that he could supply "Advantage and Marked-Back Playing Cards, by which you can tell the size and suit, by the Back as well as the Face." Monsieur Grandine assured prospective purchasers that these cards "are an exact imitation of the fair Playing Cards in use, and are adapted for bluff or poker, Seven-Up, Forty-Five, Euchre, Cribbage, Vingt-et-Un, or Twenty-One, Loo, and all other games of cards, where knowing just what your opponent holds in his hand would enable to win. Square and marked cards cut to order for Stocking Hands, for every game. Also Faro Boxes, Lay-Outs, and Tools. Roulette-Wheels, Keno-Sets, Ivory Goods, Rouge-et-noir or Red and Black, Roulette, Feather and Anchor, Over and Under Seven, Eight and Ten Dice, and Faro Cloths, and every variety of sporting Implements and Materials."

This proud manufacturer likewise had for sale superior Sleeve Machines, for holding out, or playing extra cards, "the most perfect piece of mechanism ever invented for this purpose. This article works in the coat sleeve noiselessly, admits of holding the hands in the most natural manner, requires no false movements, and weighs about *four ounces*." Right and left snap roulette wheels, the "breast-works," or "vest hold-outs" and the "bug," a contrivance for playing extra cards, were declared to be of the finest quality, and made by reliable and skilled workmen.[11]

Three-card monte throwing became generally popular in 1837. Few games attracted coneys and gulls as did this one. This was a perfect game for throwers, cappers and strippers to work. Three walnut hulls or thimbles and a pea, or three cards with different faces were sufficient equipment. Dealers or throwers were always careful to let their victims see the faces of the cards or the position of the pea, and by the simple trick of jostling the gull, or by tapping him on the shoulder, the capper was able to divert his attention for a moment and the position of the card or pea was changed.[12]

Outstanding of the sharpers traveling through the western country were George Devol, Price McGrath, Elijah Skaggs, the "preaching faro player," and John Morris. George Devol and John Morris have left their memoirs, and from these a fairly complete story of frontier gambling can be reconstructed. Elijah Skaggs was a gentleman of action and shrewdness if not of breeding and upbringing. He was born in western Kentucky when that region was the haunt of the ba'r and painter. His elementary training consisted of intensive study in such pleasing diversions as card playing, running quarter horses, cockfighting, and butchering neighbors. At twenty, young Skaggs deserted the plow handles for faro tools, and the butternut for broadcloth. Price McGrath, a Woodford County, Kentucky, boy, left a tailor's shop and a tedious task of sewing and ripping to become a past master at games of chance in any form.[13] Later in life he became owner and master of the famous McGrathiana Stud at Lexington. Here he entertained regiments of Kentucky Colonels. He fed them, liquored them, and then relieved them of spare cash. McGrathiana thoroughbreds won large purses for the poor tailor boy, and honor for the stud.

Wherever two people, excluding too-conscientious preachers, deacons and women, were assembled in the West, prospects for gambling were good. The table, cards and dice boards were frequent topics of conversation, and western figures of speech were highly flavored with terms which came from "fighting the tiger," or other forms of gambling. The Ohio and Mississippi Rivers with their many tributaries and port towns were veritable channels for keard-slickers, who "euchred" thousands of clumsy fool farmers and river tradesmen out of hard-earned cash. In many cases gamblers were in cahoots with steamboat captains, and passengers were stripped by trickery and could get no assistance from the officers of the boat. When situations became too stormy, and dirkings and shootings were threatened, captains pulled their craft into woodyards so gamblers could escape and await the coming of another boat and another flock of gulls. When captains were on the level, as they were in most cases, and a tricky gambler was caught redhanded, the boat was pulled into the bank at the boggiest point and the culprit landed bag and baggage. In the 1830's the captain of the boat *Sea Serpent* dumped a dignified trickster who called himself Major Montgomery up to his waist in the muck and mire of a canebreak. Major Montgomery had made a slight social blunder when he dropped a significant card out of his coat sleeve in a sociable game. The Major had already garnered a large sum of collateral, and this he had to re-distribute. The captain ordered the yawl lowered, and a soot-stained fireman crammed the long-tailed and bewhiskered blackleg into it amid oaths that made even the rugged captain blush. When the Major was safely deposited amid the cane, the crawfish and the moccasins, the fireman bantered him with, "I say, Mr. Jack-of-Knaves, looks rather wolfy in these parts." "Shut your black mouth, you scoundrel," replied the Major. "I say, stranger," continued the fireman with provoking good humor, "would you swap them buffalo robes on your cheeks for a pair of coonskins?" The fireman left the "beached" old reprobate with the parting shot: "Halloo! my hearty, when you want to be rowed up Salt River again just tip me the wink; and remember Mr. King-of-Clubs, don't holler till you get out of the woods, or you'll frighten all the varmints."[14]

Moral forces in many of the western states became more militant in their warfare on amusements. They forced legislation through general assemblies which attempted to close gaming houses of all sorts. In Kentucky the legislature passed a law in 1831 which outlawed billiard and pool houses.[15] This crushing blow put the boys out on the street and considerably at the mercy of their wits for entertainments. At Louisville the smart gamesters devised ways and means of circumventing a law which was specific in its application to the game of billiards, and which forbade the use of pockets in any game. By the early 'forties the needs for amusement in the Falls City were served. Pockets were legally eliminated but an ingenious dodger of the statutory moral taboos of the sovereign state of Kentucky ripped off the cloth at the pocket positions and widened the table to the "reg'lar" width. A beautiful silver peg was driven down in the center, and billiard rules of play were adopted.

With this new and "moral" equipment the idle billiardmen of the Falls City now enjoyed a satisfactory substitute for the outlawed pocket iniquity. No one, however, was so careless as to give the deception away by calling the game pool or billiards—it was *Kentucky*.[16] When Phineas Taylor Barnum brought his Swedish nightingale to America, the Kentucky gentlemen, like chivalrous harness-makers, furniture-designers and other skilled artisans, honored the "little woman" by changing the name of *Kentucky* to *Jennie Lind*. A correspondent, perhaps George D. Prentice, to the New York *Spirit of the Times* said, "As the matter now stands you can go into three or four saloons in town, enjoy yourself for an hour or two, and think, according to your previous education, you are playing billiards, when bless your innocent eyes, you are really playing 'Jennie Lind.' Where's Barnum? There is nothing to undeceive you except a little pin about as long and as thick as your finger, setting in a solitary state down at the foot of the table, and strangely reminding you of Pompey's pillar in reduced circumstances."

Occasionally innocent foreign visitors stumbled into western gambling centers, or into gaming halls such as billiard and pool parlors, and they were scalped before they got out. Many travelers' journals refer to the prevalence of gambling. Even Maria Wakefield, a gentle visitor, goes into a lengthy tirade against the vice. She cautions young women of the West against marrying men who gamble, for, said she, they could never be happy.

No traveler found himself so thoroughly taken in, however,

as a Cockney who was on his way to the Mississippi Valley. This verdant Britisher took matters a bit too literally and allowed himself to be shown through a "menagerie" which lacked the ordinary collection of ferocious wild beasts. After a confusing conversation with the "keeper" of the menagerie the Englishman asked what animals were kept in this museum of animal life. The gambler replied that because of certain legal restrictions he was limited to the "Crock, a Guyascutus, and a tiger." These were indeed strange animals, except, possibly the tiger, and the Englishman said they must be purely American for he had never "read of them, either in Cuvier, Botta, or Goldsmith. But of the tiger I have seen some noble specimens."

There was some difference, however, between the royal Bengal tiger, and the popular beast of the frontier. The green visitor was invited to fight the native American animal a few rounds that evening after dark. That night there was spread before the zoological dilettant the strangest assortment of bloodless "animals" he had ever beheld. For fun he went a few rounds with the Ohio Valley striper, and in a short time the Cockney was three hundred dollars ahead of the game and was accepting numerous drinks of brandy on the menagerie. His battling the tiger, however, cost the reckless Briton five hundred pounds and the severest headache of a lifetime. He observed that "if any man ever gets me to henter an *American menagerie* where the hanimals have such queer names, and a look at them cost such a lot of money, may 'ell fly away with me—that's hall."[17]

Many an American son lost equally as much as the English traveler did on the tiger. He was a ferocious beast which ate up many a year's work between Pittsburgh and New Orleans. The little "black box" and its tools were heartless instruments of amusement. They seemed never to have had any scruples about their failure to pay off. It was the chance taking and animate fool whose head ached the next day, not the tiger's.

On the frontier, taverns, courthouse grounds, stagecoach

waiting rooms, steamboats, and even church grounds, were never free of gambling. Wherever there was a general assembly of people there were gamblers—innocent and otherwise. Nevertheless this disobedience to the scriptures was one of the frontier's earliest sins, and it enjoyed tremendously its continuous sinning.

The gambler and his victims, having, perhaps, guilty consciences, were anxious to tell their stories. Not only have Morris and Devol left splendid accounts of their activities, but the garden-variety greenhorn gamblers have contributed many fine yarns about how they were skinned by the smart boys who enticed them to light among their traps.

Three-card monte, or guessing which walnut hull covered a pea, was the most treacherous of frontier games of chance. Strangely enough these base scoundrels, the three-card monte players, found gulls to pick at every steamboat landing or around every courthouse. The editor of the New Orleans *Picayune* has left a splendid account of how these blacklegs worked their rackets on innocent upriver boatmen and farmers.

## A Stronger Game Than Thimbles

Some time since a Kentuckian arrived at Natchez with a boatload of produce. Having deposed his "plunder" and received his pay, he went from the river up to one of the banks to get his bills converted into specie. The amount, some four or five hundred dollars he tied up in an old red bandana handkerchief, and started back for the river. His movements were closely watched, by a practical professor of the Thimble Rigg, who, considering that the Kentuckian did not understand the game, thought him a fair subject. He was grievously mistaken in the end, however, as the sequel will show. Walking up alongside of the flatboatman with much familiarity he accosted him with:

"How are you stranger? How do you come on?"

"Pretty fair, thank you, how do you rise?"

"About the same. You have lately come down I take it."

"Yes, a few days since."

"Have you been over the city much—seen the curiosities about town?"

"No, I hain't much time to spare—want to get back."

"Well, you ought to look around a little. S'posing you take a short walk with me out in this direction," pointing to a part of the river bank where there were no houses. "Come, I will show you some of the curiosities with pleasure."

Anxious to see what the fellow was up to, the Kentuckian, a shrewd sensible man, consented to accompany his new acquaintance. They soon came to a lonely and unfrequented part of the bluff overlooking the river. Here the rascal recommended a halt, and a set-down was agreed to. After some commonplace conversation, he hauled out a set of thimbles and commenced sliding them backward and forward, lifting them, and displaying the little ball.

"This is a great game," said the gambler.

"It looks interesting," returned the Kentuckian.

"I don't exactly see into it," continued the Kaintuck, who all the time was as well up to it as the other.

"It's very interesting after you once get the hang of it," said the rascal.

"I should think so, very."

"S'posing we strike up a small game just to pass away the time?" inquired the stranger.

"I have no particular objections," rejoined the Salt River man.

Things were now in a fair way, and the greedy thimble player looked with an eager eye toward the handkerchief of Mexican castings before him, shortly, as he thought, to become his own. He calculated on baiting his victim a little, letting him win once or twice in order to make the grand haul he contemplated more sure. Having arranged his thimbles, he said, "Now, what'll you bet you can tell which the ball is under?"

"I'll bet you ten dollars it's under the middle one."

The money was put up, the thimble raised, and the Kentuckian won of course. The gambler appeared vexed at his loss, but soon had everything arranged for another stake.

"What will you go this time?" said the fellow.

"I'll go twenty this pop," returned the Kaintuck.

The thimble was raised and with the same success. The gambler cursed his luck, said fate was against him, that he never handled the things so clumsily in his life, and intimated that a child might beat him. He was still willing, however, to "go it again," and soon had everything fixed for a last trial.

"How much you bet this time?" said he to the Kentuckian.

"I'll go the entire pile and quit," returned the Kaintuck.

"What! the whole of it?" said the greedy knight of the thimbles, his eyes sparkling with delight in anticipation of so much booty.

"Every cent in the pile," said the Kentuckian coolly. "I go the whole pile or nothing."

"Well, I haven't got that much money about me," retorted the gambler, "but there's my watch—that's worth so much"—at the same time putting it in among the money which was now spread open in the handkerchief. "There's a diamond breastpin—that's worth so much"—putting that in also. In this way, and by staking what money he had he soon had an amount which the Kentuckian considered a fair stake.

The gambler now commenced arranging his tools with greater care than usual, while the Kentuckian set to work at the different corners of the handkerchief, lifting them up apparently to get all the money and valuables in the center. He was evidently bent upon playing a stronger game than the gambler, but one which the latter never saw until it was too late. One by one the gambler placed his thimbles, and one by one the Kentuckian gathered each of the four corners of the bandana in his hand. Before him was a high and very steep bluff, almost perpendicular—one which no one could ascend and one which not a soul but a Kentuckian would dare go down. He well knew that the gambler would win this time, and he also knew that he would never dare follow him in a tumble down the bluff.

"All fixed?" said the gambler.

"All fixed," said the Kentuckian as by a sudden twist he wound the corners round his wrist, gathered himself up, and rolled off the precipice like a turtle off a log, taking his own money besides the watch, breast-pin and money of the gambler. The latter was thunderstruck, and gazed at his victim, who was rumbling and tumbling down the precipice, with the same feelings of the British troopers when they saw old General Putnam riding down the stone steps at Cow Neck. Safe and sound, under the hill, the Kentuckian landed, jumped upon his feet in an instant, and sang out to the disappointed gambler, who still stood on the high bluff some hundred feet above him:

"How are you now? Sorry to leave you in this unceremonious way; but business must be attended to. When you want to get up another game of thimbles, and run your rigs upon a chap that has slept all his days on the Mississippi, just drop on board my boat. You'll find me at home."

This was the last he ever heard of the thimble player. The rascal well knew that he could get nothing on board the flat-boat except a lynching, and wisely kept away.[18]

A writer known as "A. L." tells an ingenious story of how a Kentuckian "came it over" a shifty Frenchman with large velvet sleeves.

### A New Dodge in Playing Poker

A long-legged, saturnine-looking Kentuckian was playing poker with an individual who seemed to be an odd combination of jew-face and creole manners, and moreover, had the peculiar pronunciation of some of his vowels that distinguishes many citizens of New Orleans. He was dressed in a large loose brown sack, with velvet cuffs, turned up somewhere in the neighborhood of a quarter of a yard. Though the two fellows was [sic] as different as could be, it seemed to be a toss-up which was the greatest rogue, and accordingly, the game seemed to run nearly equal. If anything, it was rather against the Kentuckian, and the players watched the game for a long time in silence.

"Hot day!" observed he of the cuffs, at last, raising his eyes to his opponent's and scanning them reflectively.

"Well, stranger, that's a fact; it's hot as hell in dog days. Let's liquor. *I never begin to play till I get a drop of something.* Hallo, steward, a couple of brandies?"

The brandies were brought, and as the other turned to receive his the Kentuckian moved the candle a little, so dexterously as not to be perceived. He put his glass to his mouth and drained it at once.

"Strong as a nigger's sweat!" said he. As he spoke he brought his glass down with force enough to drive the few remaining drops up in the air and down again on the table.

The game now re-commenced in very different style: when the cards proved in favor of the Kentuckian he was always sure to have had a heavy bet placed on them, but when against him he had a mere nothing staked. This went on until the New Orleans man seemed to have his eyes sharpened by his losses, and he noticed that the Kentuckian did his dealing in rather an odd position—elbows squared and holding the cards lightly by their sides. Soon after he observed his eyes occasionally fixed on a drop of the brandy that lay directly before him, and now the mystery was explained. As he dealt *he had seen each card reflected in the drop!*

"Sir-r-r!" said the velvet cuffs, rising with immense dignity. I'd have you know that I am a man of honor, Sir, and never deal with those who take unfair advantages!"

"Keep cool, stranger!" answered the Kentuckian, sweeping the last stake into his pocket, "keep cool! Your 'honor' won't stop you making it up out of somebody that's greener than yourself, and the next time that anybody tells you he 'never begins to play till he gets a drop of something,' you'll know what he means."[19]

Perhaps no traveler on the Mississippi River or through the West saw more of the other side of life than did Sol Smith. "Old Sol" was a philosophical actor who could hold a hand in any company. On one occasion he allowed himself to be roped into a tricky game, and by rare good fortune he was saved from his sharp-playing companion.

## A Friendly Game of Poker

On the evening of our second day out from New Orleans I found myself seated at a card table with three of my fellow passengers, playing at the interesting game of poker. Card playing was a very common amusement then (1835), and it was not unusual to see a half-dozen tables occupied at the same time in the gentlemen's cabin of a Mississippi boat. I had sat down at the game for *amusement,* but on rising at ten o'clock I found my amusement had cost me sixty dollars! "This won't do at all," said I, thinking aloud; "I must try it again tomorrow." "Of course you must," replied one of the poker players, who happened to be an old acquaintance of mine from Montgomery, Alabama, where he had been a jailer for several years, and where he was considered a very respectable citizen. "You must not give it up so," he continued, following me out on the guard; *"tomorrow you'll get even."* I entered into conversation with my old acquaintance, whose name was Hubbell or Hubbard, I don't remember which—we'll call him Hubbard—and he advised me by all means to try another sitting on the morrow. I suggested to him that a slight suspicion had crossed my mind that some of our card party might possibly be blacklegs—in other words—*gamblers.* He answered that the same thought had struck *him* at one time, but he had come to the conclusion that all had been fair. Before leaving me, my quondam friend told me that *he* had become a sporting man— he felt it his duty to inform me of it—but he assured me, upon his honor(!), he would not see me wronged. *Of course* I believed him, and it was agreed that we should try our luck again.

Next morning, soon as breakfast things had been cleared away, I found Hubbard and a *friend of his* waiting for me at one of the card tables, and I took my seat with the hope of *getting even*—a hope which has led many a man into irretrievable ruin. I felt confident of winning back my losings overnight, and my playmates gave me every encouragement that I should be successful. At it we went, playing with varying luck for about two hours. At about eleven o'clock Hubbard's friend left us for a few minutes to "get a drink," and the jailer and myself were left playing singlehanded. When the third man left, we were using the "small cards," as they are called—that is, *sixes* and under; but Hubbard immediately proposed that we should take the "large cards" (tens and over), which I agreed to, as a matter of course. One thing I here observed— my friend, the jailer, dealt the cards *without* shuffling. This made me resolve to watch him closely. Taking up my cards, I was agreeably surprised to find I had an excellent hand. "Now," thinks I to myself, "now is the time, if ever, to get even; if my adversary only happens to have a decent hand, I shall do well enough."

I commenced the game by bragging a dollar. My adversary went the dollar, and five better. I went that and ten. He immediately put up the ten, and laid down a twenty, keeping his pocketbook out, as much as to say, "I am ready to go any thing you choose to bet." After a moment's reflection (all acting), I said, "I go that—and fifty." "All right," replied the jailer, "there it is; I go that and a hundred!" I here looked at my cards again, and affected to have great doubt whether I should go the hundred. "Take back your last bet," I urged; "it is too much for either of us to lose: I begin to think I have been rash; take it back, and let us show our hands for the money already down." "No," said Hubbard; "if you mean sporting, put up your hundred, or back out and give me the money." "Can't do that," I replied; "I don't come from a backing-out country; I must have a showing for the money that's down—so there's the hundred; and, as my pocketbook's out, and my hand's in, there's another C." This new bet seemed to please my friend Hubbard mightily. He answered it without a moment's pause, and went to a hundred more! I now requested my opponent to permit me to show my cards to some of the by-standers, who were crowding around the table in great numbers to see the fun, all considering me most undoubtedly "picked up." Hubbard would not agree that I should show my hand to, or take advice from, anyone. "Play your cards," said he, reaching over, and gently compelling me to lay my cards on the table before me. "Then," said I, "you tell me if *three aces* and two *other cards* can be beat?" "Oh yes," he replied, smiling with a self-satisfied air, and using the spitbox, "they *can* be beat, certainly, but not easy." *"Not easy,* I think myself," replied I; "therefore, inasmuch as I believe you are trying to bluff me off, I go two hundred." "You do!" "Yes, I *do;* there's the money." "Anything better?" inquired my adversary, insinuatingly, and leaning over to make use of the spitbox again, all the time keeping his gray eyes fixed upon my countenance. "Why yes," I answered, "since you've got me excited, I will go something better—I go two hundred better than you." Looking me steadily in the face, he said, "Well, you're a bold fellow, anyhow, for a novice: *it takes all I've got,* by hokey, but I got it; and, if you'll let me *bet on a credit,* I should like to go back at you." (Spitbox.) Feeling confident of winning, I consented that he *might* go what he liked, on a credit, provided I should be allowed the same privilege. "Well, then," said Hubbard, a little spitefully, "I go you five hundred better—on a credit." (Spitbox again.) "The devil you do!" exclaimed I; "this looks like gambling; but, since we're in for it so deeply, I go you five hundred better on a credit." At this stage of the game the third hand returned, and seeing at a glance how matters stood, requested to look at Hubbard's cards. "No, *sir,"* interposed I, *"you must play your own cards,"* at the same time motioning my opponent to lay down *his* cards as I had laid down mine. The carpet began to suffer about this time—the spitbox was disregarded. The excitement among the passengers was great, and my ears received many a whisper that "I was licked." Hubbard took a long earnest look into my eyes, and said slowly but confidently, *"I got it—and—call you."* "I suppose I'm beat," said I (hypocrite that I was! I *didn't* suppose anything of the kind); "but turn over your papers and let us see what you've got." With one hand he gracefully turned over *four kings* and a jack, and with the other tremblingly "raked down" the pile of bank notes, gold and silver, while a groan burst out from the spectators, who all seemed to regret my bad luck. "You are lucky as a jailer," I remarked, as my friend began to smooth down the V's, X's, L's and C's. "By-the-by," he inquired, again resorting to the spitbox, and looking over patronizingly at me, "I forgot to ask what *you* had." "Well," I replied, calmly, "I think you *might* as well see my cards." "Ha! ha!—oh, I reckon you're beat, my friend," he answered; "but let's see your hand at all events." "Here are the documents," replied I; "there's *my* hand!" and I turned over my cards one by one: "there's an *ace*—and there's another—and there's another!" "A pretty good hand, young man," remarked Hubbard—"three aces! What *else* have you?" "What *else?* What else? Why, here's a *queen."* "And what *else,"* asked everybody. *"Another ace!" —Four aces!!!*

I looked over the table and discovered the face of my lately elated *friend* had lost all color; the tobacco juice was running out the corners of his mouth; the V's, X's and C's were dropped and amazement and stupefaction were strongly imprinted on his features. A shout went up from the bystanders, and all hands were invited to take champagne at my expense.

It is scarcely necessary to say that the money *bet on a credit* was never paid, nor was it *expected* to be paid. My friend Hubbard recollected he had urgent business at Vicksburg, and *left the boat.* It so *happened* that the *stranger* who had played with us also disembarked at the same burg, where they met with a singular accident, being promiscously hung, a few days afterward, by a mob! Hubbard died *game,* and *spat* upon the excited populace.

About a month after the adventure above related, I met a gentleman in Cincinnati whom I instantly recognized as one of my fellow passengers on the *Warren*. After inquiring the state of each other's health, he asked me if I had played any at the game of poker lately. "Not since the great game you witnessed on board the *Warren*," I replied. "Do not play any more," said he, assuming a serious air; "you are liable to be fleeced. I saw you were in the hands of swindlers," he continued, "and, when one of the fellows left the table, I noticed that he laid a pack of cards *he had been* shuffling near your adversary's elbow. As an experiment (passing by at the moment), *I took the top card from* the pack and shoved it under the bottom, by which means *you* got the four aces intended for his partner, while he got the four kings intended for *you;* and thus the sporting gentlemen were caught in their own trap!"

*Moral*— Poker is decidedly a dangerous game to play at, particularly with strangers; but when you find yourself in possession of *four aces, go it with a perfect rush.*[20]

## CHAPTER XIII

## *FIDDLIN'*

"RIGHT-HAND man of the Devil was a fiddler," said the frontier preachers. The Reverend John Taylor, a shepherd of the regular Baptist faith, moved out to Kentucky from Virginia, and here he found that Moses Scott "a small man of stature" had preceded him and was a captain in the ranks of Diabolus. Brother Scott had shed his cloak of moral scruples and godliness which he had worn back in the Old Dominion as a communicant of the Presbyterian faith. He now labored in the new country with marked faithfulness for the cause of Beelzebub. Scott was known throughout his section of the West as a great fiddler, and was "fond of all amusements connected with that practice. It may generally be taken for granted," said Brother Taylor, "that . . . this Scott gloried in his native strength of intellect, and connected with his wit, capacitated him to make wickedness acceptable to men." He was indeed a sore trial to the Baptist brethren. The cause of the gospel made little headway so long as the profane Scott was able to "saw out" tunes, and more than once he had turned a Baptist "night meeting" into a rip-roaring dance-party. Even conversion to the faith did no good, because as soon as a gathering took place in the neighborhood, the Devil ordered his "airthly" captain to the front, and the preachers were left without hearers. Time and again this great fiddler led the "good" people from the altar, but Satan was not to succeed forever. By providential intercession, the abominable instrument of temptation, along with its owner's house perished in flames.[1]

On the frontier where there were such numerous dignitaries as majors, colonels, doctors, preachers, professors, tavern-keepers, judges, sheriffs and governors, none ranked higher in popular affection than the fiddlers. From the beginning of the first settlement in the western wilderness, the fiddle took its place as an instrument necessary for entertainment. At the falls of the Ohio, those who remained behind after the Clark expedition had departed for Kaskaskia, relieved the monotony of long days and nights of waiting for news by dancing to the tune of the slave Cato's fiddle. These settlers had come from the valley of the Watauga, and Redstone in Pennsylvania. Their tastes ran decidedly to the vigorous reels which bore the label "Virginia." Before Christmas Day arrived extensive plans were made for a rampant breakdown, but Cato became overly enthusiastic and sawed all but one of his strings in two. He could not extract a tune from the remaining frazzled cord, and it seemed that Christmas would be a time of despair instead of rejoicing.

Fortunately relief came for the despondent victims of Cato's too vigorous rasping of his fiddle bridge. A musically inclined French fur trader landed at the foot of Corn Island, and he had with him a "violin." Also, this lone wayfarer brought with him additional strings. Cato entered into a secret bargain with the Gallic visitor by which he purchased a supply of strings at an exorbitant price measured in terms of 'coonskins.

The Frenchman stole a march on the dusky musician, however, and announced to the whites that he had a violin. This was as cheering news as if a runner had come bearing tidings that Clark had captured Vincennes. This joy was short-lived because the Latin violinist could not play "Virginia" music. He only knew how to play the polite minuet, the branle, and the pavan. These were strange dance tunes to the Americans, whose taste for music was more vigorous and could not be satisfied by the gentle French ballets. Time and again the clumsy-footed settlers tried to trip gracefully through the delicate steps and turns of the minuet or the branle only to fail. Soon the musical fur trader gave up in disgust.

Cato's moment had come. He had watched the unsatisfactory proceedings of the evening with grim delight. When his competitor had sacked his violin, Cato waltzed onto the floor with his battered old fiddle under his chin, and blasted out a rip-roaring "toe smasher" from Old Virginny. In a moment melancholic frontiersmen were swinging their gals through reels that were more uproarious than the mighty falls themselves.[2]

The West was not alone a land of "injun" fights, wars with Britishers, conspiracies with tricky Frenchmen, and disputes with stubborn Spaniards at New Orleans. There were lighter moments. "Yankee Doodle," in a letter to the editor of the *Spirit of the Times,* said that the frontiersmen showed their nobler points in their hunts, fish fries, barn dances, shuckings, raisings, housewarmings, infares, quiltings and in a thousand other pleasant ways.[3] Fiddles in the hands of masters of the heel-bruising "hoe digs" were as much instruments of construction in the West as were axes which girdled trees, paddles which propelled boats, and rifles which fetched down meat and redskins.

Sour-faced parsons of the "regular" and "missionary" Baptist faiths, dignified Presbyterian missionaries who wandered into the land along the Ohio with a feeling of Princetonian superiority, and cadaverous Methodist circuit riders who swarmed over the region like the locusts of ancient Egypt, made life difficult for accomplished fiddlers. Like the dour Brother Taylor, they concentrated their powers of prayer against these efficient "lieutenants" of hell. Even that hoary old servant of the faith, Peter Cartwright, waded into a frolic and laid prayerful hands upon the master mind. This bold defender of the Wesleyan cause in the western woods was invited by a buxom young lady to dance with her, but before he would consent to skip a step, he insisted on praying. He besought the Lord to shower fire and brimstone upon the fiddler, and he did it in such ominous tones, that the frightened fellow took to his heels and left his amusement-seeking companions in the midst of a "hellfire and damnation" Methodist experience meeting.[4]

Tunes such as "Leather Britches," "Barbara Allen," "Old Joe Clark," "Fisherman's Hornpipe," "Fair Eleanor," "Skip-to-my-

Lou," and hundreds of others—many of which have been forgotten—excited the boys and girls of the backwoods. There was no excuse like a square dance for a boy to do a little experimental hugging and kissing of the maidens in the neighborhood. Perhaps, by rare good fortune and malicious intent, a backwoods beau could confine his fondling activities to a single chosen one for a whole night of storming the puncheons.

It is a matter of distinct credit to frontier architects and builders that flimsy log cabins withstood the vociferous and acrobatic carousing which took place in them during a Saturday night of snorting. Buck-toothed, heavily-shod males dragged giggling straggly-haired and blushing gals around in a continuous whirl that would have made even the solar system dizzy. In such formations as were required in the reciprocal tunes of "Hog Drovers," "Old Sister Phoebe," and "Frog in the Middle Pond," dancers tripped in and out to meet their true lady loves, and to caress their willing lips.[5]

Fiddlers seldom hit the high mark as they did at weddings and infares. A wedding of any importance was the best excuse a frontier community ever had for dropping the lines and turning loose with all fours and forgetting its collective troubles. Fortunately several accounts of frontier nuptials have been preserved by participants in these joist-shivering debaucheries. Courtships were short, and directly to the point. The frontier swain had little or no time to go moon-gazing while holding the trembling hand of a reserved but interested female. Competition was fierce, and if he was to play a leading role in a wedding he had to speak up and get an answer with a minimum of lost motion.

If the wedding was a formal affair it was generally performed in the morning so as to get the necessary legal or religious formalities out of the way in time for dinner. There followed the "hitching," a wedding procession, and, often, a neck and neck horse race for the bottle. The winner was awarded a bottle of fresh spirits which he passed around "to supple up" the party for a gracious repast at the expense of the groom's family.

During the wedding dinner, which consisted of enough food to founder the state militia, the bottle was passed freely and frequently from one greasy mouth to another. By the time the last bone had been stripped, and the last of the cake eaten, the fiddler had taken his place. There began a breakdown dance which lasted as long as there were couples to bump into one another upon the pretense of dancing. Fiddlers were worked in relays, but it was only through frequent swiggings at the bottle that they were kept at their business throughout the night. Long before the cock crew for midnight, the bride and groom were stolen away from the party and deposited snugly beside each other in an attic room. Since there were no wedding trips, the gay wedding guests were considerate enough not to interfere with the couple's nuptial prerogatives.[6]

Celebrating marriages did not stop with the wedding night for there was the infare, a day or two after the marriage cere- mony, the house-raising, the quilting bee, and the house- warming or shivaree. Frontiersmen and their maidens needed little excuse for a frolic, and they were vigilant in seeking oppor- tunities for a night of free cavorting.[7] Fortescue Cuming saw Westerners returning from frolics everywhere he went. He said they used the term "frolic" to indicate a house-raising, feasting, dancing and weddings; and that all of these would come in the fall and winter seasons.[8]

Labor on the frontier was difficult. Woods were dense, timber was large and heavy, and in order to clear land in preparation for cultivation, tree trunks had to be gathered into piles and burned. No pioneer had sufficient man power to clear the ground and roll the logs by himself. He gave a clearing to which he invited his neighbors, and treated them to liquor, a feast, and at night to a dance. The owner of the land, in the process of being cleared, stood all the expense, and his reward of plenty of liquor, an assembling of the community's girls, and a good fiddler made his "working" a success.

Logrollings were well-attended by the men of the com- munity, and the women went along to help with dinner. In the field of labor, liquor was plentiful, songs, sometimes slightly bawdy, were sung to keep everybody in high spirits, and trials of strength took place almost with the lifting of every log. Many a strong-armed bully went to an early grave because he boasted that he could "pull" every man on the field down. These muscular backwoodsmen even asserted their manly strength by giving their weaker brethren the advantage of the long ends of the sticks.[9] Once the logs were rolled, and fields were opened to cultivation, settlers required their neighbors' services in other capacities.

House and barn-raisings were favorite types of workings. The English observer Wood said that one of "my son's neighbors had a threshing floor, and intended to add a barn to it. . . . It is built of solid logs, and covered with cleft boards. There were between thirty and forty people employed in raising the logs as they were uncommonly large, and all lifted up by 'main-strength' without aid from pullies."[10] Like logrollings, logs at barn-raisings could be lifted by main strength if there were sufficient alcoholic encouragement. One good citizen in Ohio ran into difficulty with his supply of liquor. He made the tactical blunder of taking Reverend James B. Finley into a shed room to show him a ten-gallon keg of choice Kentucky whisky. "I asked my host, who was said to be a pious man, what the keg contained?" said Finley, "and he replied that it was whisky, and that he had procured it for the purpose of raising a barn with it." Brother Finley lectured this backwoodsman at length on the evils of drinking liquor, and denounced the practice of enlivening frolics and workings by such means. Finley's parishioner became independent, and asserted "there is no law against using whisky, and I'll do as I please." This was flaunting a brazen challenge in the face of a determined circuit rider, and he asserted, "Very well, it is a poor rule that won't work both ways. If you do as you please, I will do as I please, and unless you take that keg of liquor out of this room I will leave this house, for I would rather be out in the woods than to sleep in a Methodist house with ten gallons of whisky for my roommate."[11]

Fortunately all of the frontiersmen did not frown upon ten-gallon kegs and they had few or no scruples against using liquor to raise a barn, a house, clear a field, or to enliven a dance with a neighbor's daughter. A house-raising on the frontier was a happy affair. To less selfish neighbors it meant a settlement of the country and the beginning of a better life. There was a careful division of labor, a fatigue party cleaned off the site of the house, and cut the logs, and four of the best axmen in the community stood at the corners to cut and fit the notches. A crew split puncheons, rived boards, mixed mortar for chinking and made shutters. By nightfall of the third day a new and "commodious" home was ready for occupation without an undue amount of exertion on the part of anyone. Of course, no new home which had come into existence as a result of communal labor could be occupied until it had been "warmed."

Housewarmings were generally more rampageous than were the cavortings on wedding nights. The floor of the "big room" was covered with a thick coat of bran which polished the puncheons, and by nine o'clock scuffing boots had worn the whole surface smooth and slick. Seldom did the merrymaking in a new house cease before the morning sun shone through the windows and doors.[12] Unless the fiddlers were kept merrily drunk in these celebrations they were "sawed out" in relays, and the party ended.

Once society was settled on the frontier, a large portion of it found excellent excuses for frolicking in corn shuckings, knittings, spinnings, pickings, serenades, barbecues and burgoo dinners. Thomas Nuttall was amused by a lively corn shucking which took place in Kentucky during November, 1818. He said "landing rather late, we took our lodging where there happened to be a corn husking, and were kept awake with idle merriment and riot until past midnight." Of course the Kentuckians would have to have more than a mere corn shucking to keep them entertained. They worked up their collective blood pressure by choosing sides and going into a "skull busting" political debate, as the Britisher observed "in a boisterous and illiberal style, but without coming to blows."[13]

A free and easy young woman who was not afraid to jostle the boys about could make a party. If this "knowing" young lady could drawl out in singsong fashion an endless procession of verses of such an old "toe snapper," as "William Taylor" whose claim to immortal fame rested upon the single courageous feat of "walking with his layde upon the sand," her popularity was complete. Her lips were the ones "which the huntsmen for the red ear" sought at the husking bees, and her hands were the ones held most often in the "fiddle games."

Great excitement attended the business of shucking out a neighbor's corn. The shrewd owner of the corn stacked it in two large piles, and teams were chosen to race against each other in husking the ears. A referee was selected to compromise all disputes arising out of the finding of red ears. He decided whether anxious swains had actually found red ears or whether they had bootlegged them to the party in hip pockets. Too, the question often arose as to whether rows of strawberry grains actually constituted "red" ears or not.[14]

Not all the excitement in a husking match came from anticipating a prolonged smacking of a fair neighbor's lips, but the passing of a well-filled gourd spurred the hands and aroused the spirits. Liquor flowed freely—since corn shucking was a hot and dirty task. Western neighborhoods were kept busy and happily disturbed throughout October, November and December with the business of shucking corn and kissing every girl whose face was not homely enough to reverse the course of greased lightning. Boys made resolutions when red ears evaded their persistent and vigorous search that when they became corn planters in their own rights they were going to stick to a "red" variety of seed. No place on earth encouraged the gentle art of shucking and kissing as did Ohio, Indiana and Illinois. Corn grew in these states from the beginning in superabundance, and the gals kept abreast of the corn production. Romance here was as vigorous as were the towering rows of tasseling native maize.[15]

When winter days grew short and cold, women of the frontier called upon their nimble-fingered sisters to aid them in the endless task of preparing clothing and covering for numerous offspring. Pickings, cardings, knittings, cuttings and quiltings were held in order to complete quickly the chores of the household. Quilting frames suspended from the ceiling by four cords were as necessary equipment in the big rooms of the frontier homes as were buckhorn rests for the family rifles, or ticking Yankee clocks. About these frames hovered gossiping females who worked for hours patching in small pieces of miscellaneous cloth, and at whipstitching them into place firmly enough to endure the hard usage of at least three vigorous generations. The rasping of cards, the whirring of spinning wheels, the clacking of looms, enlivened frontier homes for days at a time. At night, following these "female workings," the men gathered at the fireside, the quilting frame was hoisted to the ceiling, the cards, the wheel and the loom were shoved back, and the fiddler struck up a tune. These parties went into whirling "stomping" dances which kept up for the better part of long winter nights.[16]

Fiddles whined merrily at barbecues and burgoo stewings. Barbecues always bore the stamp of politics. These took place during the heavy campaigning seasons for offices, or at Fourth of July celebrations. There was no more famous barbecue stand in the whole West than the, now extinct, Maxwell Springs in Lexington, Kentucky. Here politicians bellowed forth platitudes which caused gullible supporters to yell approval in a volume sufficient to wake up the dead. Fiddlers were hired to entertain those who gathered for the purpose of being entertained and politically gulled.[17] Center of all attractions at barbecues was, of course, the barbecued meats. For twenty-four hours before the meeting fire-tanned men stood over burning pits of charcoal turning spits of meat to insure proper cooking. Liquor was used to wash down tasty hunks of beef, pork, mutton and, sometimes, venison. Few partakers of the viands and liquids of a western barbecue ever went home sober enough to describe the activities of the day, or to know whether the meat they had eaten was mutton or rattlesnake. They carried with them a hazy recollection of what their favorite politicians had said, a muddled opinion of a neighbor's horse, and, always, a grim memory of fist and skull fights. If by chance the adventurer of the day became overzealous in defending the cause of a candidate or a party he might easily bear painful testimony of his stand in the form of deep scratches, black eyes, and, in some cases, he might even be "snake poled" or gouged.[18]

Ol' Kaintuck developed, along with the barbecue, the burgoo suppers or stews. No one knows when this wayward daughter of Virginia made this culinary and political departure from the established institutions of the Old Dominion. Burgoo was composed of a mixture of game, venison, domestic meats and vegetables in abundance. It was cooked in large pots or cauldrons until the whole mixture was a soup. A native son invited William T. Porter to come to Kentucky for a burgoo celebration. He said, "Excuse my liberty, for you must know that us chaps in old Kentuck don't stand tiptoe on ceremony, but if a friend comes along, we ask him to take a glass of rough whisky, or go to a burgoo with us where you'll get as good a bowl of soup as you ever put to your lips."[19] Kentuckians talked horses, politics and women to a finish over steaming bowls of this meaty mixture. Sometimes raw whisky, burgoo and hot tempers left deep marks on everybody at the gathering.

The fiddlin' West was a happy-go-lucky section. Numerous frolics, and a frolicsome nature, sometimes left unfavorable impressions upon serious-minded travelers who did not understand the music, and believed the square dance the work of maniacs. Such an observer was the sophisticated Fordham who wrote in his journal "a grand ball will be given tonight, to which I shall not go, as I do not choose the risk of being insulted by any vulgar Ohioans."[20] However, this snob was impressed with the democracy of the frontier entertainments. On Christmas Day in the West he found the churchgoers attending sermons and prayers from breakfast to supper, another set cooking wild turkeys and dancing. The young men were "firing *feux de joi* almost all the preceding night." They explained that "we back-woodsmen never fire a gun loaded with *ball into* the town,— only from parts of it, out towards the woods."[21] Fordham found a judge at the dance with his daughter, and other local digni-taries who were unconscious, as he thought, of their positions long enough to unbend and do a little fancy "cake walking" with the wild boys who were firing *"feux de joi."*

If Fordham, Nuttall and their traveling compeers had met at Frankfort where a dinner was being held in honor of H. Clay they would have been shocked beyond recovery by what went on there. "Vulgar Ohioans" would not have been alone as a class had these gentlemen seen "Harry of the West" top off a night of festivity by committing "a grand terpsichorean per-formance on the table." This he "accordingly did, executing a *pas seul* from head to foot of the dining-room table, sixty feet in length, amidst the loud applause of his companions, and to the crashing accompaniment of shivering glass and china; for which he next morning paid, without demur, a bill for $120."[22]

Rowdiest of frontier musical performances were the shivarees and serenades. If the howling and shrieking band of serenaders besieged a newly wedded couple, the antics often became coarse and vulgar. It was woe unto timid grooms who did not invite the party in for a drink around, a slice of cake or an impromptu dance. If no invitation came forth and the party was ignored it did its best to tear down the place. Livestock was turned out in growing field crops, wheels were yanked off vehicles, and rocks thundered down upon roofs. At times, however, these western mummers received the worst of the deal. A noisy band of marauders went from house to house in Frankfort, Kentucky, shouting racy songs, and disturbing the peace in general. They stopped under one window which they had tangible reason to regret. One member of this party said: "They had got on very well thus far, when suddenly a *shower* came down from the third story window, and I assure the reader it was not all 'lavender water.' Then a voice from a head and nightcap roared out, 'Go home, you damned noisy rascals, and do not disturb the neighborhood with your howlings.' This was an admonition which did not have to be repeated, but seldom in the West were receptions so odious or inconsiderate."[23]

No frolic was ever complete without the fiddle or some other manly musical instrument such as the dulcimer, the banjo or the guitar. Fiddles were loaded with rattlesnake rattles. Frontiersmen claimed that the rattles from a snake added a weird, but delightful tone to a fiddle because they vibrated with the impact of the bow upon the strings.[24] Many fiddlers never seemed to realize that the instrument on which they sawed out rasping tunes was capable of producing gentler music. They had learned to play by ear, and had never heard anything except the raucous and blaring music which they and their masters played. In 1823, James Whitcomb, later governor of Indiana, was traveling between Indianapolis and Whitewater when he came, at nightfall, to a cabin on the Blue River. Strains of a fiddle greeted his ear, and when he dismounted and went into the house he found a boy, Amos Dille, scraping away on a battered old violin. When the boy had gone to care for the horse, Whitcomb picked up the instrument and began playing gentler tunes than had ever been heard in those bottoms before. When the owner of the fiddle returned he struck up "Hail Columbia." The boy became so excited that he shouted, "If I had fifty dollars I would give it all for that fiddle; I never heard such music before in my life." Young Dille examined the violin carefully, and was pleasantly perplexed; turning to his musical visitor he said, "Mister, I never saw two fiddles so much alike as yours and mine."[25]

High public officials were not above playing the fiddle in true backwoods style, and most of them could send boisterous dancers through jigging sets in fine spirit. Judge George M. Bibb, Chief Justice of the Kentucky Court of Appeals, could rasp off any tune which had ever crossed the mountains. When N. M. Ludlow's theatrical company played at Frankfort, he and Sam Drake loafed with Judge Bibb and Humphrey Marshall.

The Judge would insist on Sam Drake playing the "new short tunes," and he would follow along as "second." During the winter sessions of the general assembly, Bibb would play for the legislative dances. He kept the lawmakers in a giddier whirl with his fiddle bow than he ever did with decisions from the high bench.[26] Ludlow became very much enamored of a young Frankfort belle who was reputed to possess a fine estate, and during his company's appearance before the legislature he called upon her with serious intentions of courtship. When this adventurous caller reached the home of the young lady he was mortified to find her in the parlor with a fiddle stuck snugly under her dainty little chin playing a lusty Virginia breakdown. This sickened the theatrical caller, for like every other man on the frontier, he was convinced that the alabaster chin of a western belle should never clamp a fiddle butt.[27] Women could play fiddles without bringing discredit to themselves if they held them well down in their arms as in the manner of an awkward young mother holding a bawling first-born, or they could perform a secondary function by beating straws. No self-respecting frontier woman could "chin" a fiddle and get along smoothly in polite society.

No people ever enjoyed their frolics more than those mortals living in the Ohio Valley. Historians and dreamers may yet yearn for what might have been the "good days." Frontiersmen might not have known what was happening in Europe, nor did they know even what was happening in Washington, but they did know the measure of every waist, and the texture of the lips of nearly every girl in their community. Indians, varmints, Britishers and taxes disturbed the sons of the great valley, but they relaxed completely in their gatherings. Workings performed many burdensome tasks in the pleasantest way. Ten gallons of good corn liquor at a barn-raising relieved a powerful lot of stress and strain.

The frontier frolic, and the masters of the bow, surrendered stubbornly to the "modern ways." Bob Walker of Kentucky was one of the last of the old guard to give up. Bob was a well known red horse who hated the word "violin," and his fiddle "was his only companion; his pillow at night, and his breakfast in the morning; he lived and slept by it—he was in Ol' Kentuck what Paganini was in Europe." This fiddlin' troubadour could, in the local sense, "smell" a frolic for miles off, and he seldom missed one.

About the winter of 1829 the Dramatic Company of Louisville entertained the state legislature at Frankfort with the tear-fetching tragedy *Virginius*. The orchestra for this powerful bit of acting consisted of one anemic Frenchman who "scratched away two or three nights, much to his own satisfaction, but little to the amusement of the audience." While the Falls City dramatists were stabbing eloquent adversaries in high drama, and the Frenchman was butchering classical tunes before dumfounded representatives, Old Bob came to town. Several governmental dignitaries who had reached higher positions in cross roads politics than in musical appreciation insisted that the native son be paired with the wheezing Frenchman in the orchestra pit. Bob looked with disdain upon the Frenchman, and he despised the book music. "He would rather have been at a corn-shucking frolic than the theater. The play was *Virginius* and everything went on well until the close. Virginius dies—the ladies are seen with white handkerchiefs to their eyes—the big tear is seen to course down the cheek of manly youth—the bell rings for the curtain to descend. Slowly the little Frenchman strikes up a melancholy air on the 'pianissimo.' Old Bob looked at him and said, 'Pianna hell,' and struck with all his might 'Oh Judy put the Kettle on!' It was like magic— the sublime to the ridiculous. The curtain came down with a double shuffle—the audience yelled—the little Frenchman scratched his head—and the indignant Virginius swore vengeance against all Kentucky fiddlers."[28]

Frontier dances were ideal places for trouble to break out. On the other hand, these social gatherings were often scenes of rich comedy. One of the best observers of social customs in the West was J. S. Robb, a contributor to the Saint Louis *Reveille*. He

uses his character Jim Sikes as the leading figure to give a good
account of a backwoods ball in Illinois.

## NETTLE BOTTOM BALL

Well, it are a fact, boys, that I promised to tell you how I cum
to git out in these platte diggins, and I speculate you mout as
well have it at onst, case it's been troublin' my conscience
amazin' to keep it kiver'd up. The affarr raised jessy in Nettle
Bottom, and old Sam Stokes' *yell,* when he swar he'd "chaw me
up," gives my meat a slight sprinklin' of ager whenever I think
on it.

You see, thar wur a small town called Equality, in Illinise,
that some specelators started near Nettle Bottom cos thar wur a
spontaneous salt lick in the diggins, and no sooner did they git
it agoin' and build some stores and groceries thar, than they
wagon'd from Cincinnate and other upstream villages, a pacel
of fellers to attend the shops, that looked as nice, all'ays, as if
they wur goin' to meetin' or on a courtin' frolic; and, "salt their
picters," they wur etarnally pokin' up their noses at us boys of
the Bottom. Well, they got up a ball in the village, jest to inter-
duce themselves to the gals round the neighborhood, and invited a few on us to make a contrary picter to themselves, and
so shine us out of site by comparison. After that ball thar wasn't
anythin' talked on among the gals but what nice fellers the
clerks in Equality wur, and how slick they wore their *har,* and
their shiny boots, and the way they stirrupp'd down their
trowsers. You couldn't go to see one on 'm that she wouldn't
stick one of these fellers at you, and keep a talkin' how slick
they looked. It got to be parfect pisen to hear of, or see the
critters, and the boys got together at last to see what was to be
done—the thing had grown perfectly alarmin'. At last a meetin'
was agreed on, down to old Jake Bents'.

On next Sunday night, instead of takin' the gals to meetin'
whar they could see these fellers, we left 'm at home, and met at
Jakes's, and I am of the opinion thur was some congregated
wrath thar—whew! wan't they?

"H-ll and scissors!" says Mike Jelt, "let's go down and lick the town, *rite strait!*"

"No!" hollered Dick Butts, "let's kitch these slick badgers comin' out of meeting', and tare the hide and feathers off on 'em!"

"Why, d—n 'em, what d'ye think, boys," busted in old Jake, "I swar if they ain't larnt our gals to wear *starn cushions;* ony this mornin' I caught my darter Sally puttin' one on and tryin' it round her. She tho't I was asleep, but I seed her, and I made the jade repudiate it, and no mistake—quicker!"

The boys took a drink on the occasion, and Equality town was slumberin', for a short spell, over a con-tiguous yearthquake. At last one of the boys proposed before we attacked the town, that we should get up a ball in the Bottom, and jest out-shine the town chaps, all to death, before we swallowed 'em. It was hard to gin in to this proposition, but the boys cum to it at last, and every feller started to put the afarr agoin'.

I had bin a long spell hankerin' arter old Tom Jones's darter, on the branch below the Bottom, and she *was* a critter good for weak eyes—maybe she hadn't a pair of her own—well if they warn't a brace of movin' light-houses, I wouldn't say it—there was no calculatin' the extent or handsomeness of the family that gal could bring up around her, with a feller like me to look arter 'em. Talk about gracefulness, did you ever see a maple saplin' moving with a south wind?—It warn't a crooked stick to compar to her, but her old dad was *awful*. He could jest lick anythin' that said *boo,* in them diggins, out-swar satan, and was cross as a she *b'ar,* with cubs. He had a little hankerin' in favor of the fellers in town, too, fur they gin him presents of powder to hunt with, and he was precious fond of usin' his shootin' iron. I detarmin'd, anyhow, to ask his darter, Betsey, to be my partner at the Nettle Bottom ball.

Well, my sister, Marth, made me a bran new pair of buckskin trowsers to go in, and rile my pictur, ef she didn't put stirrups to 'em to keep 'em down. She said *straps* wur the fashion and I should ware 'em. I jest felt with 'em on as if I had somethin' pressin' on me down—all my joints wur sot tight together, but Marth insisted, and I knew I could soon dance 'em off, so I gin in, and started off to the branch for Betsy Jones.

When I arriv, the old feller wur sittin' smokin' arter his supper, and the younger Jones' wur sittin' round the table takin' theirs. A whoppin' big pan of *mush* stood rite in the centre, and a large pan of milk beside it, with lots of corn bread and butter, and Betsy was helpin' the youngsters, while old Mrs. Jones sot by admirin' the family collection. Old Tom took a hard star' at me, and I kind a shook, but the *straps* stood it, and I recovered myself, and gin him as good as he sent, but I wur near the door, and ready to break if he show'd fight.

"What the h-ll are you doin' in *disguise?*" says the old man—he swore dreadfully—"are you comin' down here to steal?"

I riled up at that. Says I, "Ef I wur comin' fur sich purpose, you'd be the last I'd hunt up to steal off on."

"You're right," says he, "I'd make a hole to light your innards, ef you did." And the old savage chuckled. I meant because he had nothin' worth stealin' but his darter, but he tho't 'twas cos I was afear'd on him.

Well, purty soon I gether'd up and told him what I cum down fur, and invited him to cum up and take a drink and see that all went on rite. Betsy was in an awful way fur fear he wouldn't consent. The old 'oman here spoke in favor of the move, and old Tom thought of the licker and gin in to the measure. Off bounced Betsy up a ladder into the second story, and one of the small gals with her, to help put on the fixups. I sot down in a cheer, and fel a talkin' to the old 'oman. While we wur chattin' away as nice as relations, I could hear Betsy makin' things stand round above. The floor was only loose boards kivered over wide joice, and every step made 'em shake and rattle like a small hurricane. Old Tom smoked away and the young ones at the table would hold a spoonful of mush to thur mouths and look at my straps, and then look at each other and snigger, till at last the old man seed 'em.

"Well, by gun flints," says he, "ef you ain't makin' a josey—"

Jest at that moment, somethin' gin way above, and may I die, ef Betsy, without anythin' on yearth on her but one of these *starn cushins,* didn't drop rite through the floor, and sot herself, *flat into the pan of mush!* I jest tho't fur a second, that heaven and yearth had kissed each other, and squeezed me between 'em. Betsy squealed like a 'scape pipe,—a spot of the mush had spattered on the old man's face, and burnt him, and he swore dreadful. I snatched up the pan of milk, and dashed it over Betsy to cool her off,—the old 'oman knocked me sprawlin' fur doing it, and away went my *straps.* The young ones let out a scream, as if the infarnal pit had broke loose, and I'd jest gin half of my hide to have bin out of the old man's reach. He did *reach* fur me, but I lent him one with my half-lows, on the smeller, that spread him, and maybe I didn't leave *sudden!* I didn't see the branch, but as I soused through it, I heerd Tom Jones swar he'd *"chaw me up,* ef an inch big of me was found in them diggins in the mornin'.'"

I didn't know fur a spell whar I was runnin', but hearin' nuthin' behind me, I slacked up, and jest considered whether it was best to go home and git my straps strait, and leave, or go see the ball. Bein' as I was a manager, I tho't I'd go have a peep through the winder, to see ef it cum up to my expectations. While I was lookin' at the boys goin' it, one on 'em spied me, and they hauled me in, stood me afore the fire, to dry, and all hands got round, insistin' on knowin' what was the matter. I ups and tells all about it. I never heers such laffin', hollerin', and screamin', in all my days.

Jest then, my trowsers gin to feel the fire, and shrink up about an inch a minit, and the boys and gals kept it up strong, laffin' at my scrape, and the pickle I wur in, that I gin to git riley, when all at onst I seed one of these slick critters, from town, rite in among 'em, hollerin' wuss than the loudest.

"Old Jones said he'd chaw you up, did he?" says the town feller. *"Well he all'ays keeps his word."*

That minit I biled over. I grabbed his slick *har,* and maybe I didn't gin him *scissors!* Jest as I was makin' him a *chawed speciman* some feller holler'd out, —"Don't let old Jones in with that ar *rifle*." I didn't hear anymore in that Bottom, —lightnin' couldn't a got near enough to singe my coat tail. I jumped through that winder as easy as a b'ar 'ud go through a cane-brake; and cuss me if I couldn't hear the grit of old Jones's teeth, and smell his glazed powder, until I crossed old Mississippi.[29]

Kentuckians were masters at political strategy. Perhaps Henry P. Leland's account of a particular bit of political trickery is one of the best political stories coming from Kentucky. This yarn rests upon fact; the long man was John C. Breckenridge and the short one was Robert Letcher. Political wireworkers were certain that music had charm, and they often used this knowledge to good advantage.

## Heading Off the Music

Insure me a brass band and I'll insure your election. And so widely during the last election was music called in to aid oratory, that this answer serves as a good endorsement to the poet's note that "Music hath charms to soothe the savage breast," and attractions to "go to the polls and Vote Early."

The forty horsepower music on elections being thus settled by common consent, leads us to believe that "too much credit cannot be awarded" to the Kentuckian who faced his political opponent's music as follows:

Both were candidates for the office of Governor of Kentucky, and "stumped" the state together quite harmoniously until they reached one of the counties in the "hill country." Here it was necessary to make a decided demonstration, and accordingly the two candidates fairly spread themselves to catch all the votes possible—scaring up the American Eagle, and calling down the shade of Washington; pitching out profuse promises, and pitching into each other's party politics, in a manner decidedly refreshing to the hearers. On the first day's canvass, victory hung suspended by the tail feathers over the rival forces, but the second day fell slap into the lap of the shortest and stoutest candidate, leaving his long and lean opponent "no kind of a show." In vain the long man pumped up the waters of drink. But round the short man elbowed and crowded a mass of thirsty voters, drinking in his tones with delight. Why this attraction? Had he a barrel of old bourbon? No; he had a fiddle! Getting the start of long man he had addressed the voters in a short speech, and then, for the first time, bringing out a fiddle, retired a short distance from the speakers' stand, in order to let his opponent reply, playing, however, such lively airs, that he soon drew the entire assemblage away, and left the other side of the question unattended to, unheard.

For three days in succession short man and the fiddle carried the day, in three successive mass meetings, in as many towns in the hill country, and long man's chances for a single vote in those parts grew remarkably slim. In vain a long consultation was held by the latter with his political friends.

"Get the start of him at the next meeting and speak first," advised one.

"Raise a fiddle and play them choones!" said another.

"Yell him down," shouted a third.

The long man followed the advise of the first counsellor, and got the start in voice, but the noise of the fiddle run him neck and neck; he would have listened to his second monitor, and raised a fiddle, only he knew it would fall through, as he couldn't scrape a note; and as for his third adviser, he told him that "yelling down" short man was simply ridiculous.

Affairs grew desperate with long man, when, on the third meeting, he saw, as usual, the entire crowd of voters sweeping off after short man and his fiddle, leaving only one hearer, and he a lame one, who was just about to hobble after the others.

"Can it be possible that freemen—citizens of this great and glorious country—neglecting the vital interests of their land, will run like wild men after cat-gut strings? Can it be possible,

I say?" And the lame man, to whom long man was thus elo-
quently discoursing, answered, as he too cleared out:

"Well, it can, old hoss!"

Despair encamped in the long man's face, as he watched short
man, at a distance, playing away for dear life and the Guberna-
torial chair on that "blasted" old fiddle; but suddenly a ray of
hope beamed over his "rueful visage," then another and another
ray, till it shone like the sun at midday.

"Got him now, sure!" fairly shouted the long man, as he
threw up his arms, jumped from the stand, and started for the
tavern, where he at once called a meeting of his political
friends, consisting of the landlord and one other, then and there
unfolding a plan which was to drive his rival "nowheres in no
time."

The fourth meeting was held. Short man addressed the crowd
with warmth, eloquence and bluntly vacating the stand for his
adversary, and striking up a lively air on the violin, in order to
quash his proceedings; but, though as usual, he carried the
audience away, he noticed that they were as critical as numerous. One six-footer, in homespun, walnut-dyed clothes, with
wild-looking eyes and a 'coonskin cap, eyed every movement
of the fiddle-bow, with intense disgust, finding utterance at last,
in:

"Why don't you fiddle with that t'other hand o' yourn?"

"T'other hand!" shouted a chorus of voices. "Fire up with
that t'other hand!" Faster played the short man, but louder
and louder shouted the crowd, "T'other hand, t'other hand!"

"Gentlemen, I assure you—"

"No more honey, old hoss. We ain't b'ars!" shouted the man
with the 'coonskin cap.

"T'other hand, t'other hand!" yelled the crowd; while even
from the distant stand where the long man was holding forth
"to next to nobody" for some listeners, seemed to come a faint
echo, "T'other hand, t'other hand!"

Short man began to be elbowed, crowded, pushed; in vain he

tried to draw the bow; at one time his bow-arm was sent up to the shoulder over the bridge, at another, down went the fiddle, until he shouted out:

"Gentlemen, what can I do but assure you that—"

"T'other hand!" roared 'coonskin, shouldering his way face up to the short man, "we've heard about you! You fiddle down thar in that d—n Bluegrass country, 'mong rich folks, with your right hand and think when you git up in the hills 'mong pore folks, *left-hand fiddlin's* good enuf for them; you've cussedly missed it! Left-hand doin's wont run up hyar; tote out your right, stranger, or look out for squalls!"

The short man looked out for squalls, threw down the fiddle and the bow, oh! oh—jumped on his horse and put a straight horse tail between him and his enraged "fellow citizens."

"It's a fact," says the long man, "my opponent's being left-handed rather told against him up in the hill-country and whoever circulated the story, up there, that he always fiddled with his right hand down in the Bluegrass country, *headed off his music* for that campaign."[30]

## CHAPTER XIV

# FOOLIN' WITH THE GALS

No people ever had a higher regard for their women than the American frontiersmen. Women, in a sense, were trail breakers in the American West. Even the Indians realized this for when the women and children appeared west of the mountains they knew that white settlement would be permanent. Woman was symbolical of all that the backwoodsman wanted for his land; she was the necessary element of happiness in his life. Yet peculiar conditions on the frontier made the life of women a bit of a comedy at times, and a tragedy at others. Facilities for separation of the sexes did not exist, and familiarities, of course, were common. Women played their part well in frontier life, and they accepted conditions as they found them without grumbling. No American woman has ever enjoyed more independence than the backwoods belle.

The frontier home was the hub of western civilization. Home to the Westerner meant a plot of land, a log cabin, a wife and a rapidly growing family.[1] Many frontier accounts have emphasized the importance of the family, and the vanity of the parents when their cabins became a veritable bedlam because of fretting young ones.

The heads of households considered themselves the patriarchs of small kingdoms, and to satisfy their vanities they often sent from three to five wives to the cemetery before them because they overtaxed their physical systems in bearing children. Margaret Dwight Bell was one of the few women to write of her hardships, or of life on the frontier. She was born in Connecticut in 1790, and went to Ohio in 1810. In 1811 she was married and in 1834 she died. During her twenty-three years of married life she bore a brood of thirteen children. There were other women on the frontier, however, who had more children to show for their time than the literate Mrs. Bell, but even a brood of thirteen born in such a short interval of time required much attention.[2]

Proud husbands in some cases satisfied their vanities by making testimentary injunctions that kept their widows in mourning for a "proper" length of time. Provisions were made in many regions for funeral services to be preached several months after a burial in order that a "grieving" widow would not ride to the graveyard behind her husband's corpse, and ride back in the embrace of a prospective husband. In communities where delayed funerals were customary, the date and conditions of the funerals were provided for in the deceaseds' wills. The delay was always a "decent" one and varied in length according to the selfish inclinations of the departed brethren.

Sometimes widows went to these funerals and grieved loudly, not over the deceased, but in disgust at the long time which had intervened between the burial and the funeral. No self-respecting widow looked at another man, or in any way broke faith with her dead husband, at least openly, because if she did she was disgraced in the eyes of the community. The delayed funeral of the frontier (a custom which still prevails in parts of Tennessee and Kentucky) was a great social institution. Here courting on a grand scale was the order of the day. Close relatives relieved themselves of emotional storms, jockeys traded horses, gamblers won and lost handsome sums, sheriffs and constables served writs and warned people to public "workings," candidates pressed their causes, and preachers were free to preach rip-snorting denominational sermons. In one case a sweat-begrimed parson asked from the pulpit if any of the sorrowing brethren had any seed peas for sale.[3] Generally the will of the deceased prescribed the texts, and the preacher warped it into a plea for his own particular belief.

Anxious relatives sometimes had sermons preached for members of their families who had moved out on the frontier, and from whom they had not heard for a long time. In Tennessee a native son had been lost to his relatives for many years after his removal to Texas, so they had his funeral preached. The parson opened his sermon with the statement that "the last time we hearn from him he was very sick, an' seein' as how he's never writ any more, the breathering, friends and relatives consider it onsafe to wait any longer about the funeral, an' so the time has arriv' accordin' to previous apintment, to preach the funeral."[4]

Of all the amusements on the frontier none were more exciting than weddings. Courtships were short, and marriages were whirlwind affairs. People poured into the home of the bride from miles around, and following the ceremony, if the groom lived near by, a dinner took place at his home. Wedding dinners were the outstanding feasts of the frontier; not even logrollings or barn-raisings equaled them. Of course the dance which followed the dinner was the major attraction. Tables and benches were shoved back, the fiddlers struck up a breakdown tune, and the hymeneal celebration was under way. Before the hour grew late a group of "sniggering" gals led the bride away to her bridal chamber (which most often was in the loft of the house), and within a short time a group of boys dragged the self-conscious groom up the ladder to be placed snugly in bed beside his bride. Amid giggling and suggestive references to the couple in the loft, the dance went on with much excitement and frequent swigs at the bottle. Many wedding dances continued until sunup. On the day following the wedding an infare was held, and again a round of frivolities was initiated. If at the end of the infare the community was still anxious for entertainment, there remained the noble excuse of giving a house-raising and a dance. At these gatherings, many of which took place around log heap fires, there were girls enough to make the meeting interesting. Strangers were invited to "step up and meet our gals." Perhaps there were not always enough girls to go around, but what there were of them were lively and made frontier life exciting.[5]

Not all of the weddings were "big" affairs, for often back-woods girls and boys appeared before preachers and justices of the peace and demanded that they be "hitched-up" without undue ceremony. A witness recalls having seen his father per-form a marriage for which he received a pair of shuck collars, and a swig of bad liquor. When the pair had been "made as one" the groom pulled forth a bottle of homemade liquor from his shirt bosom and sealed the bonds with a drink "all-around."[6] Much joking, and a considerable amount of quib-bling occurred over payment of the standard fee of "one silver dollar." Justices of the peace and ministers sometimes rode long distances on rented horses only to be paid a dollar—a sum which did not begin to pay expenses.[7]

It has always been true that a frontier country had more men than women, and several times in American history groups of single girls have been imported to satisfy the demand for wives. Virginia colonists imported the tobacco brides, Louisi-anans welcomed the casket brides, and Kentucky had an immi-gration of many women in 1780. As the frontiersmen pushed deeper into the West there arose a demand for wives. A company of forty-one women traveled from the eastern com-munities to Iowa to offer themselves as brides to the adventurers who were pushing the line of settlement westward. No time was lost in getting married. "When a steamboat load of ladies is coming in at the wharf," said a bystander, "the gentlemen on shore make proposals to the ladies through the speaking trumpets something like the following: 'Miss with the blue ribbon in your bonnet, will you take me?' 'Hallo thar, gal, with a cinamon shawl; if agreeable we will jine.' The ladies in the meantime get ashore and are married at the 'hotel.' The parties arranging themselves as the squire sings out 'sort your-selves, sort yourselves!' "[8]

Girls were scarce on the frontier, and once arrangements were made for weddings they were practically assured that they would not be left at the altar. There was nothing strange, however, in a woman changing her mind, since she ordinarily had many other choices, but for a man to breach his promise to marry was unusual indeed. Such a case, however, occurred in Union County, Indiana. A hunchback son of that region changed his mind and failed to show up at the appointed time. As a result his fiancée sued him for breach of promise, and hauled him into court to defend himself against some novel charges of damage. The maiden, a handsome young woman who carried herself well, and displayed an attractive set of teeth when she smiled, claimed that she and her family had been injured to the amount of five thousand dollars. An itemized bill of expenses was submitted which included one hundred suppers, which required one turkey and six chickens, several large dishes of beans and potatoes, a boiled ham, and turnips and boiled cabbage in profusion. Damages were likewise assessed for several calico dresses, one white muslin and one gingham dress with broad stripes.

Lawyers for the plaintiff bemeaned the faithless and deformed lover who had caused the beautiful belle of Union County to be embarrassed and disappointed at the altar. They carefully pointed to the long and tedious hours of labor on the part of the family in preparation for the nuptial ceremonies. The daughter had exhausted herself at sewing, and the mother, the best cook in the county, had worked her fingers to the bone baking an overstock of her famous custard pies. With these damaging charges before the jury the plaintiff rested their case. These were all "fixed" facts, and there was little for the defense council to say; however, he did point out that the suppers were eaten by the guests, and that the girl was attractive enough to find a husband at any time she chose, therefore she could wear the dresses in courting another man. No loss, said he, had resulted from his client's failure to marry the plaintiff. When the judge read the charge to the jury it was clearly evident that he was favorably inclined toward the handsome maiden, and that worthy body of peers quickly returned a verdict assessing eight dollars for the dresses and three dollars and fifty cents for the suppers. It is hard to say whether the jurymen in this case underestimated the culinary attainments of the old lady, or meant to convey the idea that the injured parties were fortunate in having escaped an alliance with the defendant.[9]

An Illinois Sucker sized up the frontiersman's regard for womenfolks when he told a justice of the peace that it was all right to marry him to a fourteen-year-old girl. "It is all right," said the Sucker, "girls are like new potatoes; they are old enough as soon as they are big enough."[10] This seems to have been a universal rule throughout the early West. Single women were about as scarce in most frontier circles as was regard for the Sabbath. Girls did not have to wait longingly for suitors, because they could take their pick. If their choices were bad they could leave their beds and board and seek greener fields. / The frontier was a single woman's paradise and a married woman's hell. Many marriages were made in haste, and separations were common. Early newspapers carried weekly notices that women had deserted their "bed and board" for more romantic pursuits. When a woman walked out on her husband he felt it his "bounden" duty to "post" her by inserting an ad in the paper disclaiming responsibility for her deeds and especially her accounts. Such a case was that of Christopher Mattocks who believed it his duty to inform a virtuous public that "Whereas my wife Mary Mattocks, has without any just cause eloped from my bed and board, and has taken up with a certain William Gibson, I hereby warn all persons from crediting her on my account, as I am determined to pay no debts of her contracting." Occasionally indignant husbands made horrible mistakes and "posted" their wives without having all the facts in hand. Malachi Brown became overanxious and told the public "Whereas my wife Sally Brown has eloped from me without cause, I do forewarn all persons from having any dealing with her on my account, as I am determined to pay no debts of her contracting." When Sally returned home, however, and righteous neighbors informed the hasty Malachi that he had posted an innocent woman, he had publicly to admit the next week that "In justice to the character of my wife, Sarah Brown, who by misinformation and ill advice, I published in your last Saturday's paper, I have to inform you and the public, after having investigated the matter fully it is sufficiently proven to me that the charge against her is ill-founded, and I do hope this publication will wipe off a stain my last made on an innocent character."[11]

Occasionally there appeared heart-rending appeals such as that from Terrence Smith who was detained in the Bourbon County, Kentucky, jail. Poor Terrence pleaded that "Whereas my wife Christina, has lately craved security of the peace against me, on which account I am now confined in the gaol of this county; and as I understand (and I have good reason to believe) that she takes advantage of my confinement, to dispose of my property and run me in debt, I do hereby forewarn any person from dealing with her, or receiving any property from her on any pretense, as I shall prosecute all such with the utmost rigour of the law."[12]

Mrs. Terrence Smith was indeed a cautious woman, and in flirting around outside of the marital "coop" she made certain that there would be no embarrassing impasses with Terrence. In an adjoining county a brazen wife was more reckless and took her amorous adventures where she found them without locking her husband in the county jail. This woman, the "Widder" Conklin, had hardly left one husband's bed and board before she established another domestic base of operation. She successfully ensnared the timid and unsuspecting Jonathan Dan, Jr., in matrimony. Jonathan made the horrible mistake of not investigating the Widder's history, and so in a remarkably short time he was proclaiming to interested neighbors that "Whereas about three months since I took to my bed and board the reputed Widow Demarias Conklin, whom I supposed to be as *chaste* as an *icicle* and as *virtuous* as the *Goddess Diana*— and whereas since my inter-marriage with the said reputed widow, I have learnt she has other husbands living, on whom I presume all her love and affections are placed, as she exhibited none towards me—and whereas the said Widow Conklin has frequently wandered from the path of rectitude and conducted herself in such unbecoming manner that my breast has been filled with jealousy, my days with trouble, and my nights with sorrow—and whereas I wish to lead the life of a good and peaceable citizen, instead of being hen-pecked and tormented with an insatiable wife, whose conduct is a disgrace to her sex. Now, therefore, be it known, that without the formalities of the law, I have separated myself from my unruly rib, and all the good people are cautioned against trusting her on my account, as I will hereafter pay no debts of the contracting of the said Widow Conklin. I have no objection to her being harbored by any of my fellow citizens, but as to paying any of her debts I will not. I now enjoy myself remarkably well being out of the reach of tongs, broomsticks and ladles, and sleep quietly in my own shop, having none to molest or make me afraid."[13]

Other female pioneers harassed their husbands in unusual ways. They were wayward, they were coquettish, and sometimes they were downright mean. The frontier was hard on women, and the backwoods belle cannot be blamed if at times she ran away to more caressing arms and softer beds. Hundreds of marriage disputes were dragged before frontier legislatures.[14] Grounds upon which divorces were granted were numerous, and many of them unusual. Peyton Chapman of Adair County, Kentucky, sought deliverance from his wife, Nancy, who had deserted him, but who took fiendish delight in returning from time to time for the purpose of "harassing and perplexing Peyton and destroying his property."[15] Other husbands were dumfounded to find that they had married women whom they believed to be chaste, but who were in an advanced state of pregnancy. Joshua Pyke was intermarried in July, 1819, with the "lovely Lucinda Woodward," "under the expectation and belief that she was a virtuous and chaste woman, and that he was induced to said marriage by the purest and unfeigned love and attachment to her; but to his utter astonishment and confusion after his marriage rites were celebrated, he discovered that she was sometime advanced in a state of pregnancy by another man."[16]

Pregnancy, however, was not always reason enough for turning back from the altar. An Illinois magistrate was asked to perform the marriage ceremony for a couple, but when he discovered that the fair bride gave evidence of being with child he called the groom, whom he believed to be ignorant of the fact, aside, and informed him of the state of affairs. The groom was liberal in his views, and asked that the ceremony proceed, since single girls were so scarce.[17]

Occasionally frontiersmen found themselves thoroughly "sold" by wandering females. None, however, were ever left quite so completely undone as was that son of Tennessee who went traveling in search of adventure along the highways of his native state. This wandering blade fell into the company of a whimpering female with an infant in her arms who was being driven from her father's hearth. She explained to her gallant companion that she had brought disgrace upon a fair family name because of her lewd conduct. This, however, was not necessarily a point of social maleficence which put her in bad standing in the eyes of the young Tennessean. As the editor of a western newspaper said, "This gentleman and lady, both being of the same mind, immediately formed a social acquaintance and passed the afternoon very pleasantly."

As evening approached, the gallant young man, noting the self-assurance of his fair and sporting companion, proposed that they pass the night at a near-by tavern as man and wife. This pleased the frolicsome daughter who had already disgraced an honorable name, and she agreed readily to the arrangement. When the gay couple reached the tavern, the woman went to her room, being careful to keep her infant's face concealed. The bell rang for supper, but she pleaded a stomachache and was unable to come to the table. While the deceptive female remained in her room with her ill-gotten child, her gay young Galahad treated himself to a hearty supper. Soon after the meal a bed was prepared and the couple retired. During the night the baby began crying loudly and awakened everybody in the house. The slumbering "father" was aroused from his peaceful dreams, and before he could adjust himself to the strange commotion, the tavern-keeper's wife was pounding on the door asking what was wrong with the child. Before the confused youth could answer this question his hostess asked, as is natural with women, what sex the child was. After some delay the answer came that it was a boy. While concerned friends awaited without the door the prodigal "blood" gathered up his "son" and comforted him with "hush, my dear—our Mumma will soon return again." He wondered, however, just what had become of "our Mumma." By some strange seventh sense he knew that she was embarrassingly absent at a crucial moment.

Finally the door was opened and the landlord and his lady were admitted to the chamber of the clumsy adventurer. The landlady took the child and danced it on her knee, congratulating her guest as she did so upon having such a fine offspring. Upon minute examination, however, the child was found to be a mulatto! Horror of horrors, the woman had fled leaving behind her a bawling half-breed child, and a penniless and horseless lover, to mourn the day on which he had formed an illicit coalition with a morally sporting female.[18]

Somewhat after the fashion of the "sawed" Tennessean, John Robert Shaw, the amorous well-digger, found himself deserted by a scheming female. Shaw was a man who was often tormented by the famous western ailment called "bottle fever." He was led into a silly trap by a shrewdish matron and her daughter in Lexington, Kentucky. This sentimental well-digger had lived through many romantic adventures before he removed to Kentucky from Pennsylvania, but in practicing his gentle art of blasting wells and building rock fences he had impaired his faculties. His hearing was permanently injured, and his eyesight was rapidly failing. On court day in Fayette County he got "half seas over," and as he said "dashing thro and fro among the crowd I happened to meet with an old

woman and her daughter, informing them I had been a
widower nine years, and my attachment always being great
for women, I promised them considerable presents provided the
young one would grant me certain favors, to which she agreed.
I accordingly carried them to the store, where the young one
first supplied herself with a handsome gownd pattern, and
immediately slipped out the door; after which the old one
received her fee, observed me talking to the storekeeper, she
took advantage and stepped out at the blind side of me, leaving
me as usual in the lurch."[19]

Not all the marital frivolities of the frontier were committed
by the gals. The frontier was the great "burying ground" for
past mistakes, or for philandering on a grand scale. Exploiting
husbands could desert wives as long as new settlements could
be found between Virginia and Missouri. Frequent notices
appeared in western newspapers warning "ALL UNMARRIED
WOMEN" that certain runaway and sporting husbands were
loose on the frontier and for them to beware. These philan-
derers started their connubial exploits in Virginia and moved
westward as rapidly as they were able to squander their wives'
property. In 1816, Lucy Botewright of Virginia advertised:
"That whereas a certain Powhatan Botewright, lately from the
state of Virginia, did agreeably to the laws of this state, marry
Miss Lucy Utley, who at the time of her marriage with the said
Botewright, had by her a considerable quantity of money, a
part in specie and a part in Kentucky notes, and said Botewright did on the last day of January, 1816, taking advantage
of his wife's absence who had gone to one of the neighbors, and
packed up his clothes and all the money, and made his escape:—These are to caution all women not to intermarry with
said Botewright, as she is determined to prosecute, if he marries
contrary to the laws of this state or any of the United States."[20]

The next year Mary Dodd found herself in a like predicament. Mary had made the serious mistake of marrying the
suave Jesse Dougherty who had whispered bewitching words
in her ear. Later she found that Jesse had a marked fondness

for her property. She "posted" him in the public press by warning: "And beware of the swindler Jesse Dougherty, who married me in November last, and sometime after marriage informed me that he had another wife alive, and before I recovered, the villain left me, and took one of my best horses— one of my neighbors was so good as to follow him and take the horse from him, and bring him back. The said Dougherty is about forty years of age, five feet ten inches high, round shouldered, thick lip, complexion and hair dark, grey eyes, remarkably ugly and ill-natured, and very fond of ardent spirits, and by profession a notorious liar. This is therefore to warn all widows to beware of the swindler, as all he wants is their property, and they may go to the devil for him after he gets that. Also, all persons are forewarned from trading with said Dougherty, with the expectation of receiving pay from my property, as I consider the marriage contract null and void agreeably to the law; you will therefore pay no attention to any lies he may tell you of his property in this county. The said Dougherty has a number of wives living, perhaps eight or ten, (the number not positively known), and will, no doubt, if he can get them have eight or ten more. I believe that is the way he makes his living."[21] Women dragged trifling husbands before the state legislatures seeking divorces from them on the grounds of philandering, or for having a string of wives all the way across the frontier.[22]

Exploitation of women by rascals who either made love or married them for the sole purpose of gaining possession of their property seems to have been at least a frontier threat. One legislature adopted laws which prevented "forcible and stolen marriages" for the purpose of abuse. These statutes were specific in providing that "Women, as well as maidens, as widoms, and wives having substances for the lucre of such substances, have been oftentimes taken by misdoers, contrary to their will; and afterwards married to such misdoers, or to others by their consent and defiled."[23] Frequently legislators were presented cases involving many irregular angles of matrimonial differences. Bigamy and exploitation were certainly evils of the frontier West, and statutory measures were necessary to curb them.

Not a large proportion of the women, by any means, were unfaithful wenches who committed the "original sin" with all comers. Of course for the most part, the frontier women were as solid and staunch in their virtues as was the virgin forest. Frontiersmen came to regard them as such, and at their public gatherings where toasts were drunk by the hundreds, one of the first subjects was *the fair*. It was a tender sentiment indeed that a bull-voiced Kentucky toastmaster roared out:

> "THE FAIR—The World was sad, the garden
> Was Wild
> And man the hermit sighed
> Till woman smiled."[24]

On another occasion a frontier toastmaster drank wishfully to the *"fair of Kentucky*—enlightened, virtuous and amiable— may each meet with a friend qualified to appreciate her worth."

Cordial friends, however, occasionally *borrowed* each other's wives and sometimes were so unthoughtful as to forget to return them. At Louisville, in 1800, a jovial fellow was in the habit of inviting his friends into his home to enjoy the conviviality of a dutiful wife and a well-laden table. Among others there came a pious Methodist preacher who had more fondness for the loving caresses of his neighbor's wife than respect for Biblical commandments against such indiscretions. After enjoying his gracious host's hospitality for several weeks, this revered "man of the Word," "started off one fine summer's morning, taking with him, probably through mistake or inadvertence, *his friend's wife!* The host missing this article of domestic furniture upon his return home, and suspecting whither it might have gone, put boot in stirrup and dashed off in pursuit. He soon overtook the *soi distant* [sic] Reverend

Gentleman and demanded his property." The preacher made a proposition that he would trade his saddle mare, and would throw in the bridle and saddle, for immediate possession of the adulterous wife. The disgruntled husband being a good and "reasonable" Kentuckian whose love of fine horseflesh far outweighed his appreciation of wifely companionship consented readily to the trade. The preacher led his feminine prize away, while the husband rode happily back to Louisville to bestow his attentions and affections upon the docile mare.[25] Few frontiersmen in like predicament, however, were so fortunate at salvage.

Sometimes wandering and wayward husbands returned to their deserted wives and reclaimed them after years of separation. A western Enoch Arden went back to Louisville to resume marital relations with a wife who had given him up years before for dead. His "grieving" wife had not wasted much time, however, awaiting his return for she had married and buried two other husbands, and when the wandering benedict returned she was hotly in pursuit of a fourth. When he appeared on the scene in a good state of health, the long separated couple flew into each other's arms. A minister was called in and the two were rejoined in the bonds of matrimony.[26]

A tenderer aspect of the romantically inclined West was the pleasure of "courting" on horseback. Riding was conducive to lively conversation, and timid lovers were not faced with the embarrassment of running out of something to talk about. As a courting couple rode along the roads and trails, the scene changed just often enough to keep the conversation alive. To a young swain who drives a modern automobile, trees, rocks and streams mean nothing as points where he will make his proposal, but to the amorous gentleman of the nineteenth century in the West, mounted on horseback they meant everything. Many a timid horseback rider marked the spot where he intended to make his proposal, and rode toward it with fear and trembling. One western lover declared to his fair equestrian companion that "I had determined not upon any account, to pass that tree, without making known to you a devoted attachment which you have no doubt guessed sometime since. But I am such an outrageous coward that I could not summons the courage even to speak."²⁷ With this frank admission the timid frontier lover proposed and received a favorable answer. At least the early western swains had some advantages over their twentieth century descendants. The horse knew the way home, and when roads were constructed a horse and buggy did not require the exacting attention of a steering wheel.

Sons of the West loved the gals, and when they had to be away from them they felt an insatiable longing. It is with a plaintive note that a frontiersman wrote home from the Mexican War that "I miss one thing very much out here, and if you have a chance you must send me one—that is the Daguerreotype likeness of some pretty girl. I am not particular which one. Almost all the boys have one with them excepting myself, and it puts me to considerable trouble borrowing them so I will not *forget how our girls look*. If you can find a young lady who will send me a copy do so by all means, and if I reach Mexico I will reciprocate the favor."²⁸ This was the sentiment of the whole frontier; it didn't want to forget the gals. Even though they were scarce, there were always enough to keep the boys interested and excited.

When a backwoodsman loved a girl it was with all his heart. When he was away from her he put a powerful strain on his imagination trying to conjure up visions of her. A Kentuckian undertook to relieve himself of this anxiety, and to do some vicarious courting besides by having a miniature made of his gal.

### THE KENTUCKIAN AND A MINIATURE

Daniel Long was a tall specimen of humanity, as his name implies, hailing from Kentucky; he stood about six feet eight in his stockings, and was wanting in flesh, although he made up for it in stature. He had great staring eyes, of that peculiar color which generally appertains to the feline tribe; a nose commonly termed a "pug"; a huge mouth, which, as the facetious Dr. Valentine observes, would go round his head, if it was not for his ears: these ornamental appendages were concealed by a dense shock of hair, of the reddest hue imaginable.

He was very decently clad, and one evening while on his visit to one of our eastern cities, he sauntered along the principal streets of ——. His attention was soon arrested by the display of some miniatures in a window; attached was a card informing the passers-by that the artist was to be found at certain hours, accompanied with a polite invitation to the public in general to walk up to his studio and examine the collection on hand, to which there was "free admission."

Our hero accepted the invitation forthwith, and made his way up the stairs, and opening the door found himself in the presence of the painter; he made an awkward bow, which was responded to by a courteous salutation from the other.

"I say, mister," thus Dan opened the conversation, "did you paint all them pictures in the winder down there?"

"Yes, sir," replied Mr. Easel.

"Wall," he continued, "they're darn nice-looking, and you are an almighty smart chap, I swan. How long does it take a feller to do 'em up slick, eh?"

"It depends on the style and size."

"Now look here, stranger, there's a gal what loves me, and I love her, and we both on us love t'other; I'm agoing to marry her, I am; what'll you have for paintin' her picter!"

"If you wish a low-priced article, I can accommodate you at twenty-five dollars; but should you desire a more finished one, in my best style I increase my price to fifty—"

"Oh darn your fifty," the Kentuckian interrupted; "I say, mister, you may begin it right away."

"Very well, sir; when will the lady be ready for her first sitting?" inquired Mr. Easel.

"Her what?" ejaculated Dan.

"Her first sitting," rejoined the artist. "When shall I first have the honor of seeing her!"

"Seeing her," our hero replied—"seeing her! Why, stranger, she's way out West—she won't be here at all."

"And how am I to make a likeness, never having seen her, or knowing anything of her?" asked the bewildered painter.

"Didn't you tell me, stranger, that you painted them picters down thar, and if you painted them, you kin paint her; she's an all-fired purty gal as ever I see, or you see, or anybody else see; jist paint her as purty as you can do."

"But, my dear sir, are you not aware that there are different styles of beauty? Here are two pictures," continued Mr. Easel, "of different persons, though both are considered beauties; the one a blonde, the other a brunette; you perceive there is a remarkable distinction between them."

Daniel stared at them, and, after a moment, exclaimed, "Wal, I'll jis' look round your shop, an' see if I can't scare up somethin' that's like her, anyhow."

And in accordance with this original idea, he ran his eye over every one of the paintings with which the studio was adorned, but without finding anything which could compare with his Dulcinea. At last he turned toward Mr. Easel with a sorrowful glance, and was about to speak, when he spied a pair of plaster casts, and vaulting over toward the mantelpiece on which they rested, he exclaimed,

"By golly, thar she is now! 'ceptin' she's all white."

The cast was an Apollo!

Mr. Easel looked at him in perfect amazement, revolving in his mind whether his visitor was a fool, madman, or one playing off a practical joke. He remembered too that it was not the first of April. While he was thus undecided, Mr. Long began again:

"Now, Mr. Painter, here's ten dollars to begin with; do you paint her like that 'ere stater, only make her look somethin' like flesh and blood, and dress her up slick. If I didn't know she war alive this moment, I'd swore that is her ghost."

"But, sir," responded the painter, looking at the note and finding it genuine, "that is a cast of the celebrated Apollo, and—"

"Never mind," struck in Dan, "whether its Polly or Nancy; I say it's my gal, and jist you get to work and have the picter done agin' I go home."

The painter then inquired her complexion, color of hair, eyes, and promised to exert himself to the utmost of his power. Dan left; the artist was in a genuine quandary, but he resolved to try, at all events, and succeeded in making a very good-looking picture. Our Kentucky friend came in every day to see how his gal's face was gittin' on, and to correct mistakes.

At last the miniature was completed, paid for, and Dan set off homeward bound, and in a few days arrived safe and sound. Alas! for the inconstancy of the female sex. Mr. Long found that a Mr. Short had supplanted him in affections for his lady-love, and made her Mrs. Short.

"Cheated, humbugged," screamed Dan, "fifty dollars for your paintin' that ain't worth fifty coppers to me now. Oh! California is all that's left to me!"[29]

The West indeed was the land for a romantic female who liked to have men paying strict attention to her whims and fancies. The following account is a good presentation of frontier conditions as far as single women were concerned.

### Sophy and the Fellers

I got here two weeks ago, and here I shall certainly end my days. Mr. Garrison that came out with me left me at Shekigo, and I was glad on it, for I never did see a feller stick to a gal as he did to me, and it warn't for nothin', nether—but he didn't talk of marryin' me, but was jest hangin' round me, but I told him to keep his distance—that's the way to use such fellers. I've a notion that hees in a fix with a gal down in Kaintuck—and now, I wouldent look at him now, for I've had five fellers to spark me since I cum here, and another wants to cum, but I give him the bags. One of my sparks has got three quarter secshuns and hous, is six foot tall, and four yoke oxen, and is a widdorer, and wants to marry me next week, but I shall wait a little and see if

I can do enny better, for between us, widdorers are so quear, and talk rite up so, they alwis friten me—but howsumever I s'pose they don't mean more than uther men. This cuntry is very large and so is men and the prarys they say is rollin' but I don't see but they are as still as any uther plase. Meeting is scarcse here and wheat dont fetch but 2 and 6—hay and potatoes they almost give away, and sich lots of children—the unfeelin' mothers feed their babys on pork and potatoes on account of milk sickness in this country, a puty way to grow babys I guess you'll think.

Now you must come out, I know you'll make your fortin here. Jim sez ther's only one gal on the hill of big prayry, with golden hair like yourn, and she got an offer every day in the week after she got here. Now she's got a husband, a nise hous and farm and a pare of twins. You can't help liking the country—tell Amy if she'll come here she wont have to keep awishing and a lucking for the fellers as we used to in Westbrook—out her theyr rite arter you before you think of it. Tell mother I hope she'll come to see me as soon as I get to housekeepin' and if she thinks on it she may bring them little red socks in the till of my chest. When you cum be shure and go with the steamboat *Cheespeak,* Captain Dilsy, at Bufferlow—he is the nicest man on the water, was so good to us all. I almost luv him if he *is* a marryed man. Give my luv to Jane, and ask her how she and Bill gits on, and if hees popped the question yet. She may have him for all me—I can do better. I can pick my likin's 'mong the fel'ers here. Nobody cant help likin' this country. No more from your lovin' Cousin till death.[30]

Kentuckians of the early period took their love affairs seriously. To take liberty with their fair ladies was to invite trouble quickly.

## A Kentucky Row

At a ball in Frankfort the other evening a young gentleman it is said took an undue liberty with a lady's pretty ringlet. The lady made her complaint to a gentleman with whom she was dancing. Thereupon the last named gentleman knocked the first named gentleman down in the ballroom. The fight extended until, as we are told, fifteen or twenty persons were engaged in it. Fists, pistols, and knives of all sorts were flourished, and some blood was spilt, though, nobody was killed. Two of the persons who took part in the affair, have since arrived here (Louisville) with the intention of settling their affair on the Indiana shore.

It is said that an English officer, sojourning for a short time in Frankfort, was remarking, the day before the affray that he had heard much of Kentucky "rows" and that it was his most anxious desire to see one. When the ballroom fight got well under way, a gentleman who had heard the expressed wish of the officer ran to his room and told him what was going on. The officer ran to the ballroom, but, the moment he entered the door, a tremendous stray fist knocked him down. He scrambled to his feet ensconced himself in a corner where he thought he could look on in security. He had not been there many minutes, however, before a big fellow mistaking him for another, rushed at him, exclaiming, "This is the very scoundrel I have been looking for." The officer darted like lightning from the room. And strange to say he has not since been heard to express the slightest curiosity to see a Kentucky row.[31]

## CHAPTER XV

# YANKEES B'GAD

THE West came to know that ingenious Yankee who invented the "wag-on-the-wall" clock as both its benefactor and general aggravator. The frontier was a fertile market for clocks and "notions," and a continuous stream of New England peddlers poured down the Ohio River from Pittsburgh after 1790 in search of backwoods customers. Flatboats loaded with clocks left Pittsburgh, and horseback traders with four clocks attached to their saddles rode through the country selling them at twenty to forty dollars each.[1] Names such as Eli Terry and Seth Thomas became virtually as famous in the West as those of leading pioneers.

Yankee traders were shrewd, and they were past masters at driving trades which were always favorable to themselves. They were so much better traders than the backwoodsmen that the latter came to look upon them as cheats, cutthroats and thieves. Even newspaper editors took editorial notice of the eastern tradesmen and denounced them as calumniators of the first water. They accused the Yankee of duping the honest people of the West by taking valuable products in exchange for useless and inferior "notions." John Bradford, at Lexington, Kentucky, denounced all Yankees as crooks. He said, "Yankees are educated by charity, and come to the West to turn peddlers, editors, clockmakers, tinners and robbers." A murder had recently been committed on the Ohio River and Bradford accused *Yankees* of this fiendish deed through his editorial column.[2]

Hatred of Yankees was universal throughout the frontier before 1812 because of their shrewdness in trade, but after that date it was because of the New Englanders' attitude toward the war with England, Easterners were dubbed "damned bluelight," and "blue-bellies," who were too good to fight for their country.[3] A stonemason told Henry Bradshaw Fearon that "there is nothing in America but rogues and damned Yankees—it may be well enough for getting pork and whisky, and wages, it would be a good enough country if it was free from dirty, cheating Yankees."[4] False rumors caused the Westerners to believe that the Yankees were busily engaged in the manufacture of "cute notions" which included wooden nutmegs, pit coal, indigo, and gin made by putting pinetops in whisky. Even tavern-keepers were dubious of Yankee patrons because they were afraid the sons from the land of "bluelights" would outtalk them.[5] So notorious had the peddler tradition become that boatmen often answered greenhorns, when they were asked concerning their cargoes, that they had on board pit coal, indigo, wooden nutmegs, straw baskets and Yankee notions.[6]

Kentuckians hated Yankees, and frequently foreign visitors speaking with strange accents were asked two and three prices for services and goods. The traveler Faux was mistaken for a Yankee and when he was ferried over the Ohio River at Cincinnati the boatman charged him a dollar instead of the standard fee of a quarter. This caused the irate Faux to observe that the "Yankees are the smartest of fellows, except the Kentuckians. Suaveness and impudence are characteristic of these men."[7]

"A Kentuckian," said the traveler Fordham, "suspects nobody, but a Yankee, whom he considers as a sort of Jesuit."[8] This observer might have broadened his observation, and said that this was true of frontiersmen in general. Perhaps nobody in the whole western country was so conscious of the regard with which the natives held the "bluelights" from the East as the Yankee himself. At Winchester, Virginia, an Easterner on his way to the West was offered a wager by the landlord of the tavern where he was stopping that he could not pull a Yankee trick on him. This gave the traveler an idea, and the next morning before he left he succeeded in selling at a good price the coverlets off his bed to the boasting Boniface, and then had the audacity to collect the wager.[9]

Stories of wooden nutmegs persisted throughout the western country. The Vincennes *Sun* published a story about the "nutmeg and button" business in that locality. This report made the claim that a Yankee had sold all the Wabash merchants buttons sawed the easy way, that is, they were sawed crosswise of the grain and would split easily. An account, purporting to come from a purchaser, commented to the effect that "those buttons that were made of sassafras were tolerable good; but those made of elm and beach warn't worth a damn."

Whether these stories were true or not mattered little to the public. Most people believed the Yankee a rascal, and they put nothing past him when it came to thinking up clever or crooked schemes. A Yankee peddler appeared in a small Kentucky town with harness and leather goods for sale. He asked an aged Kentuckian if he wished to buy a horse collar. "Hog's tallow?" asked the startled native. "Horse collar!" shouted the peddling Yankee. Again the Kentuckian shouted, "Hog's tallow?" and vehemently the salesman repeated, "Horse collar!" So thoroughly convinced was ol' Kaintuck that here was a hawk-billed Yankee who was trying to make a perfect idiot of him that he shouted back, "Damn you and your hog's tallow too, so clear out with it, I don't want any of it." An enterprising Yankee, however, might have sold "hog's tallow" in Kentucky without difficulty if only he had declared that it had a high medicinal value.[10]

Yankees, of course, were to blame for much of the existing prejudice against them. Timothy Flint, an informed Easterner, said that he could recite a score of Yankee tricks, but that he was certain three-fourths of them were not committed by Easterners. Wherever Flint and his family stopped for the night they were first asked if they were Yankees, and when they said yes there was a lengthening of visages. It was only through his appearance and profession, said Flint, that he and his family were able to travel and receive courteous treatment. They were told many times of the petty impositions and cheating of the Yankee. Landlords talked by the hour of tricky Jonathans who walked off without paying for rooms and meals.[11]

Traveling through the West, Easterners felt themselves superior and criticized without restraint the service which they got, and the crude conditions of living which they found. They were incessant talkers, and anything west of the mountains to them was unworthy of consideration. They inspired a sort of terror, wrote Flint, "and as that terror procures a certain degree of respect, many a blockhead from the southern and middle states has wished to shine his hour, as a wise man, and has assumed this terrific name; and thus the impression has finally been established, that almost all the emigrants who pass down the river are Yankees."[12]

Another Yankee condemned the practice of talking and asking endless questions on the part of his fellow Easterners. This traveler, J. H. Ingraham, found on board his steamer from New Orleans to Natchez, a girl from Vermont who was on her way to the West. She asked Ingraham one question after another, and hardly waited for an answer. This incessant quizzing finally exhausted the patience of the schoolmaster-author and he declared that "traveling Yankee ladies are certainly, unless young and pretty, a little annoying."[13]

Yankees floated southward with their store boats on which floated red flags for groceries, and yellow ones advertising dry goods. Enterprising New England merchants operated fleets of arks and broadhorns that floated annually down the river to sell goods and to collect products for the New Orleans market. Once these products, taken in exchange for Yankee notions, were sold in New Orleans, the peddlers sailed around the coast to New England to start their circuits all over again.

This southern trade often infuriated local tradesmen who did everything possible to destroy transient businessmen. B. V. Marsh voiced the sentiment of all western merchants when he warned his readers in an editorial-advertisement to beware of Yankees. Heading his plea in favor of local merchants, Marsh began, "Clocks—Yankees, Peddlers and Economy. Amid the gigantic strides the world is now making in the arts and sciences . . . nutmegs, mahogany hams and Yankee clocks, this last mentioned article has reached such perfection in its manu-facturory that the very best article, a brass 8-day Yankee clock, from any of the Eastern Clock factories can be had . . . to sell for $12 to $15. Peddlers charge from $35 to $40.

"Desirous of putting a stop to these impositions of these itiner-ant clock peddlers who have been long practicing in conjunction with their fraternal kin, who now go about the country with their knapsacks, vending rusty needles, rotten thread, brass jewelry, and other worthless wares, together with some remote members of the same family, who deal in slopshop secondhand clothes and half-made new ones, of old and rotten goods, made and fixt up to sell and unfit to wear, I have, with a view to open-ing the eyes of the community to this system of humbuggery, obtained from the factories an assortment of superior Yankee Clocks, which I am now offering for about one-third the price for which the peddlers sell the same article.

"And just recollect when you want a clock, that my clocks and my prices will spread a contagion among the Yankee clock peddlers as fatal to their trade as was the cholera to good health."[14]

The average Westerner believed that New England was filled with swindling clock peddlers who were entirely void of conscience.[15] So definite was this feeling that even a British traveler gained the impression that "the whole race of Yankees, peddlers in particular, are proverbial for dishonesty. These go forth annually in thousands to lie, cheat, cog, swindle, in short, to get possession of their neighbor's property in any manner it can be done with impunity. Their ingenuity in deception is confessed very great. They warrant broken watches to be the best timekeepers in the world; sell pinchback trinkets of gold; and have always a large assortment of wooden nutmegs, and stagnant barometers."[16]

A Kentuckian in the wild mountain county of Clay mistook

Charles Fenno Hoffman for a "trading" Yankee. This hillbilly looked at Hoffman's rifle and inquired if he had any more left. Another native asked him what price he set upon it, for he believed a Yankee had no use for a gun. One of these gawky mountaineers asked the somewhat undiplomatic question: "Are there any gentlemen among the Yankees? Well, you see, stranger," said the hillbilly, "I thought they were all peddlers; but how come you deny your country if it isn't after all among the leavings of nature's work?"[17]

The editor of the *Western Monthly Review,* himself a Yankee, was somewhat more charitable to the itinerate merchants than the native son above. This writer said: "A Yankee is a Yankee over the globe; and you might know him, if you met him on the mountains of the moon in five minutes by his nationality. We love and honor him for it, wherever it is not carried to a blinding prejudice."[18] The popular conception of the Yankee in the West was of an individual who never fit his clothes. His legs were long and his trousers short. His waist was slender, but too long for coat and trousers to meet. Long skinny arms stuck far beyond coat sleeves, and his elbows had a way of gnawing out.[19] He had a hatchet face with a hawk-bill nose, and a high rasping voice. The characteristics which the editor of the *Western Review* had in mind, however, were his go-getting qualities.

"Halloo! Horse!" said an old tavern-keeping Boniface, slapping on the shoulder a broad-backed fellow that stood in the doorway. "Where's Yankee and Dutchie? The bacon and greens are smoking on the table, and I must take a glass of cool liquor with them before we sit down. Ah! there's my stout rifle cracker; come along, Dutchie my boy. . . . Yankee, my tall fellow, a glass of old peach with us before dinner; smack! how it relishes! down with it all; it won't harm a hair of your head; I've washed my mouth with it these forty years. And now, boys, in to dinner while the bacon's hot."[20] These Westerners were interested in what they believed to be a genuine live "blue-bellied" Yankee. They fully expected him, however, to strike up a trade which would "skin" them out of their houses and homes. A Yankee to them was like a rattlesnake, a dangerous but exceedingly fascinating varmint.

Frontiersmen sought trouble by displaying greenhorn curiosity about travelers who came among them. Sharpers were quick to take advantage of such situations and to engage in tricky transactions. The provincial inhabitants were seldom able to discriminate between foreigners and Yankees. An Englishman and his son, traveling through the West were hailed continually with, "What goods do you sell?" When the natives were informed that these travelers had nothing for sale they were asked, "What onder arth are you if you ain't peddlers?" One woman ran after them and begged them to stop and show their goods, and when she was told they were not peddlers she philosophized that "if you h'ant got nothin' to sell, I reckon you must be tailors, and that you are going about tailoring?"[21] The most romantic moment in the lives of many frontiersmen was that occasion when a Yankee opened his pack and displayed gaudy calico, brass clocks, shiny jewelry, glistening knives and razors, and loudly ticking watches. These pack peddlers knew more about practical sales psychology than half the high-pressure professors in modern business schools. They never forced sales upon their gawky customers, but led them on with subtlety until the customers were begging the peddlers to sell their notions.[22]

James Flint was amused at times, and annoyed at others by the general belief in the sparsely settled sections of the back country that everybody who came by with a pack was a peddler selling goods. Wherever he stopped the backwoodsmen asked where he had come from and where he was going. They wished also to know whether he carried goods or plunder in his pack. If the former, they were anxious to see them, if the latter, they knew that he was traveler and pumped him of information of all sorts.[23]

The clock peddler led the itinerate Yankee traders in business throughout the West. He was the supersalesman of the whole drifting mercantile population from New England. A traveler said, "Yankee clock peddlers, they are everywhere, and have contrived, by an assurance and perseverance that have been unrivaled from the McAbees down, to stick up a clock in every cabin in the western country. Wherever we have been in Kentucky, Indiana, Illinois, Missouri or Arkansas, in cabins where there was not a chair to sit on, there was sure to be a Connecticut clock. The clock peddler is an irresistible person; he enters a log cabin, gets familiarly acquainted with its inmates in the shortest imaginable time, and then comes to business: 'I guess I shall have to sell you a clock before I go.'

" 'I expect a clock's of no use here; besides I h'ant got no money to pay for one.'

" 'Oh, a clock's fine company here in the woods; why you couldn't live without one after you'd had one a while, and you can pay for it some other time.'

" 'I calculate you'll find I ain't a-going to take one.'

"Turning to the wife the Yankee began 'Well, Mistress, your husband won't take a clock; it is most surprising; he hadn't ought to let you go without one. Why every one of your neighbors is a-going to git one. I suppose, however, you've no objection to my nailing one up here, till I come back in a month or so. I'm sure you'll take care of it, and I shall charge you nothing for the use of it at any rate.' "[24] By this easygoing method the peddler sold his clock because no family ever allowed a Yankee to take one off the wall when they got used to it, and the shrewd rascal knew just how long it ordinarily took a frontier family to form an attachment for a clock.

So definite was the feeling against the Yankee in certain communities of the West that many New England immigrants were careful never to divulge their place of origin. They were eager to be called Buckeyes, Hoosiers, Kentuckians and Suckers as quickly as possible.[25] Many peddlers sold out their supply of goods or they ran amuck with highly restrictive peddler laws and were forced out of business.[26] They found settling fertile farms and building homes and barns more appealing than driving carts or packing large bundles of goods through a wild and sparsely settled country.

A traveler in Arkansas was much impressed by the effort which a Yankee was making to prevent his nationality from being known. He claimed to be a Spaniard and had adopted the name Don Bigotes. This visitor, who discovered Jonathan under the pretense of being a Spaniard, said that "I was seated opposite to a dignified person with a well grown set of mustachios, a round-about jacket, with other vestments made in Spanish fashion, and a profusion of showy rings on his fingers." Don Bigotes had spread the information that he was from New Spain, but he gave himself away to the stranger when he committed an un-Spanish-like trick by bolting his food and dashing out of the dining room. Suspecting the ring-jangling Don of duplicity, the British traveler followed him to his place of business where he found him seated cross-legged working away with needle and thread at the tailor's trade. After a brief conversation the Englishman discovered that Don Bigotes of New Spain was a Yankee named Patterson from Connecticut who was out to make his fortune in the quickest possible way. "Such is the plastic nature of Jonathan," said the visitor, "his indomitable affection for the almighty dollar, and his enterprise in pursuit of it, that it is far from being impossible that there are lots of his brethren at this time in the interior of China, with their heads shaved and long pigtails behind them, peddling cuckoo clocks and selling wooden nutmegs."[27]

Judge John Dean Caton of Chicago was very much pleased when a group of Hoosier wagoners from the Wabash Valley mistook him for a Kentuckian or a Tennessean. Among these ox-driving backwoodsmen was an old patriarch called Uncle Jake. Uncle Jake told young lawyer Caton, "These Yankees that are coming in here in bigger flocks than the locusts that eat up the 'Filistens, hip and thigh,' will be stealing corner lots and running off with 'em in less nor a month and then they will be after you to chase 'em. Chase 'em! Why, them fellers will slip through a knothole where you could not squeeze a flaxseed. But they will pay you all the same. There's your hog and hominy, young man!" To these Hoosier wagoners everyone from east of Ohio was a Yankee, and they considered them sharper if not more honest than horse thieves and counterfeiters.[28] Mark Fletcher, clerk of the Circuit Court of Kane County, Illinois, impressed a cross in one side of the Bible and a silver dollar in the other. Protestant Hoosiers and Suckers he swore upon the opened Bible, Catholics he swore upon the sign of the cross, and Yankees upon the imprint of the dollar.[29]

Wherever there was a settled community the Yankee was certain to find it. He came most often as a trader to purchase native products and to sell manufactured goods, but occasionally one of them settled in the country. They were keen judges of good land and were quick to sense an opportunity. As they drove over impossible trails through dense forest, or over the western prairies they paid strict attention to natural resources and returned to take advantage of them. A western newspaper quoted Daniel Boone in his latter years as saying that "I first moved to the woods of Kentucky. I fought and repelled the savages, and hoped for repose. Game was abundant, and our path was prosperous, but soon I was molested by interlopers from every quarter. Again I retreated to the region of the Mississippi, but again these speculators and settlers followed me. Once more I withdrew to the licks of Missouri, and here at length I hoped to find rest. But I was still pursued, for I had not been two years at the licks before a damned Yankee came and settled down within a hundred miles of me!"[30]

Although there was honest antipathy against the Yankee in the frontier country, occasionally a good-natured anecdote found its way into western newspapers. Perhaps the best-known of these is the purported conversation between a Yankee and a Kentucky congressman. These gentlemen were traveling together when they met a drove of mules being driven to market. The Yankee asked, "Do you know what animals these are?" "Indeed I do," replied the Bluegrass congressman, "they surely must be some of your constituents." "No doubt," answered

Jonathan, "and I suppose they are on their way to Kentucky to be employed as schoolmasters." In this case it is hard to say who was being joked the hardest, the Kentucky congressman, the Yankee schoolmasters, or the people in the West who employed graduates of the eastern colleges as academy masters and preachers.[31]

Doubtless the Yankee did skin pioneers by the thousands, and perhaps his clocks and notions were not always as represented, but he was an interesting part of the frontier's population. He was a persevering and ingenious "crittur" who could drive a two-horse wagon through a virgin forest and locate every settler's cabin from Powell River to the Arkansas, and he could sell merchandise without difficulty. He was the brunt of many crude jokes, he tolerated good-naturedly the old fiction of wooden nutmegs, mahogany hams, tricky clocks and pine-top gin. When Westerners called him Jonathan, "a damned blue-belly" and a "bluelight," he accepted all this with a Yankee's good humor. Yankee blood was a fine leaven which was needed on the frontier, and from which the West profited on a large scale.

So thoroughly was the "clock, nutmeg, pit coal and pine-top gin" tradition of the Yankee established on the frontier that western yarns were nearly always colored with it. Edmund Kirke relates a story which covers the frontier attitude toward the hawk-bill traders of the East.

## A RANTANKEROUS YANKEE

"Well, Stranger, I reckon I owes ye one now, I never knowed nary uther Yankee but onst an' he war 'bout so smart as ye is, fur he sold dad a clock. Shill I tell ye 'bout it?"

"Yes, but finish the moon story first."

"It hain't a minnet long, an' I kin end the moon in a jiffen. Ye sees, dad hed nary clock, an' couldn't tell when the sun riz— he had a great reespect fur the sun, nuver got up afore it in all his life—so, when a peddler come 'long with a whole wagin-load uv clocks, he war drefful put ter't ter hev one. They wus the eight-day kine, all painted up slick, an' worronted to gwo till the eend uv time. The peddler axed ten dollar fur 'em, an' dad hadn't but three. I hed two thet I'd bin a savin' up, an' dad wanted ter borre 'um, but I wouldn't a lent 'um ter him ter save his soul, fur I know'd he'd nuver pay in nuthin' but promizes, an' fur his age, dad war the most promizin' man ye uver know'd on. Wall, I buttoned up my pocket, and dad eyed the clocks; an' sez he ter the peddler: 'Stranger, I'd loike 'un uv them mightily, but rocks is sca'ce, jest now; I hain't got on'y three dollars in the wurle.'

" 'Hain't ye!' said the peddler; 'wall thet's a all-fired pity; but bein's ye's a monstrous nice sort of man, an' bein's I allers kind o' took ter sech folks as ye is, ye kin hev a clock fur yer three dollars. But I wouldn't sell 'un ter nary uther man for thet money, nowhow.'

"Wall, dad tuck the clock, and the peddler tuck the money and mosey'd off.

"Dad sot druffel high on thet clock. He took on over it fur all the wurle, jest like a chile over a new playthin'. He got up airlier, an' sot up later then I uver know'd him afore, jest ter yere it strike, but arter a few days it stopped strikin', and nuver struck agin! Dad wus sold—an' sold, too, by a rantankerous Yankee; an' dad allers 'counted (but mind, Stranger, I doan't guv this as my 'pinion) thet a Yankee ar a lettle the measliest critter in all creation. Wall, not more'n a month arter thet, as dad an' I wus a wuckin' in the corn patch 'un day, who shud come 'long the road but the Yankee peddler. As soon as dad seed him he sez ter me, sez he: 'Bullets an' blisters, Tom! but thar's thet outdacious Yankee! Now, ef I doan't strike better time on his noggin then his dingnation clocks uver struck in all thar lives, I'll pike stret fur kingdom come, ef I hes ter gwo afoot.' Bilin' with wrath, dad moseyed fur the peddler; but he hedn't more'n got inside 'o hearin', 'fore the Yankee bawled out: 'I say, Mister, ye's got a clock as b'longs ter me. It woan't gwo, an' I want's ter get it, an' guv ye 'un as wull gwo. I hed jest 'un bad one in the lot, an' I'se bin a sarchin' fur it 'mong nigh onter a hun'red folks I'se sold clocks ter, an' hain't found it yet, so ye mus' hev tucken it; I knows ye did, case I sees it in yer eye.'

"That mellored dad ter onst, an' ter own the truth, it guv *me* a sort o' good 'pinion ov the Yankee. Wall, dad and he swopped clocks, an' the peddler stayed ter dinner—an' the old man 'udn't take a red fur't, he was so taken with him. As he wus a gwine ter leave, the peddler ope'd the hind eend uv his wagin, an' takin' out a peck measure, heapin' full of whot 'peared the tallest oats thet uver grow'd, he sez ter me, sez he: 'Tom, ye an' yer farder hes bin 'mazin clever ter me, an' I nuver loikes ter be obligated ter nobody, so yere's some o' the finest plantin' oats ye uver know'd on; take 'um; they'll grow ye a monstrous tall crop, as big as oak trees.'

"Now ye sees, I hed a four-year-old mar I'd raised up with my own han's. I sot drefful high on har, an' she got drefful high on oats, an' I'd bin a savin' up them two dollars s'pressly ter buy seed ter make a crap fur her privat' eatin'. So, when I seed them oats o' the peddler's they filled my eye, loike the camel filled the eye of the needle in Scriptur'. He hedn't guv'n me 'nuff ter gwo no distance in plantin', but bein' he war so gen'rous loike, I couldn't ax him ter guv more, so I sez ter him: 'Stranger, wouldn't ye sell a bushel o' them oats?'

" 'Wall, Tom,' he sez; 'bein's it's ye, an' ye an' yer farder is such monstrous clever folk, I doan't know but I'd sel ye the *whole* on 'um, fur the fact ar' they's too hearty loike fur mu hoss; ye see the feller's got a sort o' weak stomach, an' can't 'gest 'um. I guess thar's nigh on ter five bushel, an' bein's they hain't uv no use ter me, ye shill have the hole on 'um, fur them ar' two dollars o' yourn.' Now, I figger'd on my fingers, an' foun' thet warn't more'n forty cents a bushel; an' oats, sech as war raised in our diggins—an' they warn't no way nigh so nice as them—went fur sixty, so ye kin reckon I tuck 'um, an' ye mought b'lieve it rained big blessin's on thet peddler 'bout time he druv off. He'd altered my 'pinion o' Yanks' 'pletely, an' I tole him he orter make hisself inter a wild munag'ree, an' travil the whole southin' kentry, jest ter show folk whot the Yankees raaly is; fur I know'd ef he done it they'd swap thar 'pinions jest as I hed, an' thet ye know would do a might heap t'ards perpertratin' the Union. Wall, arter he war gone, I tuck the five bushel inter the house, an' kivered 'um up keerful in the cock-loft; but, feelin' mighty gen'rous loike, on 'count uv my big bargin', I thor't I'd give the mar a sort o' Christmas dinner o' the peck measure full. So I put 'um afore her, an' she smelled on 'um ravernous mad fur a minnet, but then she turned up her nose, an wouldn't luck at 'um agin.

" 'She found them too hearty loike; I suppose,' I said, re-straining a strong inclination to laugh.

"I s'pose she did, an' I reckon they *would* hev bin raather hard o' 'gestion, fur they wus *shoe pegs!*"

"Shoe pegs?"

"Yas, shoe pegs! The durnation Yankee hed been a scowrn the hull district, an' found no 'un green 'nuff ter buy 'um, but me."[32]

A Yankee who had visited his old home in Bangor to recuper-ate from his trying experiences in the Mississippi Valley wrote a friend of a quarrel which he had overheard on his return trip. This altercation occurred between a Yankee farmer and a tour-ing dandy, and the yarn itself is a fine example of Yankee bluff and shrewdness.

### Kicking a Yankee

The dandy trod on the Yankee's toes and threatened on top of this insult to pitch him out of a steamboat cabin.

"You'll kick me out of this cabing?"

"Yes, sir, I'll kick you out of this cabin!"

"You'll kick *me*, Mr. *Hitchcock*, out of this cabing?"

"Yes, sir, I'll kick *you*, Mr. Hitchcock!"

"Well, I guess," said the Yankee, very coolly, after being

perfectly satisfied that it was himself who stood in such imminent peril of assault, "I guess, since you talk of kicking, you've never heard me tell about old Bradly and my mare, there, to hum?"

"No, sir, nor do I wish—"

"Wal, guess it won't set you back much, anyhow, as kicking's generally best to be considered on. You see old Bradly, is one of these sanctimonious, long-faced hypocrites, who put on a religious suit every Sabbath morning, and with a good deal of screwing manages to keep it on till after sermon in the afternoon; and as I was a Universalist, he allers picked me out as a subject for religious conversation—and the darned hypocrite would talk about heaven, hell and the devil, the crucifixion and prayer without ever winking. Wal, he had an old roan mare that would jump over any fourteen-rail fence in Illinois, and open any door in my barn that hadn't a padlock on it. Two or three times I found her in my stable, and I told Bradly bout it, and he was 'very sorry'—'an unruly animal'—'would watch her,' and a hull lot of such things, all said in a very serious manner, with a face twice as long as old Deacon Farror's, on Sacrement day. I knew all the time he was lying, and so I watched him and his old roan too; and for three nights regular, old roan came to my stable about bedtime, and just at daylight Bradly would come, bridle her and ride off. I then just took my old mare down to a blacksmith's shop, and had some shoes made with 'corks' about four inches long, and had 'em nailed to her hind feet. Your heels, Mister, ain't nuthing to 'em. I took her home, give her about ten halter, and tied her right in the center of the stable, fed her well with oats about nine o'clock, and after taking a good smoke went to bed, knowing that my old mare was a truth-telling animal, and that she'd give a good report of herself in the morning. I hadn't got fairly to sleep before the old 'oman punched me and wanted to know what on airth was the matter out at the stable. Says I, 'Go tu sleep Peggy, it is nothing but Kate—she is kicking off flies, I guess!' Purty soon she punched me agin, and says she, 'Mr. Hitchcock, du get up and see what in the world is the matter with Kate, for she is kicking most powerfully.' 'Lay still, Peggy—Kate will take care of herself, I guess.' Wal, the next morning, about day-light, Bradly, with bridle in hand, cum to the stable, and, as true as the book of Genesis, when he was at the old roan's sides, starn and head, he cursed and swore worse than you did, Mister, when I came down on your toes. Arter breakfast that morning, Joe Davis cum to my house, and says he, 'Bradly's old roan is nearly dead—she's cut all to pieces and can scarcely move.' 'I want to know (says I) how on airth did it happen?' Now Joe Davis was a member of the same church with Bradly, and whilst we were talking up cum that everlastin' hypocrite, and says he, 'Mr. Hitchcock, my old roan is ruined!' 'Du tell,' says I. 'She's cut all to pieces,' says he; 'do you know whether she was in your stable, Mr. Hitchcock, last night?' Wal, Mister, with this I let out: 'Do I *know* it?—(the Yankee here, in illustration, made a sudden advance upon the dandy, who made way for him un-consciously, as it were). Do I know it, you no-souled, shad-bellied, squash-headed old night-owl you!—you hay-hookin', corn-cribbin', fodder-fudgin', cent-shavin', whittlin'-of-nuthin' you!—Kate kicks like a mere dumb beast, but I've reduced the thing to a *science!*'" The Yankee had not ceased to advance, or the dandy, in his astonishment, to retreat; and now, the motion of the latter being accelerated by an apparent demonstration on the part of the former to "suit the action to the word," he found himself in the "social hall," tumbling backward over a pile of baggage and tearing the knees of his pants as he scrambled up, a perfect scream of laughter stunning him from all sides. The defeat was total;—a few moments afterward he was seen drag-ging his own trunk ashore, while Mr. *Hitchcock* finished his story on the boiler deck.[33]

Back-country sheriffs took their official duties seriously. Sel-dom did they worry about peddler's licenses, however, until a Yankee appeared on the scene; then they became most offi-cious.

### Waking Up the Wrong Passenger

The high sheriff of an almighty small settlement in Indiana who had arisen to that tall niche in official duty from the mere lees of pettifogging, knowing the law, and feeling his oats, determined to do his duty up to the handle; and under these circumstances he hit upon all trangressors of the statutes of his country, with the "dead set" of a 'possum on a June bug. Fate, an old sorrel horse, with a Yankee wagon stowed with notions, brought an adventurous son of New England out upon the aforesaid high sheriff's beat, and as the sheriff was particular pandemonium on hawkers and peddlers without license, he no sooner espied a peddler's wagon, or a Dutchman with a pack, than he would "drop all," and board such craft plum! For the sake of abbreviation, we shall call the high sheriff Nickem. Nickem one morning, sees an old sorrel, hitched to a "yaller" wagon, coming up the road; so out he sallies, and soon overhauls the wagon and contents.

"Fine mornin'," said Nickem, reining up his nag in front of the peddler's wagon.

" 'Tis pooty fine, I guess, fur yeour wooden country," said the peddler.

"What you got to sell, anything?" said the sheriff.

"Guess I hev, a few notions, one sort or uther. What'd yeou like to hev? Got some rale slick raze-surs, and some prime strups; an article I guess you want, but wait til you see it, Squire, by the look o' your beard. And here's some rale genoowine paste blackin'—make them old ceow-hide beoots o' yourn shine like a dollar."

"Thank you," said Nickem, "I don't use blackin'; grease is better, we allow, out this way. But what's that stuff in the bottles thar—is it good to take?" continued he, pointing to a lot of labelled bottles.

"Well I guess, Squire, it is sort o' good; its balm o' Columby; good for the 'har,' and cures the belly ache; all nation fine stuff for assistin' 'poor human natur',' as the poet says, in the affairs of life. And such stuff for expandin' the ideas, and causin' 'em to flow spontanacueously! Knew a feller once who took a bottle on a 4th July, a-n-d scissors! didn't he make a speech! Dan'l Webster and Henry Clay got ashamed of themselves, and went clear hum! Fact, by golly!"

"What d'ye ask for it?" inquired Nickem.

"A dollar a bottle's the price, Squire, but see'n its yeou, guess I'll let yeou hev it fur sev-en-ty-five cents. Cheap as dirt, ain't it?"

"Well, I reckon I'll take a bottle; thar's the change," said Nickem.

"And there's the balm of Columby. Haint nothin' else in my line t'day, Squire?" said the composed and vivacious Yankee.

"B'lieve not, oh! yes, now I think of it, stranger, have you got a license for peddling in this State?" said Nickem, coming to business.

"Guess I hev, Squire, may be yeou'd like to see it?"

"Well, stranger, see'in as I'm the high sheriff of this county, I reckon I shall trouble you to show your license."

"Oh! certain, certain, Squire, yeou kin see it; there it is all fixed up in black and white, nice as wax, aint it?"

"It's all right, perfectly right," said Nickem, folding up the document and handing it back to the peddler, and he added, "I don't know, now that I have bought this stuff, that I keer anything about it. I reckon I may as well sell it to you again; what'll you give for it?"

"O! I deon't know that the darn'd stuff's any use to me, but see'n its you, Sheriff, guess I'll give yeou about thirty-seven-and-a-half cents for it," quietly responded the trader. The high sheriff handed over the bottle, and received the change, when the peddler observed:

"I say, yeou, guess I've a question to ask just neow, *hev you got a peddler's license about yeour trowsers?*"

"Me? No, I haven't no use for the article, myself," said Nickem.

"Haint, eh? Well, I guess we'll see abeout that, pooty darn'd soon.—Ef I understand the law, neow its a clear case, that yeou've been a tradin' with me, hawkin' and peddlin' Balm o' Columby, on the highway, and I shall inform on yeou—I'll be darn'd ef I don't!"

Reaching the town, the Yankee peddler was as good as his word, and the high sheriff was *nicked* and fined, *for peddling without a license!* The sheriff was heard to *say,* "You might as well try to hold a greased eel as a live Yankee!"[34]

The razor-strop Yankee was about as common a species of nuisance as the frontier produced. He ran his clock-peddling brethren a close second when it came to disposing of merchandise. This gentleman of trade dealt with a highly specialized clientele but this fact seldom limited his activities.

### Razor-Strop Trade

"I calculate, sir, I couldn't drive a trade with you today," said a true specimen of a Yankee peddler as he stood at the door of a merchant in St. Louis.

"I calculate you calculate about right, for you cannot," was the sneering reply.

"Well, I guess you needn't get huffy about it. Now here's a dozen genuine razor strops, worth two dollars and a half—you may have 'em for two dollars."

"I tell you I don't want any of your trash, so you had better be going."

"Wal, now, I declare! I'll bet you five dollars if you make me an offer for them ere strops we'll have a trade yet."

"Done," replied the merchant, placing the money in the hands of a bystander.

The Yankee deposited the like sum—when the merchant offered him a picayune for the strops.

"They're your'n," as he quietly fobbed the stakes. "But," he added with great apparent honesty. "I calculate a joke's a joke, and if you don't want them strops, I'll trade back!"

The merchant's countenance brightened.

"You're not so bad a chap after all; here are your strops—give me the money."

"There it is," said the Yankee, as he received the strops and passed over the picayune. "A trade's a trade—and now you're wide-awake in airnest; I guess the next time you trade with that pic, you'll do better than buy razor strops."

And away walked the peddler with his strops and the wager, amid the shouts of the laughing crowd.[35]

There is no more appropriate place to leave the reader of this narrative than in a razor-strop trade with a Yankee. At least the reader knows how the trade ended, and who got the pic-ayunes and the wager. I do not intend to leave him in the lurch as a wag in Cincinnati left one of that city's editors. In the 'forties there came to the desk of a Porkapolis editor the begin-ning of a whirlwind love story. So good was the story, in fact, that the editor immediately began publication before he knew whether the whole manuscript existed or not. The opening installment was cleverly organized, and it ended with the hero suspended from the limb of a tree over a yawning chasm by the seat of his pantaloons. Week after week went by with both the editor and his readers wondering when the rest of the serial would appear. Finally it became evident that the editor had been "singed" and his patrons began writing in to know how the story ended. This was embarrassing, but not beyond solution for the "cornered" scribe. He informed his tormenters that, "After hanging to the treacherous tree for four or five weeks, his pantaloons gave way, and Charles Melville rolled headlong into the yawning precipice. He fell a distance of five miles, and came down with the small of his back across a stake, which jarred him so that he was compelled to travel in Italy for his health, where he is at present residing. He is engaged in the butchering business, and is the father of a large family of chil-dren." Unlike the unfortunate Cincinnati editor I hope I have left neither the frontier nor the reader suspended over a yawn-ing precipice.

NOTES

# THE BACKWOODS

[1]Gilbert Imlay, *Topographical Description of the Western Territory*, 1-86; John Filson, *The Discovery, Settlement and Present State of Kentucky*, 57; William Faux, *Memorable Days in America*, 334.

[2]William Calk's Journal, original in possession of Mrs. Price Calk, Mt. Sterling, Kentucky.

[3]A. B. Faust, *The German Element in the United States*, I, 364.

[4]Mann Butler, *History of the Commonwealth of Kentucky*, 1836 ed., 455-456.

[5]E. C. Barker, *Life of Stephen F. Austin*, 8.

[6]C. A. Murray, *Travels in North America During the Years 1834, 1835, 1836*, I, 210.

[7]*Ibid.*, 211, 214, 215.

[8]François A. Michaux, *Travels to the Westward of the Alleghany Mountains*, 70.

[9]In a sense all the foreign travelers' accounts were land advertisements. See specifically W. Winterbotham, *An Historical, Geographical, Commercial and Philosophical View of the United States*, III, 125-148.

[10] George W. Ranck, *The Traveling Church*.

[11]Joseph Doddridge, *Notes on the Settlement and Indian Wars in the Western Parts of Virginia and Pennsylvania*, 129-135.

[12]Charles Fenno Hoffman, *A Winter in the West*, II, 54.

[13]Theodore Roosevelt, *The Winning of the West*, III, 208*ff;* Frederick Jackson Turner, *The Significance of the Frontier in American History*, 26-27; Faust, I, 357-374.

[14]G. W. Featherstonhaugh, *Excursion Through the Slave States*, 81.

[15]April 21, 1820; James Flint, *Letters from America* (Thwaites, IX), 129.

[16]John Wood, *Two Years' Residence in the Settlements on the English Prairie* (Thwaites, X), 341; Flint, 232-233; Featherstonhaugh, 77; Doddridge, 137-140.

[17]W. P. Strickland, ed., *Autobiography of Rev. J. B. Finley*, 66.

[18]Featherstonhaugh, 81.

[19]George Ord, *Supplement to the American Ornithology of Alexander Wilson*, 119, 123, 156.

323

[20]Frequent notices of robberies appeared in western newspapers. The *Kentucky Gazette,* June 1, August 24, September 14, 1801; June 11, 1802.

[21]Hoffman, II, 119.

[22]The *Spirit of the Times,* April 5, 1845, Vol. XV, 61.

[23]Charles Cist, *Cincinnati Miscellany,* I, 187, 272, 318.

[24]Timothy Flint, *Recollections of the Last Ten Years,* 64.

[25]Many of the articles appearing in the *Spirit of the Times* are in the very best dialect. James Flint, 288.

[26]N. M. Ludlow, *Dramatic Life as I Found It,* 76.

[27] Estwick Evans, *A Pedestrious Tour,* 1818, 284.

[28]James Flint, 118.

[29]O. H. Smith, *Early Indiana Trials and Sketches,* 28.

[30]The *Spirit of the Times,* quoting the *Cincinnati Chronicle,* June 27, 1846, XVI, 208.

[31]James Flint, 168.

[32]Isaac Weld, *Travels Through the United States of America,* I, 235; James Flint, 168.

[33]Michaux, 79.

[34]Weld, I, 235.

[35]James Flint, 291.

[36]Hoffman, II, 121.

[37]Auguste Levasseur, *Lafayette en America, 1824 et 1825,* II, 379-381.

[38]W. E. Connelly and E. M. Coulter, *History of Kentucky,* I, 294; Benjamin Casseday, *History of Louisville,* quoting Bedford County *Gazette,* 1814. It was reported that the three shocks of the earthquake frightened the people into building a church, but when the destruction of the world failed to come they built a theater instead.

[39]Faux, 13; Robert Baird, *View of the Valley of the Mississippi,* 223-224; Wood, 255-256; John Bradbury, *Travels in the Interior of America, in the years 1809, 1810, and 1811,* 292; Richard Flowers, *Letters from Lexington and the Illinois* (Thwaites, X), 125.

[40]Frontier legend is full of shooting yarns. Sometimes to miss meant death. Fortescue Cuming, *Sketches of a Tour to the Western Country,* 30-31.

[41]Wood, 289; the *Kentucky Gazette,* April 16, 1805. A party killed 8,800 squirrels in Madison County, *ibid.,* March 18, 1801. A party in Mercer and Lincoln counties killed 5,442, and bet they could kill double the amount on the next day.

[42]F. H. Herrick, ed., John J. Audubon, *Delineations of American Scenery and Character,* 60-61.

[43]Bernard Mayo, *Henry Clay*, I, 150.

[44]The *Kentucky Gazette*, March 4, 1816.

[45]The *Kentucky Reporter*, April 23, 1814, October 21, 1818; Cist, I, 349, 354, 861.

[46]Connelly and Coulter, I, 295.

[47]Weld, I, 192; Murray, I, 211-215. As a legal evidence of mayhem see William Littell, *Statute Law of Kentucky*, II, 13, 467. *Revised Statutes of Indiana* (1824), 79, 142-143; Fortescue Cuming, 118-119; Zadoc Cramer, *The Navigator*, 236-237.

[48]Littell, *Statute Law of Kentucky*, II, 13, 467; *Revised Statutes of Indiana*, 142.

[49]Thomas Hamilton, *Men and Manners in America*, I, 90-91.

[50]Murray, 211-215.

[51]Herrick (Audubon), 56-63; *Minute Book of the Board of Trustees of the Town of Lexington*, June 21, 1798; Francis S. Philbrick, *Laws of Indiana Territory*, 1801-1809, CXXV.

[52]Featherstonhaugh, 79.

[53]This may not be an absolute definition of this game. No contemporary has left an exact description of "long bullets."

[54]The *Spirit of the Times*, quoting the Richmond (Va.) *Times*, August 1, 1846, Vol. XVI, 273.

[55]Ralph Volney Harlow, *Growth of the United States*, quoting an English magazine for the year 1821, 311.

## *VARMINTS*

[1]W. P. Strickland, *Autobiography of Rev. J. B. Finley*, 83-84.

[2]George W. Ranck, *History of Lexington*, 83-84.

[3]G. W. Featherstonhaugh, *Excursion Through the Slave States*, 42.

[4]M. H. Henkle, *The Life of Henry Bidleman Bascom*, 67.

[5]Wm. Faux, *Memorable Days in America*, 205.

[6]The *Spirit of the Times*, July 26, 1845, Vol. XVI-XVII, 249.

[7]*Ibid.*, March 26, 1842, Vol. XII, 45.

[8]Frederick Gerstaecker, *Wild Sports of the Far West*, 259.

[9]F. D. Srygley, *Seventy Years in Dixie*, 71; Featherstonhaugh, 102.

[10]Joseph Doddridge, *Notes*, 107-108.

[11]Strickland, 94-95.

[12]William Littell, *Festoons of Fancy*, 115-118.

[13]Jonathan Carver, *Three Years' Travel Throughout the Interior Parts of North America*, 276-277.

[14]F. H. Herrick, ed., *Delineations of American Scenery and Character*, 64-67.

[15]Carver, 276.

[16]*Ibid.*, 279-280.

[17]James Flint, *Letters from North America* (Thwaites, IX), 169; Maxmillan, *Travels in North America in the Years 1832-1834* (Thwaites, XXII), 169.

[18]Featherstonhaugh, 51.

[19]The *Spirit of the Times,* March 17, 1849, Vol. XIX, 42.

[20]*Ibid.,* August 5, 1854, Vol. XXIV, 296.

[21]The *Western Citizen,* October 26, 1855.

## GREEN 'UNS

[1]Captain Frederick Marryat, *Diary in America,* one vol. ed., 44.

[2]Gershom Flagg, *Pioneer Letters* (Thwaites, XXVI), 356.

[3]The *Spirit of the Times,* August 12, 1837, Vol. VII, 202.

[4]W. H. Milburn, *Pioneer Preachers and People of the Mississippi Valley,* 402.

[5]*Ibid.,* 401.

[6]*Western Monthly Review,* 1829-1830, Vol. III, 352.

[7]Sol. Smith, *Autobiography of a Retired Actor,* 43-44.

[8]N. M. Ludlow, *Dramatic Life as I Found It,* 98-99.

[9]Smith, 47.

[10]John Morris, *The Wanderings of a Vagabond,* 16.

[11]*Ibid.*

[12]The *Spirit of the Times,* December 22, 1849, Vol. XIX, 519.

[13]The *Western Citizen,* August 13, 1831.

[14]The *Spirit of the Times,* quoting the St. Louis *Pennant,* April 25, 1841, Vol. X, 85.

[15]*Ibid.,* March 3, 1849, Vol. XIV, 20.

[16]*Ibid.,* October 23, 1841, Vol. XI, 406.

[17]H. M. Brackenridge, *Recollections of Persons and Places in the West,* 195.

[18]The *Spirit of the Times,* February 26, 1848, Vol. XVIII, 6.

[19]The *Western Citizen,* November 19, 1831; also, Charles Cist, *Cincinnati Miscellany,* II, 134.

[20]The *Spirit of the Times,* June 13, 1845, Vol. XVI, 196.

[21]The *Western Citizen,* April 3, 1848.

[22]The *Spirit of the Times,* August 30, 1851, Vol. XXI, 327.

[23]S. P. Avery, *A Harp of a Thousand Strings,* 292.

## BOOM POLES AND PADDLE WHEELS

[1]The *Spirit of the Times,* August 24, 1844, Vol. XIV, 302.

[2]The *Western Citizen,* July 24, 1846.

[3]Gilbert Imlay, *Topographical Description of the Western Territory,* 60-73; Timothy Flint, *Recollections of the Last Ten Years,* 13; François Michaux, *Travels to the Westward of the Alleghany Mountains,* 166; Seymour Dunbar, *History of Travel in America,* I, 289-294.

[4]James Flint, *Letters from North America* (Thwaites, IX), 167.

[5]Timothy Flint, 15.

[6]George Ord, *Supplement to the American Ornithology of Alexander Wilson,* 119.

[7]Timothy Flint, 30-31.

[8]*Ibid.*

[9]*Ibid.,* 36-37.

[10]J. H. Ingraham, *The Southwest,* 19; Robert Baird, *View of the Valley of the Mississippi,* 93; James Flint, 257; John Bradbury, *Travels in the Interior of America* (Thwaites, V), 211.

[11]Otto A. Rothert, *The Outlaws of Cave-in-Rock,* 43-46; Dunbar, one vol. ed., 298-300.

[12]*Western Monthly Review,* Vol. III, 1829-1830, 354.

[13]Rothert, 37-53.

[14]G. W. Featherstonhaugh, *Excursion Through the Slave States,* 62.

[15]Michaux, 31, 34.

[16]The *Spirit of the Times,* April 19, 1851, Vol. XXI, 105.

[17]Zadoc Cramer, *The Navigator,* 5th ed., 1806; Archer Butler Hulburt, *Waterways of Western Expansion, the Ohio River and Its Tributaries* (Historic Highways of America), IX, 82-99.

[18]Hulburt, quoting Harris' Pittsburgh *Business Directory* for 1827, 108-113; Walter Blair and Franklin Meine, *Mike Fink, King of Mississippi Keelboatmen,* 38-44.

[19]Hulburt, 114-116.

[20]*Western Monthly Review,* Vol. II, June, 1828, 15; Timothy Flint, 98; A. C. Quisenberry, *The Life and Times of Humphrey Marshall,* 38, quotes the *Historical Sketch Book* of New Orleans as saying that "Kaintuck was a generic name used by Creoles." The Creoles would say to their children, *"Toi tu n'es qu'un mauvais Kaintuck."*

[21]The *Spirit of the Times,* December 5, 1846, Vol. XVI, 481.

[22]Timothy Flint, 98; John Woods, *Two Years' Residence in the Settlements on the English Prairies* (Thwaites, X), 235.

[23]*Ibid.*

[24]Blair and Meine, 30-31, 105.

[25]Thomas Ford, *History of Illinois,* 98-99; James Flint, 260; John Bradbury, 211; Ingraham, 21.

[26]James Flint, 260; Ingraham, 21.

[27]Ord, 155.

[28]Benjamin Casseday, *History of Louisville,* 128-134, 141.

[29]*Ibid.,* 130.

[30]Baird, 93.

[31]*Ibid.,* 323; Gershom Flagg, *Pioneer Letters of Gershom Flagg* (Thwaites, XXVI), 43-51; James O. Andrews, *Miscellanies,* 46-52.

[32] George Devol, *Forty Years a Gambler,* 57-58, 71-72, 109-110; Andrews, 136.

[33]*Ibid.;* Benjamin Drake, *Tales and Sketches of the Queen City,* 27-37.

[34]Devol, *passim; Andrews,* 136-137.

[35]Dorothy Dondore, *The Prairie and the Making of Middle America,* 185; The *Spirit of the Times,* July 18, 1846, Vol. XVI, 248; James Hall, *Travels in North America,* 335; Josiah Conders, *A Popular Description of America,* II, 219-221.

[36]C. A. Murray, *Travels in North America,* I, 199.

[37]Captain Thomas Hamilton, *Men and Manners in America,* I, 89-91.

[38]Steamboat food early became an American tradition.

[39]C. D. Arfwedson, *The United States and Canada,* I, 96.

[40]*Ibid.*

[41]Hoffman, II, 102; Hamilton, I, 96-97.

[42]The *Spirit of the Times,* November 18, 1843, Vol. XIII, 456, quoting the Concordia *Intelligencer.*

[43]*Ibid.,* November 25, 1849, Vol. XVII, 473.

[44]*Ibid.,* February 18, 1843, Vol. XII, 611.

## SOMEBODY IN MY BED

[1]Henry Bradshaw Fearon, *Sketches of America,* 192.

[2]Scores of travelers have left vivid accounts of poor tavern accommodations. See Margaret Van Horn Dwight, *A Journey to Ohio in 1810,* 29, 35; Fortescue Cuming, *Sketches of a Tour to the Western Country* (Thwaites, IV), 59.

[3]W. H. Milburn, *Rifle, Axe and Saddle Bags,* 65; Captain Frederick Marryat, *Diary in America,* one vol. ed., 35; James Flint, *Letters from America* (Thwaites, IX), 104, 161.

[4]Cuming, 59; Fearon, 247.

[5]William Faux, *Memorable Days in America,* 185, 208, 233-237; Elias Fordham, *Personal Narrative,* 95; François A. Michaux, *Travels to the Westward of the Alleghany Mountains,* 62-63.

[6]Francis S. Philbrick, *Laws of Indiana Territory, 1801-1809,* CXXVI; Flint, 104; Dwight, 41; Faux, 211.

[7]Cuming, 222.

[8]Brother Mason, *Ten Years a Methodist Preacher,* 39.

[9]*A Letter from William H. Herndon to Isaac N. Arnold Relating to Abraham Lincoln, His Wife and Their Life in Springfield.*

[10]Benjamin Latrobe, *The Journal of Latrobe,* 25-26; Cuming, 59; Captain Thomas Hamilton, *Men and Manners in America,* I, 84.

[11]Faux, 211.

[12]For comments on the wild crowds hanging about the taverns see Hall, 152, 192; Flint, 104.

[13]G. W. Featherstonhaugh, *Excursion Through the Slaves States,* 87-88, 92, 94, 106, 115-116; Faux (Thwaites, XI), 298.

[14]H. M. Brackenridge, *Recollections of Persons and Places in the West,* 171.

[15]Michaux, 180.

[16]The *Kentucky Reporter,* July 29, 1818.

[17]Basil Hall, *Travels in North America,* 192.

[18]N. M. Ludlow, *Dramatic Life as I Found It,* 42.

[19]Featherstonhaugh, 16-18; Flint, 108-201; C. A. Murray, *Travels in North America,* I, 218-220; Michaux, 216; Cuming, 100, 222; Milburn, 65; Dwight, 40; Latrobe, 25-26.

[20]Fearon, 239.

[21]The *Western Citizen,* December 10, 1814; J. Winston Coleman, Jr., *Stage-Coach Days in the Blue Grass,* 53-72.

[22]Fearon, 248; Hall, 152; C. F. Hoffman, *A Winter in the West,* II, 216.

[23]Marryat, 35.

[24]Charles Dickens, *American Notes for General Circulation,* 383, 400. Interesting discussions of Dickens' notes are to be found in the *Spirit of the Times,* December 3, 10, 1842, Vol. XII, 469, 492.

[25]Milburn, 65.

[26]Hoffman, II, 216.

[27]Cuming, 100.

[28]The *Spirit of the Times,* December 13, 1845, Vol. XV, 489.

[29]*Ibid.,* January 4, 1851, Vol. XX, 544.

[30]*Porter's Spirit of the Times,* September 27, 1856, Vol. 1, 54.

[31]The *Spirit of the Times,* December 27, 1845, Vol. XV, 518.

[32]*Ibid.,* January 23, 1847, Vol. XVII, 508.

## *SERVANTS OF THE PEOPLE*

[1]The Lexington *Reporter,* February 25, 1818.

[2]Indiana did at one brief period hold two-day elections; Francis S. Philbrick, *Laws of Indiana Territory, 1801-1809*, 390-391.

[3]Fortescue Cuming, *Sketches of a Tour to the Western Country*, 177.

[4]*Ibid.*, 176.

[5]James Flint, *Letters from North America* (Thwaites, IX), 256.

[6]Bernard Mayo, *Henry Clay*, I, 7; Benjamin Drake, *Tales and Sketches of the Queen City*, 90-97; W. H. Perrin, *The Pioneer Press of Kentucky*, 77.

[7]Drake, 75-97; the *Kentucky Gazette*, August 8, 1809.

[8]Perrin, 77-79.

[9]Perrin states that he does not believe this an extreme account, and he knew about the Kentucky elections of an earlier date from first-hand experience.

[10]Thomas Ford, *History of Illinois from Its Commencement as a State in 1818-1847*, 105-106.

[11]*Ibid.*, 61.

[12]The *Spirit of the Times*, April 13, 1844, Vol. XIV, 81.

[13]Elias Fordham, *A Personal Narrative*, 76.

[14]Originally candidates did not seek offices openly, and it was up to their friends to work for them, but by this system the voters could find out where candidates stood on issues only through the newspapers.

[15]O. H. Smith, *Early Indiana Trials and Sketches*, 69.

[16]*Liberty Hall*, June 8, 1823.

[17]The *Spirit of the Times*, April 5, 1845, Vol. XV, 61.

[18]*Ibid.*, January 28, 1858, Vol. XXVII, 593; Smith, 122.

[19]The *Western Monitor*, August 8, 1818.

[20]Ford, 81.

[21]*Ibid.*, 32.

[22]*Ibid.*, 25.

[23]William Littell, *The Statute Law of Kentucky*, I, 336; IV, 142; Philbrick, 562-563.

[24]*Acts*, Kentucky General Assembly, January 28, 1814, 173.

[25]Compare Kentucky act of 1795, Littell, I, 336, with acts in Philbrick, 562-563.

[26]G. W. Featherstonhaugh, *Excursion Through the Slave States*, 99.

[27]The *Spirit of the Times*, quoting the Goshen *Democrat* from the Indianapolis *Journal*, April 8, 1848, Vol. XVIII, 70. The editor of the *Journal* said that he believed this an accurate account of this speech for a good many manuscript copies were handed around immediately after it was delivered.

[28]*Ibid.,* December 12, 1846, Vol. XVI, 499.

[29]*Ibid.*

[30]Timothy Flint, *Recollections of the Last Ten Years,* 215.

[31]M. H. Thatcher, *Stories and Speeches of William O. Bradley,* 71.

[32]William Littell, *Festoons of Fancy,* 46-51.

[33]Littell, *Statute Law of Kentucky,* III, 193.

[34]Private legislation was the bane of every western legislative session. Every volume of acts contains a large number of private laws.

[35]*Acts,* Kentucky General Assembly, February 9, 1838, 1837-1838, 169.

[36]*Debates,* Kentucky Constitutional Convention, 1849, 662.

[37]The *Spirit of the Times,* July 10, 1852, Vol. XXII, 252.

[38]*Ibid.,* February 11, 1843, Vol. XII, 592.

## WHERE THE LION ROARETH AND THE WANG DOODLE MOURNETH FOR HIS FIRST-BORN

[1]W. H. Milburn, *Pioneer Preachers and People of the Mississippi Valley,* 418.

[2]W. P. Strickland, ed., *Autobiography of Rev. J. B. Finley,* 166.

[3]M. J. Spaulding, *Sketches of the Early Catholic Missions of Kentucky,* 102-103; Catharine Cleveland, *The Great Revival in the West, 1797-1805,* quoting Robert Patterson to Rev. Dr. John King, 196-201.

[4]Spaulding, 102-103.

[5]Strickland, 164-170.

[6]Milburn, 56.

[7]Strickland, 294.

[8]Brother Mason, *The Circuit Rider or Ten Years a Methodist Preacher,* 23.

[9]*Ibid.,* 9-16.

[10]*Ibid.,* 16.

[11]Mary Verhoeff, *The Kentucky Mountains, Transportation and Commerce, 1750-1911,* 194-197.

[12]Richardson Wright, *Hawkers and Walkers in Early America,* 157.

[13]W. P. Strickland, ed., *Autobiography of Peter Cartwright,* 134-138.

[14]Bayard R. Hall, *The New Purchase, or Early Years in the West,* 117.

[15]Milburn, 70-71.

[16]*Ibid.,* 56-63; Brother Mason, 78, 105-119.

[17]Hall, 115.

[18]*Ibid.,* 229-230.

[19]Brother Mason, 54-56.

[20]Strickland, *Autobiography of Rev. J. B. Finley,* 268.

[21]M. H. Henkle, *The Life of Henry Bidleman Bascom,* 128.

[22]Brother Mason, 33-34.

[23]James Flint, *Letters from North America* (Thwaites, IX), 257.

[24]W. P. Strickland, *Autobiography of Peter Cartwright,* 130-133.

[25]*Ibid.*

[26]Strickland, *Autobiography of Rev. J. B. Finley,* 252-253.

[27]Brother Mason, 146-147.

[28]Strickland, 252.

[29]Brother Mason, 148-149.

[30]The *Western Citizen,* June 15, 1855.

[31]Milburn, *The Rifle, Axe and Saddle Bags,* 73-75.

[32]The *Spirit of the Times,* July 5, 1851, Vol. XXI, 240.

[33]S. P. Avery, *The Harp of a Thousand Strings,* 224-226.

[34]The *Spirit of the Times,* September 20, 1845, Vol. XV, 356.

## BENCH, BAR AND JURY

[1]G. W. Featherstonhaugh, *Excursion Through the Slave States,* 81-82.

[2]Bernard Mayo, *Henry Clay,* I, 62-65; Glyndon Van Deusen, *The Life of Henry Clay,* 18.

[3]Especially was this true in Kentucky where land lines overlapped so frequently. For a full treatment of this question see Samuel M. Wilson, *Kentucky Land Courts.*

[4]Thomas Ford, *History of Illinois,* 28.

[5]George Ord, *Supplement to the American Ornithology of Alexander Wilson,* CXX, CXXIV-CXXVIII.

[6]O. H. Smith, *Early Indiana Trials and Sketches, passim;* Basil Hall, *Travels in North America,* 167.

[7]H. M. Brackenridge, *Recollections of Persons and Places in the West,* 78; Elias Fordham, (Ogg) *Personal Narrative,* 155.

[8]*Porter's Spirit of the Times,* March 20, 1858, Vol. IV, 46.

[9]Clipping from an early Kentucky newspaper, owned by J. W. Curtiss, Blue Licks Museum, Robertson County, Kentucky.

[10]Smith, 5-7.

[11]*Ibid.;* M. H. Thatcher, *Stories and Speeches of William O. Bradley,* 50; Brackenridge, 78; Peter B. Riffe, *Celeste,* 167-177; the *Spirit of the Times,* July 2, 1842, Vol. XII, 212; Ford, 82-84.

[12]The *Spirit of the Times,* March 23, 1839, Vol. IX, 26; the *Western Citizen,* July 16, 1847.

[13]Smith, 47.

[14]The *Western Citizen,* July 16, 1847.

[15]Ford, 85.

[16]*Ibid.*, 82-84; *Memoirs of Gustave Koerner*, I, 133-134.

[17]Thatcher, 156.

[18]Smith, 160.

[19]W. P. Strickland, *The Autobiography of Rev. J. B. Finley*, 34; Featherstonhaugh, 90; Francis S. Philbrick, *The Laws of Indiana Territory, 1801-1809*, CIXXV.

[20]The *Spirit of the Times*, August 28, 1852, Vol. XXI, 336.

[21]Smith, 25.

[22]Featherstonhaugh, 90.

[23]Strickland, 110.

[24]Joseph Doddridge, *Notes on the Settlement and Indian Wars in the Western Parts of Virginia and Pennsylvania*, 186-187.

[25]James Flint, *Letters from North America* (Thwaites, IX), 197.

[26]Smith, 5-7.

[27]James Hall, *Legends of the West*, 357-360.

[28]The *Spirit of the Times*, March 23, 1839, Vol. IX.

[29]*Ibid.*, January 6, 1855, Vol. XIV, 560.

[30]*Ibid.*, August 28, 1852, Vol. XXI, 336.

[31]*Ibid.*, January 11, 1851, Vol. XX, 557.

[32]*Ibid.*, March 29, 1845, Vol. XV, 51.

[33]*The Lexington Press*, July 6, 1879.

[34]The *Spirit of the Times*, April 5, 1845, Vol. XV, 61.

## GENTLEMEN OF RANK

[1]Helen Randolph, *Mammoth Cave and the Cave Region of Kentucky*, 57.

[2]See laws providing for the organization of militia companies. Littell, *Statute Law of Kentucky*, IV, 284, 316; Philbrick, *Laws of the Indiana Territory, 1801-1809*, 413-414.

[3]George W. Ranck, *History of Lexington*, 246-252; O. H. Smith, *Indiana Trials and Sketches*, 44-46; William Faux, *Memorable Days in America*, 211.

[4]Smith, 44-46; also, the acts of the general assemblies contain hundreds of requests for aid because of military services.

[5]After the War of 1812 militia musters ceased to be of great significance. State legislatures ceased giving aid to this volunteer army, or requiring regular musters. Some general descriptions of musters are contained in John Woods' *Two Years' Residence in the Settlements on the English Prairies* (Thwaites, X), 311; James Hall, *The Romance of Western History*, 329.

[6]James Hall, *Travels in North America*, 329.

[7]James Flint, *Letters from North America* (Thwaites, IX), 201.

[8]Charles Fenno Hoffman, *A Winter in the West*, II, 45.

[9]Arthur W. Calhoun, *A Social History of the American Family from Colonial Times to the Present,* II, 332-333.

[10]Benjamin H. Latrobe, *The Journal of Latrobe,* 1-29.

[11]Hoffman, II, 59.

[12]Frances Trollope, *Domestic Manners of the Americans,* 14.

[13]*Ibid.,* 15.

[14]Faux, 187.

[15]Hoffman, II, 220.

[16]The *Western Citizen,* July 31, 1857.

[17]*Ibid.*

[18]The *Spirit of the Times,* August 4, 1849, Vol. XIX, 281.

[19]Hoffman, II, 59.

[20]John Lyde Wilson, *The Code of Honor; or Rules for the Government of Principals and Seconds,* 11-13.

[21]The *Palladium,* March 10, April 28, May 12 and September 13, 1801.

[22]Lorenzo Sabine, *Notes on Duels and Duelling,* 109.

[23]L. F. Johnson, *Famous Kentucky Trials and Tragedies,* 27-33.

[24]Niles' *Weekly Register,* August 5, 1819.

[25]Sabine, 131-132; the *Spirit of the Times,* December 15, 1849, Vol. XIX, 511.

[26]G. W. Featherstonhaugh, *Excursion Through the Slave States,* 98.

[27]Faux, 187.

[28]William Lightfoot Visscher, *Ten Wise Men and Some More,* 27-28.

[29]Basil Duke, *Reminiscences of General Basil Duke, C. S. A.,* 423-424.

[30]If there is any curiosity as to what was drunk upon the rendition of these numerous toasts the following bill of supplies for a Kentucky celebration will be enlightening: 103 gallons of whisky, 55 gallons of brandy and rum, and 159 pounds of sugar and acid for punch, *Kentucky Reporter,* May 16, 1829.

[31]*Acts,* Kentucky General Assembly, 1830, 25; *Revised Statutes of Indiana,* 145; Charles Cist, *Cincinnati Miscellany,* II, 314.

[32]M. H. Thatcher, *Stories and Speeches of William O. Bradley,* 61.

[33]The *Spirit of the Times,* October 31, 1846, Vol. XVI, 421.

[34]*Ibid.,* April 3, 1852, Vol. XXI, 76.

## LIARS

[1]Joseph G. Baldwin, *Flush Times in Alabama and Mississippi,* 3.

[2]Lunenburg C. Abernathy, *Laughable Anecdotes,* 13-14.

[3]The *Spirit of the Times*, March 17, 1838, Vol. VIII, 40.

[4]*Ibid.*, May 23, 1846, Vol. XVI, 145.

[5]James Russell Lowell, *Lectures on Hudibras* quoted by the *Spirit of the Times*, April 28, 1855, Vol. XXV, 125.

[6]Harriett Martineau, *Society in America*, II, 210.

[7]The *Spirit of the Times*, October 23, 1841, Vol. XI, 406.

[8]T. B. Thorpe, *The Big Bear of Arkansas*, title story; also, W. T. Porter, ed., *The Big Bear of Arkansas and Other Stories*, 21-22.

[9]Quoted by Constance Rourke, *American Humor*, 53.

[10]Baird, *View of the Valley of the Mississippi*, 92.

[11]The *Western Citizen*, September 4, 1846; quoted from the Louisville *Journal* by the *Spirit of the Times*, October 21, 1846, Vol. XXIV, 429.

[12]Thatcher, *Stories and Speeches of William O. Bradley*, 132.

[13]Rourke, 51.

[14]Herrick, ed., *Delineations of American Scenery and Character*, 97-104.

[15]The *Spirit of the Times*, September 7, 1844, Vol. XIV, 329.

[16]*Ibid.*, April 5, 1845, Vol. XV, 61.

[17]*Ibid.*, March 28, 1846, Vol. XVI, 58.

[18]*Ibid.*, July 5, 1845, Vol. XVI, 217.

[19]*Porter's Spirit of the Times*, December 6, 1856, Vol. I, 333.

[20]The *Spirit of the Times*, January 17, 1857, Vol. XVII, 316.

## QUARTER HOSSES

[1]François A. Michaux, *Travels to the Westward of the Alleghany Mountains*, 79.

[2]Basil Hall, *Travels in North America in the Years 1827 and 1828*, 230.

[3]James Flint, *Letters from North America* (Thwaites, IX), 136-137.

[4]The *Kentucky Gazette*, September 11, 1806.

[5]W. S. Lester, *The Transylvania Colony*, 91.

[6]Joseph Doddridge, *Notes on the Settlement and Indian Wars in the Western Parts of Virginia and Pennsylvania*, 154; William Henry Milburn, *The Rifle, Axe, and Saddle Bags*, 47-48.

[7]See weekly issues August 11 to January 1, 1792.

[8]Minute Book, Board of Trustees, Town of Lexington, Kentucky, entry April 2, 1798.

[9]*Acts*, Kentucky General Assembly, February 7, 1798, quoted by William Littell, *The Statute Law of Kentucky*, II, 62.

[10]*Ibid.*, I, 136; Francis S. Philbrick, *Laws of the Indiana Territory,* 1801-1809, 205-206; *Revised Statutes of Indiana,* 148.

[11]Philbrick, 205-206.

[12]Minute Book, Board of Trustees, Town of Lexington, April 2, 1798.

[13]For a specific charter of this type see *Acts,* Kentucky General Assembly, February 3, 1818, 517-526.

[14]*American Turf Register and Sporting Magazine,* Vol. IV, September, 1834, 15.

[15]*Acts,* Kentucky General Assembly, December 1, 1821, 299.

[16]The *Kentucky Gazette,* July 23, October 19, November 2, 1803.

[17]*Ibid.*, March 5, 1805.

[18]*Ibid.*, March 8, 1806.

[19]Benjamin Latrobe, *The Journal of Latrobe,* 27-29.

[20]C. A. Murray, *Travels in North America,* I, 220.

[21]H. M. Brackenridge, *Recollections of Persons and Places in the West,* 1862 ed., 62.

[22]A footnote by Zadoc Cramer to Cuming, *Sketches of a Tour* (Thwaites, IV), 255.

[23]Philbrick, CXXV.

[24]W. P. Strickland, *Autobiography of Rev. James B. Finley,* 197.

[25]The *Western Citizen,* March 27, 1846.

[26]The *Kentucky Gazette,* April 23, 1805.

[27]Fortescue A. Cuming, *Sketches of a Tour to the Western Country* (Thwaites, IV), 255.

[28]The *Kentucky Gazette,* September 17, 1805.

[29]*American Turf Register and Sporting Magazine,* Vol. I, May, 1830.

[30]The *Western Citizen,* February 21, 1824. See Lexington and Louisville papers, 1800-1850. Each spring a long list of stud horses was advertised. The *Gazette* ran a supplement at an early date.

[31]*American Turf Register and Sporting Magazine,* Vol. VI, November, 1836.

[32]The *Spirit of the Times,* January 3, 1846, Vol. XV, 554.

[33]*Ibid.*, March 4, 1843, Vol. XIII, 3.

[34] M. H. Thatcher, *Stories and Speeches of William O. Bradley,* 65.

## KEARDS

[1]William Littell, *The Statute Law of Kentucky,* III, 176-177.

[2]Timothy Flint, *Recollections of the Last Ten Years,* 269.

[3]William H. Perrin, *The Pioneer Press of Kentucky,* 14-15.

[4] The *Kentucky Gazette,* September 17, 1805; Robert Baird, *View of the Valley of the Mississippi,* 324-325.

[5] W. P. Strickland, *Autobiography of Rev. James B. Finley,* 164.

[6] Benjamin Casseday, *History of Louisville,* 122.

[7] Flint, 62; Isaac Weld, *Travels Through the States of North America,* I, 191; Henry Bradshaw Fearon, *Sketches of America,* 239.

[8] George Devol, *Forty Years a Gambler,* 57-58, 71-72; G. W. Featherstonhaugh, *Excursion Through the Slave States,* 115-116.

[9] John Morris, *The Wanderings of a Vagabond,* 429.

[10] *Ibid.*

[11] *Ibid.,* quoted from the New York *Eagle,* 235-241.

[12] Weld, I, 191; Morris, 429; Devol, 71-72, 109-110.

[13] Morris, 259-262.

[14] Benjamin Drake, *Tales and Sketches from the Queen City,* 27-37.

[15] Francis Philbrick, *Laws of the Indiana Territory,* 1801-1809, 370-371; *Revised Statutes of Indiana,* 146; *Acts,* Kentucky General Assembly, 1831, 124-128.

[16] The *Spirit of the Times,* February 14, 1852, Vol. XXI, 602.

[17] *Ibid.,* February 7, 1852, Vol. XXI, 602.

[18] *Ibid.,* August 10, 1839, Vol. IX, 267.

[19] *Ibid.,* March 6, 1847, XVI, 13.

[20] Sol. Smith, *Autobiography of a Retired Actor,* 111.

## FIDDLIN'

[1] John Taylor, *A History of Ten Baptist Churches,* 99-101.

[2] Reuben T. Durrett, *The Bivouac,* January, 1884.

[3] August 10, 1844, Vol. XIV, 279.

[4] W. H. Milburn, *The Rifle, Axe, and Saddle Bags,* 387.

[5] F. D. Srygley, *Seventy Years in Dixie,* 98.

[6] Milburn, 46-53; Joseph Doddridge, *Notes on the Settlement and Indian Wars in the Western Parts of Virginia and Pennsylvania,* 152-157.

[7] These parties were organized by leaders of the young people, and often it took considerable pleading to get settled parents to give permission for parties to be held in their homes.

[8] Fortescue Cuming, *Sketches of a Tour to the Western Country,* 117, 121, 209.

[9] John Bradbury, *Travels in the Interior of America* (Thwaites, V), 300-316.

[10] John Wood, *Two Years' Residence in the Settlements on the English Prairie,* (Thwaites, X), 350.

[11] W. P. Strickland, *Autobiography of the Rev. J. B. Finley,* 248-249.

[12]Doddridge, 157.

[13]Thomas Nuttall, *A Journal of Travel into the Arkansas Territory* (Thwaites, XIII), 58.

[14]Srygley, 152; The *Spirit of the Times,* July 17, 1852, Vol. XXI, 260.

[15]Wood, 300; Srygley, 153-154.

[16]*Ibid.*

[17]The *Kentucky Gazette,* June 27, July 11, 1809.

[18]Benjamin Drake, *Tales and Sketches of the Queen City,* 92; *Argus of Western America,* June 16, August 10, 1824; the Danville *Olive Branch,* September 10, 1824.

[19]The *Spirit of the Times,* July 8, 1837, Vol. VII, 164.

[20]Elias Fordham (Ogg, ed.) *Personal Narrative of Travels,* 165.

[21]*Ibid.,* 147.

[22]R. T. Coleman, "Jo Daviess of Kentucky," *Harper's Magazine,* XXI, 351-352.

[23]N. M. Ludlow, *Dramatic Life as I Found It,* 84-85.

[24]Bayard R. Hall, *The New Purchase,* 87.

[25]O. H. Smith, *Early Indiana Trials and Sketches,* 79.

[26]Ludlow, 85.

[27]*Ibid.,* 86.

[28]The *Spirit of the Times,* January 30, 1841, Vol. X, 571.

[29]J. S. Robb, *Streaks of Squatter Life,* 59-64.

[30]*Porter's Spirit of the Times,* January 24, 1857, Vol. I, 332; also, M. H. Thatcher, *Stories and Speeches of William O. Bradley,* 15.

## FOOLIN' WITH THE GALS

[1] Theodore Roosevelt, *Winning of the West,* III, 17.

[2]Margaret Van Horn Dwight (ed. by Max Farrand), *A Journey to Ohio in 1810,* intro.

[3] F. D. Srygley, *Seventy Years in Dixie,* 187-206; Edward O. Guerrant, *The Galax Gatherers,* 169.

[4]Srygley, 200.

[5]W. P. Strickland, *Autobiography of Rev. J. B. Finley,* 71; J. D. Caton, *Early Bench and Bar of Illinois,* 21; Brother Mason, *Ten Years a Methodist Preacher,* 67; Doddridge, *Notes on the Settlement and Indian Wars of the Western Parts of Virginia and Pennsylvania,* 152-168.

[6]Strickland, 71.

[7]Caton, 30-37.

[8]The *Spirit of the Times,* Sept. 14, 1844, Vol. XIV, 346.

[9]O. H. Smith, *Early Indiana Trials and Sketches,* 29-30.

[10]Caton, 24.

[11]The *Kentucky Gazette,* April 13, April 20, 1793.

[12]*Ibid.,* June 8, 1801; *Rights of Man or Kentucky Mercury,* Aug. 30, 1797.

[13]The *Argus of Western America,* May 24, 1826.

[14]Hundreds of cases of divorce occurred throughout the West. Acts of general assemblies contain hundreds of complaints.

[15]*Acts,* Kentucky General Assembly, January 4, 1824, 1823-1825, 413.

[16]*Ibid.,* February 4, 1820, 875.

[17]Caton, 21.

[18]The *Western Citizen,* August 9, 1823.

[19]John Robert Shaw, *A Narrative of the Life and Travels of John Robert Shaw, the Well Digger,* 179.

[20]The *Kentucky Gazette,* Feb. 5, 1816.

[21]Henry Bradshaw Fearon, *Sketches of America,* 244; frequently deserted women appeared before legislatures and gave similar reasons for wishing divorces. There was Jane Plummer (*Acts,* Kentucky General Assembly, 1820, 871) who sought freedom from William Plummer because he would not stay at home, "and has associated himself with play actors in different parts of the United States."

[22]See divorce proceedings before state legislatures: specifically, *Acts,* Kentucky General Assembly, February 6, 1819, 700.

[23]Francis Philbrick, *Laws of the Indiana Territory,* 1801-1809, CXXVIII.

[24]*Kentucky Gazette,* August 25, 1801, July 19, 1817.

[25]Casseday, *History of Louisville,* 109.

[26]G. W. Featherstonhaugh, *Excursion Through the Slave States,* 114.

[27]The *Spirit of the Times,* April 9, 1842, Vol. XII, 61.

[28]The *Western Citizen,* December 4, 1846.

[29]The *Spirit of the Times,* April 7, 1849, Vol. XIX, 76.

[30]*Ibid.,* May 3, 1845, Vol. XV, 107.

[31]The *Western Citizen,* January 23, 1846.

## YANKEES B'GAD

[1]Richardson Wright, *Hawkers and Walkers in Early America,* 78-79; Harriett Martineau, *Society in America,* II, 26-27.

[2]The *Kentucky Gazette,* March 31, 1820.

[3]Benjamin Drake, *Tales and Sketches of the Queen City,* 80-81.

[4]Henry Bradshaw Fearon, *Sketches of America*, 207.

[5]The *Western Sun*, March 29, 1823; Timothy Flint, *Recollections of the Last Ten Years*, 32-33.

[6]Flint, 33, 36.

[7]William Faux, *Memorable Days in America*, 337.

[8]Elias P. Fordham, *Personal Narrative of Travel*, 223.

[9]The *Western Sun*, March 29, 1823.

[10]*Ibid.*, August 17, 1822; Abernathy, 147.

[11]Flint, 32.

[12]*Ibid.*

[13]J. H. Ingraham, *The Southwest*, II, 13.

[14]The *Western Citizen*, February 27, 1846.

[15]Flint, 69; Charles F. Hoffman, *A Winter in the West*, II, 187.

[16]Thomas Hamilton, *Men and Manners in America*, I, 126.

[17]Hoffman, II, 187.

[18]The *Western Monthly Review*, June, 1828, Vol. II, 12-15.

[19]*Ibid.*

[20]Hoffman, II, 165.

[21]G. W. Featherstonhaugh, *Excursion Through the Slave States*, 91-92.

[22]*Ibid.*, 91; The *Spirit of the Times*, February 21, 1846, Vol. XV, 610, and September 26, 1846, 364.

[23]James Flint, *Letters from America* (Thwaites, IX), 312.

[24]Featherstonhaugh, 91-92.

[25]John Dean Caton, *Early Bench and Bar of Illinois*, 4-6.

[26]Hoffman, II, 203.

[27]Featherstonhaugh, 95.

[28]Caton, 4-6.

[29]*Ibid.*, 111.

[30]The *Western Sun*, June 14, 1823.

[31]*Ibid.*, December 28, 1823.

[32]Edmund Kirke, *Down in Tennessee and Back by Way of Richmond*, 112-116.

[33]William T. Porter, *A Quarter Race in Kentucky*, 161-164.

[34]The *Spirit of the Times*, May 20, 1848, Vol. XVII, 153.

[35]Charles Cist, *Cincinnati Miscellany*, II, 359.

# BIBLIOGRAPHY

# BIBLIOGRAPHY

Abernathy, Lunenburg C., *Laughable Anecdotes, Both Ancient and Modern*, Frankfort, 1832.

Andrew, James O., *Miscellanies: Comprising Letters, Essays and Addresses: To which Is Added a Biographical Sketch*, Louisville, 1854.

Arfwedson, C. C., *The United States and Canada in 1832, and 1833 and 1834*, 2 vols., London, 1834.

Ashe, Thomas, *Travels in America*, London, 1808.

Audubon, John J., *Delineations of American Scenery and Character*, edited by F. H. Herrick, N. Y. 1926.

Avery, S. P., *The Harp of a Thousand Strings*, New York, 1858.

Baird, Robert, *View of the Valley of the Mississippi, or the Emmigrant's and Traveler's Guide*, Philadelphia, 1832.

Baldwin, Joseph G., *The Flush Times in Alabama and Mississippi*, New York, 1853.

Barker, Eugene C., *The Life of Stephen F. Austin*, Nashville, 1925.

Beggs, S. R., *Pages from the Early History of the West and Northwest*, Cincinnati, 1868.

Birbeck, Morris, *Letters from Illinois*, London, 1818.

Blair, Walter, *Native American Humor, 1800-1900*, New York, 1937.

Blair, Walter and Meine, Franklin J., *Mike Fink, King of Mississippi Keelboatmen*, New York, 1933.

Brackenridge, Henry Marie, *Recollections of Persons and Places in the West*, Philadelphia, 1868.

Bradbury, John, *Travels in the Interior of America, in the Years 1809, 1810 and 1811*, Liverpool, 1817.

Bradley, J. W., *Pioneer Life in the West; Comprising the Adventures of Boone, Kenton, Brady, Clarke, the Whetzels*, Philadelphia, 1858.

Bradley, William O., *Stories and Speeches*, edited by M. H. Thatcher, Lexington, 1916.

Brother Mason, *The Circuit Rider; or Ten Years a Methodist Preacher*, Cincinnati, 1858.

Brown, Henry, *History of Illinois*, New York, 1844.

Buckingham, James Silk, *The Eastern and Western States of America*, 3 vols., London, 1842.

Buck, Solon Justus, *Travel and Description, 1765-1865* (Collections of the Illinois State Library, Bibliographical Series, Vol. II), Springfield, 1914.

Bullock, William, *Sketch of a Journey Through the Western States of America* (Thwaites' *Early Western Travels*, XIX), Cleveland, 1904.

Burnet, Jacob, *Notes on the Settlement of the Northwestern Territory*, Boston, 1847.

Butler, Mann, *A History of the Commonwealth of Kentucky*, Louisville, 1836.

Butterick, Tilly J., *Voyages and Discoveries, 1812-1819* (Thwaites, VIII), Cleveland, 1904.

Calhoun, Arthur W., *A Social History of the American Family from Colonial Times to the Present*, 3 vols., Cleveland, 1917.

*Campaign,* the Frankfort, 1840.

Candler, Isaac, *A Summary of American Observations and Enquiries During a Journey in the United States*, London, 1824.

Cartwright, Peter, *Autobiography of a Backwoods Preacher*, edited by William Strickland, New York, 1856.

Carver, Jonathan, *Three Years' Travel Throughout the Interior Part of North America*, Boston, 1797.

Casseday, Benjamin, *The History of Louisville from Its Earliest Settlement till the Year 1852*, Louisville, 1852.

Caton, John Dean, *Early Bench and Bar of Illinois*, Chicago, 1893.

Chastellux, François Jean, *Travels in North America in the Years 1780, 1781 and 1782* (in *American History Told by Contemporaries*) New York, 1928.

Cist, Charles, *The Cincinnati Miscellany, or Antiquities of the West*, 2 vols., Cincinnati, 1845, 1846.

Cleveland, Catharine C., *The Great Revival in the West, 1797-1805*, Chicago, 1916.

Coates, Robert M., *The Outlaw Years*, New York, 1930.

Coleman, J. Winston, Jr., *Stage-Coach Days in the Blue Grass*, Louisville, 1935.

Collins, Lewis, *Historical Sketches of Kentucky*, Cincinnati, 1847.

Collins, Richard H., *History of Kentucky*, 2 vols., Covington, 1874.

Conders, Josiah, *A Popular Description of America*, 2 vols., London, n.d.

Connelley, W. E. and Coulter, E. M., *History of Kentucky*, 5 vols., Chicago, 1922.

Cotterill, Robert S., *History of Pioneer Kentucky*, Cincinnati, 1917.

Cox, Sandford G., *Recollections of the Early Settlement of the Wabash Valley*, Lafayette, 1860.

Cuming, Fortescue, *Sketches of a Tour to the Western Country,* Pittsburgh, 1810.

Curtis, Henry B., "Pioneer Days in Cincinnati, Ohio," *Ohio Archeological and History Quarterly,* Vol. I, Cincinnati, 1871.

Dana, Edmund, *Geographical Sketches of the Western Country,* Cincinnati, 1819.

Davidson, Robert, *An Excursion to Mammoth Cave,* Philadelphia, 1840.

Devol, George H., *Forty Years a Gambler on the Mississippi,* New York, 1926.

DeVoto, Bernard, *Mark Twain's America,* Boston, 1935.

Dickens, Charles, *American Notes, for General Circulation,* New York, n.d.

Doddridge, Joseph, *Notes on the Settlement and Indian Wars of the Western Parts of Virginia and Pennsylvania, from 1763 to 1783,* Albany, 1876.

Dondore, Dorothy A., *The Prairie in the Making of Middle America,* Cedar Rapids, 1926.

Drake, Benjamin, *Tales and Sketches from the Queen City,* Cincinnati, 1838.

Drake, Daniel, *A Discourse on the History, Character and Prospects of the West,* Cincinnati, 1834.

———, *Pioneer Life in Kentucky,* Cincinnati, 1870.

Duke, Basil W., *Reminiscences of General Basil W. Duke, C. S. A.,* New York, 1911.

Dunbar, Seymour, *A History of Travel in America,* 4 vols., Indianapolis, 1915.

Dwight, Margaret Van Horn, *A Journey to Ohio in 1810 as Recorded in the Journal of Margaret Van Horn Dwight,* New Haven, 1920.

Espy, Josiah, *A Tour in Ohio, Kentucky and Indiana Territory in 1805,* Cincinnati, 1870.

Evans, Estwick, *Pedestrious Tour, 1818* (Thwaites, VIII), Cleveland, 1904.

Faust, Bernhardt, *The German Element in the United States,* 2 vols., New York, 1927.

Faux, William, *Memorable Days in America: Being a Journal of a Tour to the United States,* London, 1823.

Fearon, Henry Bradshaw, *Sketches of America,* London, 1819.

Featherstonhaugh, G. W., *Excursion Through the Slave States from Washington on the Potomac to the Frontier of Mexico,* New York, 1844.

Field, J. M., *The Drama in Pokerville; the Bench and Bar of Jury-town and Other Stories*, Philadelphia, 1850.

Filson, John, *Kentucke and the Adventures of Col. Daniel Boone*, Wilmington, 1784.

Finley, James B., *Autobiography of Rev. James B. Finley; Or Pioneer Life in the West*, edited by William Strickland, Cincinnati, 1854, 1855.

Flagg, Gershom, *Pioneer Letters of Gershom Flagg* (Illinois State Historical Society, Transactions, 1910).

Flint, James, *Letters from America* (Thwaites, IX), Cleveland, 1904.

Flint, Timothy, *The History and Geography of the Mississippi Valley*, Cincinnati, 1832.

———, *Recollections of the Last Ten Years*, Boston, 1826.

Flowers, Richard, *Flowers' Letters from Lexington and the Illinois* (Thwaites, X), Cleveland, 1904.

Ford, Governor Thomas, *A History of Illinois from Its Commencement as a State in 1818-1847*, Chicago, 1847.

Fordham, Elias Pym, *Personal Narrative of Travels in Virginia, Maryland, Pennsylvania, Ohio, Indiana, Kentucky*, edited by Frederick A. Ogg, Cleveland, 1906.

Gallagher, James, *The Western Sketch Book*, Boston, 1850.

Gerstaecker, Frederick, *Wild Sports in the Far West*, Boston, 1859.

Grund, Francis J., *The Americans in Their Moral, Social and Political Relations*, London, 1837.

Guerrant, Edward O., *The Galax Gatherers*, Richmond, 1910.

Guild, Jo. C., *Old Times in Tennessee*, Nashville, 1878.

Haliburton, T. C., *Traits of American Humor, by Native Authors*, 3 vols., London, 1852.

Hall, Basil, *Travels in North America in the Years 1827 and 1828*, Edinburgh, 1830.

Hall, Bayard, *The New Purchase, or Early Years in the West*, 2 vols., New Albany, Ind., 1855.

Hall, Frederick, *Letters from the East and from the West*, Washington, 1840.

Hall, James, *Legends of the West*, Cincinnati, 1857.

———, *The Romance of Western History*, Cincinnati, 1857.

———, *Statistics of the West at the Close of the Year 1836*, Cincinnati, 1836.

Hamilton, Thomas, *Men and Manners in America*, 2 vols., Philadelphia, 1833.

Harris, Thaddeus Mason, *The Journal of a Tour into the Territory Northwest of the Allegheny Mountains* (Thwaites, III), Cleveland, 1904.

Haycraft, Samuel, *A History of Elizabethtown Kentucky and Its Surroundings,* Elizabethtown, 1921.

Henkle, M. H., *The Life of Henry Bidleman Bascom,* Nashville, 1898.

Hoffman, Charles Fenno, *A Winter in the West,* 2 vols., New York, 1835.

Howe, Henry, *Historical Collections of Ohio,* 2 vols., Cincinnati, 1908.

Hudson, Arthur Palmer, *Humor in the Old Deep South,* New York, 1936.

Hulbert, Archer Butler, *Historic Highways,* Vol. IX, Cleveland, 1903.

Hunt, Gaillard, *Life in America One Hundred Years Ago,* New York, 1914.

Imlay, George Gilbert, *A Topographical Description of the Western Territory of North America,* London, 1793.

Ingraham, J. H., *The Southwest,* 2 vols., New York, 1835.

Johnson, L. F., *Famous Kentucky Trials and Tragedies,* Cleveland, 1922.

Kennedy, H. C., *A Damphool in the Kentucky Legislature,* Chicago, 1909.

Kirke, Edmund, *Down in Tennessee and Back by Way of Richmond,* New York, 1864.

Kirkpatrick, John Ervin, *Timothy Flint, Pioneer Missionary, Author, Editor, 1780-1840,* Cleveland, 1911.

*Memoirs of Gustave Koerner, 1809-1896,* edited by J. McCormack, 2 vols., Cedar Rapids, 1909.

Lafond, Andre, *Impressions of America,* New York, 1930.

Latrobe, Benjamin, *The Journal of Latrobe* (1790-1820), New York, 1905.

Lester, William Stewart, *The Transylvania Colony,* Spencer, Indiana, 1936.

Levasseur, Auguste, *LaFayette en America, 1824 et 1825,* 2 vols., Philadelphia, 1829.

Littell, William, *Festoons of Fancy,* Frankfort, 1814.

Lloyd, James T., *Lloyd's Steamboat Directory,* Cincinnati, 1856.

Ludlow, N. M., *Dramatic Life as I Found It,* St. Louis, 1880.

Mackay, Charles, *Mackay's Tour in the United States,* London, 1859.

Marryat, Captain Frederick, *Second Series of a Diary in America with Remarks on Its Institutions,* Philadelphia, 1840.

Martineau, Harriett, *Society in America,* 3 vols., New York, 1837.

Mayo, Bernard, *Henry Clay, Spokesman of the New West,* New York, 1937.

McClung, John A., *Sketches of Western Adventure,* Covington, Kentucky, 1872.

Meine, Franklin J., *Tall Tales of the Southwest,* New York, 1930.

Melish, John, *Travels in the United States of America in the Years 1806 and 1807, and 1809,1810 and 1811,* 2 vols., Philadelphia, 1812.

Michaux, F. A., *Travels to the Westward of the Alleghany Mountains in the States of the Ohio, Kentucky, and Tennessee, in the Year 1802,* London, 1805.

Milburn, William Henry, *The Rifle, Axe and Saddle Bags and Other Lectures,* New York, 1857.

———, *Pioneer Preachers and Peoples of the Mississippi Valley,* New York, 1860.

Morris, John, *Wanderings of a Vagabond,* New York, 1873.

Murray, Charles A., *Travels in North America During the Years 1834, 1835, and 1836,* London, 1839.

Nevins, Allan, *American Social History as Recorded by British Travelers,* New York, 1923.

Ord, George, *Supplement to the American Ornithology of Alexander Wilson,* 5 vols., Philadelphia, 1825.

Peck, J. M., *Forty Years of Pioneer Life,* Philadelphia, 1864.

Perrin, William H., *The Pioneer Press of Kentucky,* Louisville, 1888.

Philbrick, Francis S., (ed.), *The Laws of the Indiana Territory, 1801-1809,* Collections of the Illinois State Historical Library, Law Series, II, Springfield, 1930.

Porter, William T., *A Quarter Race in Kentucky and Other Sketches,* Philadelphia, 1846.

Ranck, George W., *History of Lexington,* Cincinnati, 1874.

Randolph, Helen, *Mammoth Cave and the Cave Region of Kentucky,* Louisville, 1923.

Riffe, Peter B., *Celeste,* Lebanon, Kentucky, 1876.

Robb, John S., *Streaks of Squatter Life and Far Western Scenes,* Philadelphia, 1847.

Rogers, James R., *The Cane Ridge Meeting-House,* Cincinnati, 1910.

Ross, H. L., *The Early Pioneer and Pioneer Events of Illinois,* Chicago, 1899.

Rourke, Constance, *American Humor, a Study in National Character,* New York, 1931.

Rusk, Ralph Leslie, *The Literature of the Middle Western Frontier,* 2 vols., New York, 1926.

Sabine, Lorenzo, *Notes on Duels and Duelling,* Boston, 1855.

Schultz, Christian, *Travels on an Inland Voyage,* New York, 1810.

Shaw, John Robert, *A Narrative of the Life and Travels of John Robert Shaw,* edited by George L. Fowler, Louisville, 1930.

Smith, O. H., *Early Indiana Trials and Sketches,* Cincinnati, 1858.

Smith, Sol., *Theatrical Management in the West and South for Thirty Years,* New York, 1868.

Spaulding, M. J., *Sketches of the Early Catholic Missions of Kentucky,* Louisville, 1844.

Srygley, F. D., *Seventy Years in Dixie,* Nashville, 1891.

Taylor, John, *A History of Ten Baptist Churches,* Frankfort, 1823.

Thwaites, Reuben Gold, *Early Western Travels, 1748-1846,* 32 vols., Cleveland, 1904-1907.

Thorpe, T. B., *Col. Thorpe's Scenes in Arkansas,* Philadelphia, 1858.

———, *The Mysteries of the Backwoods, or Sketches of the Southwest,* Philadelphia, 1846.

———, *The Hive of the Bee Hunter,* New York, 1854.

Trollope, Frances, *Domestic Manners of the Americans,* London, 1832.

Turner, F. J., *The Frontier in American History,* New York, 1921.

Van Deusen, Glyndon, *The Life of Henry Clay,* Boston, 1937.

Verhaeff, Mary, *The Kentucky River Navigation,* Louisville, 1917.

Visscher, William L., *Ten Wise Men and Some More,* Chicago, 1909.

Wakefield, Priscilla, *Excursions in North America,* London, 1806.

Watterson, Henry, *Oddities in Southern Life and Character,* New York, 1882.

Welby, Adlard, *A Visit to North America and the English Settlements in Illinois* (Thwaites, XI), Cleveland, 1904.

Weld, Isaac, *Travels Through the States of North America, 1795-1797,* 2 vols., London, 1799.

Williams, Joseph S., *Old Times in West Tennessee,* Memphis, 1873.

Wilson, John Lyde, *The Code of Honor; or Rules for the Government of Principals and Seconds.* Charleston, 1858.

Winterbotham, William, *An Historical, Geographical, Commercial, and Philosophical View of the American United States,* 4 vols., London, 1795.

Wood, John, *Two Years' Residence in the Settlement on the English Prairie in the Illinois Country* (Thwaites, X), Cleveland, 1904.

Wortley, Emmeline, S., *Travels in the United States During 1849 and 1850,* New York, 1851.

Wright, Richardson, *Hawkers, and Walkers in Early America,* Philadelphia, 1927.

## Laws and Debates

*Acts,* Kentucky General Assembly, Frankfort, 1792-1850.
*Acts,* Indiana General Assembly, Corydon and Indianapolis, 1820-1850.
*Acts,* Missouri General Assembly, Columbia, 1820-1850.
*Acts,* Illinois General Assembly, Springfield, 1820-1850.
*Report of the Proceedings of the Convention for the Revision of the* (Kentucky) *Constitution,* Frankfort, 1849.
Littell, William, *The Statute Law of Kentucky,* 1792-1819, 5 vols., Frankfort.
*The Revised Statutes of Indiana,* Corydon, 1824.

## Newspapers

*Argus of Western America,* Frankfort, 1808-1830.
*Kentucky Gazette,* Lexington, 1787-1840.
*Kentucky Observer and Reporter,* Lexington, 1830-1860.
*Lexington Reporter,* 1808-1817.
*Lexington Press,* 1871-1895.
*Liberty Hall,* Cincinnati, 1824-1830.
Louisville *Journal,* 1830-1860.
*Microscope,* Louisville and Jeffersonville, 1826-1827.
Vincennes *Western Sun,* 1823-1830.
*Western Citizen,* Paris, 1808-1860.

## Periodicals

Anderson, Hattie M., "Missouri, 1804-1828: Peopling a Frontier," *The Missouri Historical Review,* XXXI, January, 1937.
Burnet, Jacob, "Notes on the Early Settlement of the Northwestern Territory," *North American Review,* October, 1847.
Jordan, Phillip D., "Humor of the Backwoods, 1820-1840," *The Mississippi Valley Historical Review,* XXV, June, 1938.
*Porter's Spirit of the Times,* New York, 1858-1860.
*Spirit of the Times,* New York, 1836-1860.
*American Turf Register and Sporting Magazine,* Baltimore, 1830-1840.
*Western Magazine and Review,* Cincinnati, 1827-1830.